M.

O

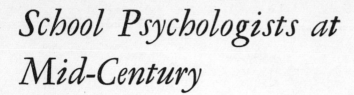

School Psychologists at Mid-Century

A REPORT OF THE THAYER CONFERENCE ON THE FUNCTIONS,
QUALIFICATIONS, AND TRAINING OF SCHOOL PSYCHOLOGISTS

Edited by NORMA E. CUTTS

American Psychological Association, Inc.
Washington, D.C., 1955

Library of Congress Catalogue Number: 55-9034

Foreword

THE Thayer Conference covered a wide range of topics dealing with the functions, qualifications, and training of school psychological workers. In this report, the need for the Conference and its actual organization have been presented first. This is followed by background material on the development of psychological services in the schools. The next chapters present the functions of school psychological workers, how these functions are carried out, and the conditions under which school psychological service is rendered. The final chapters deal with recruitment and training. The surveys of training preceding the Conference, and the kinds of training thought to be essential for different levels of service, are presented. The summary of conclusions and recommendations furnishes a brief statement of the entire report. Appendix A, written by Dr. W. D. Wall of UNESCO, shows the development of psychological services in Europe and how that development sometimes parallels and sometimes departs from the development in the United States. Appendix B, by Dr. W. Mason Mathews of the Merrill-Palmer School, Detroit, describes the work of a psychologist in a private school.

The Conference had the use of many preliminary studies which were made specially for it. The names of the individuals who conducted these are mentioned in the text. Since these studies have not been published and are not available for distribution they are not listed in the bibliography. Many unpublished reports from the Division of School Psychologists of the APA and from local and regional associations have been similarly treated. The bibliography includes the references compiled by Dr. Dale Harris, and others suggested by members of the Conference.

Members of the Division of School Psychologists at the close of the Conference expressed their appreciation to the Public Health Service of the United States Department of Health, Education, and Welfare for making the Conference possible. Appreciation was also expressed to the individual members who attended the Conference and the professional groups which provided representation. The editor is grateful to all the members, and particularly to the editorial committee, for direct contributions and for detailed and patient criticism.

NORMA E. CUTTS, Editor

New Haven, Connecticut
April, 1955

iii

Contents

Introduction

by Robert H. Felix, M.D.
Director, National Institute of Mental Health*

THE appearance of this volume is a significant event. Its importance will be readily recognized by psychologists, by educators, and by the community of workers in the mental health field.

To the psychologist, this volume summarizes a phase of the history of his discipline—the story of the growth and professionalization of one segment of the field. Developments of this kind have been a major trend in the last ten to fifteen years. This period is the one during which psychology has developed its applied function through recognizing its service value and responsibilities and during which it has matched its growth in the area of practical activities with a corresponding increase of professional sense, concern for ethical problems and self-critical appraisal of its social function and role in the culture. It should be gratifying, therefore, to the entire body of psychologists to see here an articulate and realistic appraisal of the meaning, scope, techniques, and role of professional psychology in the school setting. The appraisal of the potentialities of psychology as an applied science in the realm of education is at once reassuring and hopeful without being grandiose or self-seeking.

The educator, or more particularly the school administrator, also has reason to read this volume with gratification and perhaps with renewed hope for the future. It is the school administrator who, over the last several decades, has made possible the growth of school psychology by incorporating these services on an increasing scale into our structure of educational services. It is a just and fitting reward for those who chose to recognize the value of the school psychologist when he was a fledgling in the field of popular education to have him now respond with a sober evaluation of his own contribution and role and with a mature and sophisticated statement of what school psychology must do now and in the future to increase its contribution to our schools and our children. These pages will represent for many school administrators an experience which will surely be recognized as faith repaid.

* A component of the National Institutes of Health, Public Health Service, U. S. Department of Health, Education, and Welfare.

Those of us concerned with mental illness and its prevention and with the maintenance of mental health can also find hope and reward in these pages. The envisagement of mental illness and mental health has changed tremendously within the last century and with accelerated pace in the last decade. Treatment with small hope of success has given way in many types of illness to treatment with good hope of success. Prevention of mental illness and the maintenance of the mental health of the community have come to be terms representing considerable substance in terms of present achievement and with exciting possibilities for the future. Much of the progress has come from abandoning sole reliance upon the individual treatment of the individual case. To this approach, which still has real and significant value, has been added the practice of dealing with the entire family as the unit, whether treatment or prevention be the goal. Also, and of possibly even greater importance, it is now clearly seen that the promotion of mental health is not the responsibility alone of those who classify themselves as members of the mental health professions. On the other hand, all of the functioning groups by which a community supports and sustains itself have an impact upon the mental health of that community. Increasingly, it is recognized that mental health functions, as they involve maintenance and the prevention of illness, must be distributed in part to all of our community agencies and enterprises.

The schools have long been recognized as an influence second only to the home in determining the degree to which our citizens achieve that adult goal which the layman calls adequacy or happiness or self-sufficiency and which the psychiatrist calls maturity. The schools have long shown that they are sensitive to this responsibility, as indicated by their increasing utilization of specialized personnel such as counselors, school social workers, guidance personnel, and school psychologists.

Everyone realizes that the end is not yet. No group devoted to the improvement of mental health, as all or part of its function, can say that it knows in a final sense how to do its job. Those of us with full-time preoccupations in the mental health field welcome therefore the efforts of any group in the field to assess its contribution and to improve it. The present report grows out of a conference which was envisaged and planned by the school psychologists. It was an expression of need for clarification and redefinition of goals and function by the group itself. The National Institute of Mental Health was happy to learn of this concern and pleased that the National Advisory Mental Health Council viewed the application favorably and recommended to the Surgeon General of the Public Health Service that the grant be made. The results here reported attest to the sound judgment of the Council. The Institute, the Public Health Service, and the Department of Health, Education, and Welfare feel that, by helping others to help themselves, they have made progress in discharging their own responsibilities to our citizenry.

School Psychologists
at Mid-Century

I.

The Need to Study the Qualifications and Training of School Psychologists

THERE are now 36,000,000 children in the schools of the United States. The enrollment will increase to 45,000,000 within the next five years. Each of these children is an individual, different from all the others. Each has his own particular needs which he must satisfy and problems which he must solve if he is to grow up a well-adjusted member of society.

THE OPPORTUNITY

Authorities in public health and specialists in mental health are convinced that the schools have a major role in the promotion of good mental hygiene. The school psychologist is one of the school's important agents to this end. The schools enroll nearly all the children in the nation and so furnish each child's earliest contact with public authority. Clinical psychologists, psychiatrists, and child psychologists agree that here in the all-important early years is the place where every opportunity should be seized for the promotion of good mental health—not just the prevention of mental illness, but the achievement of wholesome personality and happy, useful living.

Unfortunately the statistics on mental illness show that, if more effective means of prevention are not exercised, a large proportion of today's children are doomed to spend at least part of their lives in institutions for the mentally ill. Mental patients now occupy more than 700,000 hospital beds, or more than one of every two hospital beds, in the United States. A total of close to 9,000,000 people have mental disorders that need treatment. Mental illness is a major factor in crime and juvenile delinquency. Uncounted thousands of all ages have maladjustments which interfere with their usefulness and happiness. Anything which can be done to prevent mental illness and to mitigate maladjustment deserves the fullest support.

Scientific investigation in psychology and education has taught us much about the development of children, relationships between in-

3

dividuals, relationships between groups, conditions favorable to learning, effective methods of instruction, and methods of evaluating what has been accomplished. Teachers and school administrators have long been applying the results of research in these areas. The school psychologist, working intimately with teachers and administrators, contributes his more-specialized knowledge to the solution of problems affecting all the children in the school. Much has also been learned about the early discovery of difficulties in schoolwork and in personality adjustment and ways of overcoming them. Some outstanding failures among young people still originate in their schooling, but, rather than discouraging us, this should emphasize the need to apply psychology in the effort to reduce such failures in the future. A psychologist who is specially trained in psychology can use his skill in assisting individual children to overcome many kinds of difficulties and to make the most of their abilities. He can help teachers use the knowledge of today to promote the best development of good mental health for all children.

THE DEMAND AND THE SHORTAGE

The number of school psychologists that would be desirable for a school enrollment of 45,000,000 children is at present a matter of guesswork. There has been so little experience with adequate service that no one can say with certainty how many could be effectively employed. Estimates of the proper ratio vary from one school psychologist for every 1,000 pupils to one for every 3,000. The materials gathered for the Thayer Conference show that, whereas a few favored districts and individual schools with enrollments of 1,000 or less are served by full-time school psychologists, there are many more where the ratio is one school psychologist to 5,000 or more children. And there are still more places where no school psychologist is immediately available.

Even the ratio of one school psychologist to every 3,000 children indicates a potential demand for more than 15,000 school psychologists. But these figures are academic. The important fact is that there are now, and will be for the immediate future at least, far too few qualified school psychologists to meet current demands.

The membership in the Division of School Psychologists of the American Psychological Association (Division 16 of the APA) gives an idea of the present situation. In 1948, Division 16 had 88 members, of whom 31 were Fellows and 57 Associates. In 1954 there were 314 members, of whom 81 were Fellows and 233 Associates. The 1954 requirements for membership were, for Associates the M.A. degree and two years' experience as a school psychologist, and for Fellows the doctor's degree and five years of experience. Obviously many people working in the field of school psychology have not joined Division 16.

A nation-wide survey was made by the Committee on Certification and Training, Division 16, during the school year 1953-1954 in preparation for the Thayer Conference. This survey was conducted under the chairmanship of Dr. Beatrice Lantz. One thousand and two individuals were found to be serving as school psychological personnel, but it was quickly apparent that not all of these had functions that were primarily in school psychology. Even among the 628 who were reported as working as school psychologists some lacked the special training which is ordinarily required. But other surveys show that the number of school psychological personnel is considerably larger than either the membership in Division 16 or the Conference survey would indicate. Within the past two years the following figures have been obtained from widely scattered states and metropolitan areas: 206 in New York State, 98 in Ohio, 62 in Chicago, 44 in Milwaukee County, 40 in Connecticut, 21 in Washington, D.C., 18 in Iowa, and 16 in Providence, R.I., a total of 505 in these 8 areas alone. The fact remains that there is an acute shortage of qualified school psychologists.

THE LIMITED OPPORTUNITIES FOR TRAINING

One reason for the shortage of school psychologists is the limited opportunities which exist for their training. A survey by questionnaire of universities and colleges which might be expected to offer training was conducted for the Conference by Dr. Bruce Moore. The responses made it evident that although courses and even degrees were offered, there were few real programs; or they were still very nebulous.

Eighteen institutions submitted fairly complete information, although not all have formalized programs. In ten of these institutions, the program of training was offered jointly by the department of psychology and the department or school of education; in seven, by the psychology department; and in one, by the department of education. Only five of these institutions have formal programs leading to the doctorate, but in five additional universities it is possible for a student to work out a special program for either the Ph.D. or the Ed.D. All of the eighteen appear to offer training at the subdoctoral level.

The responses to the questionnaires showed an interest in training programs for school psychologists. Some institutions asked for help in making plans. When the program at the University of Illinois was established in 1953, it was reported in the *New York Times* as of special interest and the first of its kind.

INADEQUATE CERTIFICATION AND CLASSIFICATION

A Conference survey by Dr. T. Ernest Newland showed that only 20 states and the District of Columbia have certification regulations governing school psychological personnel. In other words, at the time of the survey, anyone might be employed to give "psychological" service in the schools of more than half of the states. He might perform any kind of service and be called by any title. The Conference survey of school psychological personnel revealed 75 different titles. In the states where the duties and qualifications of school psychologists are prescribed by law or by certification, the requirements differ so radically as to make it very difficult to plan training that would be satisfactory in all localities. One of the purposes of the Conference was to suggest standards of training and certification which would be generally acceptable.

THE NEED TO MAINTAIN STANDARDS

School psychologists are in a position to see both the demand for qualified personnel and the lack of such personnel to meet the needs. They are concerned lest psychological services deteriorate because poorly-trained workers are drawn in to fill the vacuum. The well-trained and conscientious school psychologist believes it to be important to the public and to his profession that his fellow psychologists in his school system and in neighboring school systems shall be well-trained and give good service. Poor service by unqualified people calling themselves school psychologists not only brings the whole profession into disrepute but, more serious, endangers children. If parents and administrators are disappointed in their expectations, the available funds will certainly be allotted to other purposes. It is essential that school psychologists and school superintendents recognize the urgency of the situation. It is not too much to say that the improvement of mental health and mental hygiene in the United States rests in a major way upon the work of the schools and therefore in part upon the qualifications and training of those who become school psychologists. This idea underlay the organization and the deliberations of the Thayer Conference.

II.

The Organization of the Thayer Conference

SEVERAL studies of the functions, qualifications, training, and certification of school psychological workers have been made by the Division of School Psychologists of the APA. Considerable progress has been made in studying the field, but it has not been possible to reach agreement on certain of the major issues.

The lack of sufficient well-trained personnel to meet the demand for psychological services in the schools and the paucity of training opportunities presented a situation which seemed so urgent to Newland that he asked a few school psychologists to meet while the APA was in session in Washington in September, 1952. Following this meeting, the Committee on Certification and Training, Division 16, proposed a conference to study the qualifications and training of school psychologists.

The plans for the conference were based on the experience of the clinical psychologists with the Boulder Conference in 1949. The clinical psychologists were faced with a demand from the Veterans Administration for many more clinical psychologists to work in improving the mental health of veterans of World War II. The situation required that universities develop goals and policies, find or train staff members, and expand their facilities for training clinical psychologists. In 1947 a committee of the APA recommended a plan for a graduate training program. In 1949 the APA held a conference at Boulder, Colorado, supported by the United States Public Health Service. Seventy persons responsible for training clinical psychologists met for two weeks to review the training being given and to make plans for future training. A report of the conference, edited by Professor Victor C. Raimy, of the University of Colorado, was published in 1950 in a volume called *Training in Clinical Psychology* (149). The Boulder conference and its report established a precedent which school psychologists thought would be valuable to follow as a means of setting generally acceptable standards for the functions, qualifications, and training of school psychologists.

A proposal for a conference on school psychology was presented

8

to the Education and Training Board of the APA in October, 1952, by Dr. Frances A. Mullen, President of Division 16. She requested that the E & T Board sponsor the conference and obtain funds to finance it. With the approval of the Board of Directors of the APA, the E & T Board submitted the proposal to the Public Health Service, United States Department of Health, Education, and Welfare. In June, 1953, the Public Health Service agreed to the proposal and made the funds available.

Upon the agreement of the Public Health Service, Professor E. Lowell Kelly, chairman of the E & T Board, immediately appointed a steering committee, consisting of five persons nominated by the E & T Board and five persons nominated by Division 16. These members were:

Edward S. Bordin, University of Michigan
Dale B. Harris, Institute of Child Welfare, University of Minnesota
Nicholas Hobbs, George Peabody College
Noble H. Kelley, Southern Illinois University
Samuel A. Kirk, University of Illinois
Beatrice Lantz, Los Angeles County Public Schools
Bertha M. Luckey, Cleveland Public Schools
Bruce V. Moore, Education and Training Board
Frances A. Mullen, Chicago Public Schools
T. Ernest Newland, University of Illinois

The E & T Board gave the Steering Committee the task of planning the Conference, together with the necessary preliminary activities and the publication of a report. Dr. Max M. Levin and Dr. Jerry W. Carter, Jr., of the Public Health Service, worked with the Committee as observers and consultants and attended the Conference as guests. Moore, Mullen, and Newland served as an executive committee.

CHOICE AND QUALIFICATIONS OF PARTICIPANTS

The Steering Committee selected the participants so as to ensure a balanced representation of areas of the country, psychological fields of interest, school psychological service at various levels, and experience in training school psychologists. Every effort was made to secure participants who, because they were working as school psychologists or because their work had bearing upon the functions of school psychologists, would be sensitive to the many problems in this area. The final list consisted of 48 persons, including a classroom teacher, a school physician, a school social worker, and a psychiatrist who is serving in a child-guidance clinic. In addition, Dr. Jack R. Ewalt, Commissioner, Department of Mental Health, Massachusetts, and Professor of Psychiatry, Harvard Medical School, and Dr. Palmer L. Ewing, Superintendent of Schools, Buffalo, New York, addressed the Conference and attended the opening sessions.

Of the participants, 9 are now school psychologists, and 12 others had served as school psychologists in the past. Others have or have had as their primary responsibility: 9, supervision of school psychologists; 17, training of school psychologists; 12, special education; 11, school administration; 16, classroom teaching; 11, teacher education; and 1, educational research.

Sixteeen of the participants are now clinical psychologists and 14 others have served as clinical psychologists in the past. Other fields of psychology were represented by 11 from educational psychology, 6 from experimental psychology, 13 from child development, 11 from counseling, 13 from private practice, and 14 from mental health.

Fifteen of the participants are located in public schools, 1 in a private school, 2 in state departments of education, 22 in colleges or universities, 3 in the National Institute of Mental Health, 1 in a department of health, 1 at the Crippled Children's Commission, 1 in the Department of Education, UNESCO, Paris, 1 in the central office of the APA, and 1 in private practice.

The geographical representation was from Massachusetts to California, and from Florida to the State of Washington, with one participant from Canada and one from Paris, France. All the divisions of the APA were represented except the Division on Esthetics and the Division of Psychologists in Public Service. Several participants were members of more than one division of the APA. In all there were 97 memberships in the divisions. The largest numbers of members were in the following divisions: Clinical and Abnormal Psychology—27; School Psychologists—16; Childhood and Adolescence—14; Counseling Psychology—12; Educational Psychology—8. Thirty-six of the participants were Fellows of the APA, 6 were Associates, and 6 non-APA members. Thirty-two were Diplomates of the American Board of Examiners in Professional Psychology: 28 in Clinical Psychology, 3 in Counseling Psychology, and 1 in Industrial Psychology. Sixteen were non-diplomates.

The highest degrees obtained by the participants were as follows: Ph.D., 39; M.A., 4; M.D., 2; E.D., 1; M.S., 1; Ph.B., 1. These degrees were obtained from 24 institutions. The largest numbers were from the University of Iowa, 7; Ohio State University, 5; Teachers College, Columbia, 5; University of Chicago, 5; University of Minnesota, 4. There were one or two from seventeen other universities, widely scattered from Connecticut to California. The major subjects listed for degrees were: psychology, 27; educational psychology, 6; clinical psychology, 3; child development, 3; exceptional children, 2; psychology and guidance, 1; psychology and child welfare, 1; education, 1. The major subjects for the degrees held by the two physicians, the school social worker and the classroom teacher were in their respective fields.

OBJECTIVE OF THE CONFERENCE

The objective of the Conference was stated as the production of a definite statement about the functions, qualifications, and training of school psychologists. It was hoped that such a statement would carry sufficient prestige to influence:

1. The school psychologist in working out his own role in schools.

2. The employer of the school pyschologist, who may need guidance in the criteria for selecting qualified psychologists, defining their duties, knowing what outcomes to expect, and providing the situation in which a school psychologist can grow while employed.

3. University departments of psychology and education providing training for school psychologists.

4. Other professional persons who may be insufficiently aware of the services to be expected of a well-trained school psychologist.

It was the function of this Conference to determine:

1. The realistically possible and desirable role of the psychologist in the schools.

2. The duties and functions of such psychologists.

3. The knowledge, skills, and competencies required of the person who is to carry out those duties.

4. The outlines of a desirable and realistic training program.

Mullen reported to Division 16 in a newsletter in June, 1954:

It is not hoped or desired that the conference will attain complete agreement on all issues, although through the discussion process much synthesis of conflicting views may take place. Consensus will be sought where possible. Whenever differences of opinion remain after thorough exploration, the published report of the conference will seek to present both sides and to clarify the issues, not merely to present a majority point of view.

SELECTION OF TOPICS

Division 16 submitted a list of topics for discussion in the proposal for the Conference. The Steering Committee, using this list as a basis, evolved eleven main topics. Individual members of the Committee grouped specific questions under each of the eleven topics and sent them to the Chairman of the Steering Committee. He combined these into a four-page sheet. This was printed and sent to the 296 school psychologists who were members of Division 16 at that time. It was sent also to an approximately equal number of persons named by state directors of school psychological and special-education programs, persons named by each of the state and regional psychological associations, and other interested persons. They were asked to criticize, revise, and simplify the tentative list of topics, to indicate the more important of the critical issues and any that needed little attention, and to make comments and suggestions. After six weeks, 175 responses had been received. From these responses a list of issues and propositions on the functions, qualifications, and training of school psychologists was drafted by Moore, revised by the Steering Committee, and circulated to the participants two months before the Conference (see Appendix C).

PREPARATION OF MATERIAL PRECEDING THE CONFERENCE

The advance preparation for the Conference consisted of "grass roots" discussions, surveys, collection of pertinent reports, and assembling of a bibliography. Discussions on the issue involved were held during the 1953 APA convention, at a number of state and regional psychological meetings during the year, at the 1953 and 1954 conventions of the International Council for Exceptional Children, and at meetings of school administrators. The following surveys were made:

Newland collected facts about state certification and about laws concerning the work of the school psychologists.

Moore made a survey of the training now being offered in colleges and universities.

Lantz, chairman of a committee of the Division of School Psychologists, assisted by area chairmen Gertrude P. Driscoll, Bertha M. Luckey, George Meyer, Frances A. Mullen, and Thelma G. Voorhis, sent out a questionnaire to members of the Division and to key people throughout the country who might know of, or where to find out about, psychologists now at work in the schools. Three thousand five hundred questionnaires were distributed. Of the returns, 628 proved to be usable for analysis. The survey provided information about the following items: number of school psychological personnel; level of school organization in which they served; number of years of experience; ranking of the functions of the school psychologist in order of their importance; training; and certification.

Each Conference member was sent a list of questions which he was requested to ask one or more superintendents in his area. This provided information about what 29 individual superintendents and two groups of superintendents from 17 states and one Canadian city thought of the functions, qualifications, and training of school psychologists.

Harris compiled a bibliography and abstracts of pertinent materials and of appropriate reports of committees or surveys which had been made previously. Dr. Ethel Cornell used these materials to compile a list of the functions of school psychologists mentioned in the literature.

PLAN OF OPERATION AT THE CONFERENCE

The Conference was held at the Hotel Thayer, West Point, New York, from August 22 to August 31, 1954. The first day was devoted to organization and to the addresses by Ewalt ("Potential Impact of the Public-School Psychologist on Community Mental Health"—see Chapter V) and Ewing ("The Public School's Expectation of the School Psychologist"). One evening Dr. William D. Wall, Department of Education, UNESCO, spoke on "School Psychological Services in Europe" (see Appendix A). Another evening the school social worker, the classroom teacher, the physician, and the psychiatrist discussed their work in relation to the school psychologist and what they saw as his functions.

A whole day was devoted to a discussion of each of the five issues which had been circulated to the participants two months previously. These issues were: definition of the functions; specification of competencies; selection, training, and experience; administrative and professional relationships; and professional development, recognition, and accreditation.

The participants were divided into four groups, and each group discussed the same one of the five issues. The participants were assigned to different groups each day. One participant was assigned to be chairman of his group, another to be secretary. The duties of chairman and secretaries were rotated so that each member of the Conference shared in these responsibilities. The chairman of each group reported briefly at the beginning of each afternoon session, so that everyone might know about the thinking of all the groups. After each day's discussion, the chairman and secretary of each group met with a member of the Steering Committee, who was assigned the task of preparing a brief summary of the work of the four sections on that particular issue.

It was evident at the end of the sixth day that there was remarkable agreement on many of the aspects of the functions and training of school psychologists. There were some difficult issues on which common understanding and agreement had not been reached. These were listed by the Steering Committee, and the list was mimeographed and distributed. During the seventh day the participants read the reports of the preceding days with these critical problems in mind. If they thought any statements were not clear or if they disagreed with any of them, they were encouraged to write their revisions as concisely and forcefully as possible. Some of these revisions have been used by the editor as a basis for statements of conflicting points of view. The last two days were devoted to the discussion of these critical issues. A summary of the conclusions of the Conference is presented in Chapter XVIII.

A GROWING FIELD

The Conference members were aware that they were breaking ground in a new field. The remark was frequently made that all recommendations were tentative and could not be made for any extended period. There was full realization that varied developments will take place as school psychologists, administrators, and the staffs of training institutions exert pressures, are subjected to pressures, meet opportunities, or find satisfactions at certain levels of achievement. School psychology is a fast-growing field and will change rapidly with changes in psychology, in education, and in society as a whole.

The discussion about the functions and training of the school psychologist outlined such broad qualifications and competencies that no one person could possibly have them all. The Conference dealt with ideals. It set up requirements for the field rather than for an individual.

Appreciation of the Pioneers

The members of the Conference, during their discussions, gave complete recognition to the fact that many of the fine school psychologists today could not meet current training requirements. For example, the number of psychologists who had a period of internship 30 or 40 years ago or as late as World War II is very limited. There was every appreciation of the work which the pioneers had already done. Some of these pioneers requested the Conference. They see the necessity of increasing the knowledge and skill of those coming into the profession. They see the need for continued in-service training on the part of everyone in the field. It is the intent of this report to maintain the spirit of professional improvement which has characterized the teaching and psychological professions.

Higher standards should be introduced in such a way as to encourage, stimulate, and motivate psychologists to want to raise their own competence in every possible way. If changes are not thoughtfully planned and carefully executed in every detail, some now employed in the schools may feel threatened, insecure, and bewildered. Not only will this create problems for the individual, but it will also reflect badly on the field of school psychology itself. Procedures taken by those who employ school psychologists should be so planned that it will not appear that the raising of standards is an expression of the inadequacy of the training of those who are employed at present. Actual experience should be given the credit it so frequently deserves. The raising of standards must be recognized as a continuous process and must always remain flexible enough to allow for individual differences.

III.

The Development of School Psychology

DURING the Conference's discussions of the functions of school psychologists, one group agreed that "It might be desirable to have a section on historical perspective." They thought this would serve to show the continuing development of the profession in serving accepted aims of education and the need and possibility of raising standards of psychological service in the school. Such a history might prove helpful to psychologists, to university committees planning the training of school psychologists, and to teachers and school administrators. This chapter therefore calls attention to the various movements in psychology and education which have contributed to the profession of school psychology, and shows how this profession serves the generally accepted aims of education. The rather full bibliography will serve to help interested readers supplement this necessarily brief treatment.

THE DEVELOPMENT OF SPECIAL CLASSES

The development of school psychological services is closely connected with the development of special classes for children who are markedly different from the majority of children, and particularly with classes for mentally retarded children. Many state boards of education have long subsidized such classes provided the selection of the children is based at least in part on a psychological examination. This arrangement encouraged cities to employ psychological examiners and thus stimulated the growth of other psychological services.

Soon after separate grades became the rule in the United States, ungraded classes were established for truants and "incorrigible" children. New Haven, Connecticut, set up a class in 1871 to provide for "scores of contumacious aggressors" who were running wild on the streets and becoming a "public nuisance" (14). These ungraded classes were soon found to be too ungraded. Some of the children were truants and incorrigible, but there were also children who did not speak English and children who were mentally retarded. By 1898 the New Haven superintendent was recommending a centrally located

16

school for children who were "abnormally deficient mentally, or feeble-minded" (15).

There is some doubt as to the exact dates at which the first special classes were opened but no doubt about their rapid growth. As far as can be ascertained, Providence started a class in 1896, Springfield in 1897, New Haven in 1898, Boston in 1899, Chicago in 1900, New York City in 1900, Philadelphia in 1901, and Los Angeles in 1902 (cp. 82, pp. 185-186). The Office of Education reports that by 1922 there were special classes for mentally retarded children enrolling a total of 23,252 pupils in 133 cities in 23 states (139, p. 7). By 1953 the figures had grown to 113,565 pupils in 1,244 cities in 48 states (142, p. 19).

These same reports show the development of special classes for other types of exceptional children. For example, in 1932 the number of mentally gifted children in special classes was reported as 1,834. By 1953 there were 22,916 in such classes.

THE FIRST PSYCHOLOGICAL CLINIC

Some people think of clinical psychology as a development in the field of mental health—or illness—entirely separate from education. That this is far from the truth is shown by Dr. Lightner Witmer's account of the first clinic (33, pp. 342-349). Witmer was in charge of the psychological laboratory which his first instructor in psychology, James McKeen Cattell, had established at the University of Pennsylvania. He was interested in retardation and as early as 1889 had tutored a boy who was deficient in English. Witmer writes:

The second case to attract my interest was a boy fourteen years of age, who was brought to the laboratory of psychology by his grade teacher. He was one of those children of great interest to the teacher, known to the profession as a chronic bad speller. His teacher . . . was at that time a student of psychology at the University of Pennsylvania; she was imbued with the idea that a psychologist should be able, through examination, to ascertain the causes of a deficiency in spelling and to recommend the appropriate pedagogical treatment for its amelioration or cure.

With this case, in March 1896, the work of the psychological clinic was begun. At that time I could not find that the science of psychology had ever addressed itself to the ascertainment of the causes and treatment of a deficiency in spelling. Yet here was a simple developmental defect of memory; and memory is a mental process of which the science of psychology is supposed to furnish the only authoritative knowledge.

It appeared to me that if psychology was worth anything to me or to others it should be able to assist the efforts of a teacher in a retarded case of this kind (33, pp. 344-345).

The boy was given both mental and physical examinations. Witmer found that the chronic bad spelling was due to defective eyesight. When this defect had been corrected, the boy was able to learn to spell. In the spring of 1896 Witmer saw several other children who were retarded in general or in some special subject. He worked with individual children for a certain number of hours each week, thus establishing the clinic which is still in operation.

In December, 1896, he presented a paper before the APA in which he described a scheme of practical work in psychology:

The proposed plan of organization comprised:

1. The investigation of the phenomena of mental development in school children, as manifested more particularly in mental and moral retardation, by means of the statistical and clinical methods.

2. A psychological clinic, supplemented by a training school in the nature of a hospital school, for the treatment of all classes of children suffering from retardation or physical defects interfering with school progress.

3. The offering of practical work to those engaged in the professions of teaching and medicine, and to those interested in social work, in the observation and training of normal and retarded children.

4. The training of students for a new profession—that of the psychological expert, who should find his career in connection with the school system, through the examination and treatment of mentally and morally retarded children, or in connection with the practice of medicine (33, p. 346).

In 1907 Witmer wrote:

While the field of clinical psychology is to some extent occupied by the physician, especially by the psychiatrist, and while I expect to rely in a great measure upon the educator and social worker for the more important contributions to this branch of psychology, it is nevertheless true that none of these has quite the training necessary for this kind of work. For that matter, neither has the psychologist, unless he has acquired this training from other sources than the usual course of instruction in psychology. In fact, we must look forward to the training of men to a new profession which will be exercised more particularly in connection with educational problems, but for which the training of the psychologist will be a prerequisite.

For this reason not a small part of the work of the laboratory of psychology at the University of Pennsylvania for the past ten years has been devoted to the training of students in child psychology, and especially in the clinical method. The greater number of these students have been actively engaged in the profession of teaching (33, p. 349).

EARLY TESTS

School psychology has been closely connected with the development of the testing movement. In 1896, four years after the APA was founded, a committee called "the Committee on Physical and Mental Tests" gave a report. They had drawn up a series of tests which they regarded "as especially appropriate for college students tested in a psychological laboratory. The same series would also be suitable for the general public and, with some omissions and slight modifications, for school children" (80, p. 43). The suggested tests were presented in five printed pages in outline form under 27 headings. It was stated that the whole series could be given in one hour.

Thorndike published his *Mental and Social Measurements* in 1904 (173). He said in the preface: "It is the aim of this book to introduce students to the theory of mental measurements and to provide them with such knowledge and practice as may assist them to follow critically quantitative evidence and argument and to make their own researches exact and logical." It was planned for students of economics, sociology, and education as well as students of psychology.

THE FIRST PUBLIC-SCHOOL DEPARTMENT OF CHILD STUDY

In the annual report of the Chicago Board of Education in 1898, Dr. W. S. Christopher, Frank J. Loesch, and other board members reported a survey of the physical and mental condition of school children which they had made. The results demonstrated the need for a continuing Department of Child Study. This was established in 1899, only three years after Witmer's clinic was started. Dr. Fred W. Smedley was appointed the first director, with a staff of two assistants. They made surveys of all pupils in the schools.

The annual report of the Chicago Board of Education for the year 1899-1900 declared that "the child-study investigation in the Chicago schools has met with much favorable criticism both in this country and in Europe," and that with the possible exception of the Pedagogic Laboratory in Antwerp, Belgium, Chicago's board was the first public board of education "to establish in the school system under its charge a special . . . Department of Child Study and Pedagogic investigation" (129).

On April 4, 1900, Smedley was authorized to open a "Psychophysical laboratory" on Saturdays in the central office, since he and his staff were busy in the schools on other days. Backward and difficult children were to be brought to the laboratory by their principals. One principal took fifteen pupils to the laboratory and "after obtaining the results of a thorough investigation of them, very wisely asked that an ungraded room be established in her school for their benefit" (127).

From 1902 to 1935 Dr. Daniel P. Macmillan was the director of the clinic. During these years, procedures for the individual study and diagnosis of children were developed rapidly by the psychological profession and became standard elements in the child-study program. The Bureau contributed to the establishment of provisions in the Chicago Schools for many other types of handicapped children. In the late Twenties, clinics were established to experiment with psychological testing and counseling techniques on a broad scale in the high schools and in their contributing elementary and junior high schools.

THE SCHOOL AND THE JUVENILE DELINQUENT

Throughout 1954, various newspapers and magazines published articles describing the schools as a hotbed of juvenile delinquency. A reader might easily believe that juvenile crime was a new phenomenon, the product of modern methods of education. The least of the implications is that the schools should do something about it.

We have seen how the "scores of contumacious aggressors" wandering the streets of New Haven in 1871 resulted in the establishment of an ungraded class to which truants and incorrigibles were assigned. Similar classes were conducted in New York City until recently. And the school truant officer, with his policeman's badge, was a staff fixture in most city school systems. He frequently doubled as a probation officer. Now New York and other cities try to have cases involving truancy and delinquency handled by staff members who are trained social workers. These modern "truant officers" collaborate closely with the school psychologists. The emphasis is not on simply enforcing attendance but on discovering and remedying the causes of the child's difficulties. A psychological examination is routine procedure.

Much of the credit for this change in attitude goes to Dr. William Healy and Dr. Augusta Bronner. Healy was the director of the first clinic established in connection with a juvenile court, the Chicago Juvenile Psychopathic Institute, which was organized in 1909 (89,

p. 809). The plan of organization was the work of Miss Julia Lathrop (later Chief of the Children's Bureau in Washington). Bronner was a psychologist on the staff. Healy and Bronner worked together at the Cook County Institute when this was opened in 1914, at the Judge Baker Guidance Center in Boston, and at the Yale Institute of Human Relations. In 1917 Healy wrote:

. . . there are many besides parents who fail to understand the foundations on which delinquent careers are built. Teachers, pastors, and physicians, to whom the laity go so frequently for advice on mental and moral questions, have not always adequate knowledge of the springs of conduct. These things are not taught as yet in theological and medical schools, and are only just finding a place in psychological departments of universities and teachers' colleges. It would seem, however, that the phase of applied psychology which has to do with human behavior should be essential in all these disciplines (**89,** p. 6).

THE DEVELOPMENT OF THE BINET TESTS

The growth of special classes for mentally retarded children resulted in a continuing demand for better means of selecting such children, not only in this country but in Europe. In Paris, Alfred Binet and Henri Simon had been trying out mental tests with school children. It was natural that they should be asked to devise some way of identifying retarded children. Their work resulted in the three Binet-Simon Scales published in 1905, 1908, and 1911.

In 1908 Dr. Henry H. Goddard, Director of Research at the Laboratory, The Training School at Vineland, New Jersey, translated the 1905 Binet Scale and made some adaptations for American children (**72**). In 1910 he published a translation of the 1908 Binet Scale. In 1911 he published his own version of the 1908 Scale for use with children in the United States (**83**). He had developed this in working with 2,000 public-school children in Vineland, New Jersey. Hundreds of teachers, psychologists, and social workers were interested in the tests and visited the Laboratory. They heard lectures by Goddard and saw him demonstrate the tests. Many research students worked for a year at Vineland under Goddard's direction, and so may be said to have been the first "interns" in psychology.

Dr. Lewis M. Terman's 1916 Stanford Revision of the Binet-Simon Intelligence Scale was for many years the individual intelligence test most widely used. It is instructive to note Terman's background. He took his B.A. in 1898 from the Danville Normal College, Danville,

Indiana, and was a fellow in psychology and education at Clark University, where he took his Ph.D. in 1905. Both before and after taking his doctor's degree he served as a high-school principal. A host of teachers, administrators, and psychologists owe their first acquaintance with the ideas and ideals of intelligence testing to Terman's revisions of the Binet and to his books, particularly *The Measurement of Intelligence* (171).

Some individuals who undertook the use of Binet tests in the schools were psychologists with a knowledge of the tests which had been developed earlier. They used the Binet tests in an appropriate setting of case-study material and tests, such as the Sequin Form Board and the Pintner-Paterson Performance Scale. Other individuals were teachers who were interested in the tests and devoted time and study to acquiring an adequate knowledge and background for psychological work.

An acquaintance with Binet tests was also acquired by some teachers who stopped with the knowledge obtained in a six-weeks course in a summer session. They were then authorized to give Binet tests to select candidates for a special class. This was often their own class. IQ's were sometimes accepted as established facts by those educators and testers who had little psychological training and little understanding of the variations and limitations of test scores. There are some teachers who are still working in the same way. One might label this "arrested development." This sort of testing has made the term "Binet tester" one of opprobrium to the well-trained psychologist or educator. This use of the Binet should not blind us to the advance made in understanding children and helping to solve problems in education which this and other tests have brought about and extended to all children.

Another heritage from the early days of Binet testing is hard to overcome. The tests were used originally with mentally defective children. Though psychological work has developed far beyond this, many parents and possibly a few teachers still associate psychological examinations with retardation only.

GROUP TESTS

The value of individual intelligence tests was demonstrated and the possibility of adopting the technique for group administration occurred to psychologists. Dr. Arthur S. Otis was one of those who was experimenting in 1916-17. The urgent need for large-scale evaluation of men's abilities was precipitated by World War I, and a committee of psychologists, using the Otis material, devised the group tests used in the United States Army (122). The dramatic success of this battery of tests, called the Army Alpha Examination, gave great impetus to the use of standardized group tests. Within five years, about fifty such tests were published. Publication and wide use of group tests has continued since that time.

Educational-achievement tests were devised during the same years by many of the psychologists who worked on the group intelligence tests. They had been preceded by other tests and scales such as the Stone Arithmetic Reasoning Test, 1908, Courtis Arithmetic Computation Test, 1909, the Thorndike Scale for Measuring the Handwriting of Children, 1910, the Ayres Spelling Scale, 1915, Woody Arithmetic Scales, 1916, and Monroe Diagnostic Arithmetic Tests, 1917 (104, pp. 316, 323; 158, p. 5). The tests were generally devised by psychologists, but they were commonly used by educators.

The entire testing movement served to point out the wide range of abilities and achievement in children. Schools became more than ever conscious of the differences and increased their efforts to provide for them. Remedial teachers were appointed to work with children with special disabilities. In some cities remedial work with children progressed to the point where special clinics, such as the reading clinics in Chicago and in New York City, were established.

THE TERM "SCHOOL PSYCHOLOGIST"

The July-August, 1942, number of the *Journal of Consulting Psychology* was devoted to the school psychologist. The first article (169, p. 173) speaks of the term "school psychologist" as about twenty years old. The psychologist is described as brought into the schools to give Binet tests and group intelligence tests developed from those used in the first World War. It mentions that the first use of the term "school psychologist" probably appeared in the published literature in 1923 (98). In an article (179, p. 310) in the November-December, 1942, number, Wallin corrects the impression given in the earlier article that case work and the use of psychological tests were recent developments in school psychology. He cites the work of school psychologists in Chicago, the establishment of the child-study department in the Rochester public schools in 1907 and the Cincinnati public-school psychological laboratory in 1911.

Dr. Arnold Gesell says of his own appointment as a school psychologist: "In 1915 the Connecticut State Board of Education appointed a School Psychologist to make mental examinations of backward and defective children in rural, village, and urban schools, and to devise methods for their better care in the public schools. Connecticut was the first state of the Union to create a position of this kind" (57, p. v).

The Mental-Hygiene Movement and the Child-Guidance Clinic

A Mind that Found Itself (27), by Clifford Beers, was published in 1908. As a direct result, the Connecticut Mental Hygiene Society was founded in that year, and the National Mental Hygiene Society the following year. The first number of the *Mental Hygiene* magazine was published in 1917. The first article describes the National Committee's surveys of the public care and treatment of the insane and feebleminded. "The time has now probably arrived when this National Committee, besides following up work already begun, may well give serious attention to plans for the extension of its work to other domains" (24, p. 4). The first two numbers of this volume have articles about a survey of a school group to discover the number of subnormal children, lines of investigation for the discovery of borderline defectives, an evaluation of mental tests, and methods of discovering children who need special care. The first number of the second volume has an article on the mental health of the normal child.

The mental-hygiene movement and the emphasis on the importance of the early years of life and the "whole child" served to focus attention on the school as the first institution where work in mental hygiene might be done and on the work which the school psychologists were already doing. As a result some mental-hygiene and family-welfare societies collaborated with school psychologists to secure psychiatric and social-work service for children.

In 1922 the Commonwealth Fund announced a five-year demonstration program for the prevention of juvenile delinquency. Dr. George Stevenson says the term "child-guidance clinic" was not coined until 1922 although some of the essentials of the clinic plan had been started in Witmer's clinic (1896) and Healy's Chicago Institute (1909). The first clinic in the demonstration program opened in St. Louis in 1922. The staff consisted of one psychiatrist, one psychologist, and one psychiatric social worker, the team concept which has become so familiar. In Minneapolis, in 1923, the public-school visiting teachers did case work in a clinic. When the demonstration there was completed in November, 1924, three projects arose: a child-guidance clinic under the direction of the Board of Education; a child-guidance clinic in St. Paul; and a mental-hygiene demonstration for the state conducted by the University of Minnesota. The professor of psychology of the university served as a staff member (160).

Stevenson, in discussing the service of the psychologist to the clinic, says:

Having been trained, usually, as an educational specialist, he comes to the clinic with a better knowledge of the techniques of learning and of teaching, a greater familiarity with the way schoolmen think and act, and more awareness of the possibilities and limitations of the school, than either of the other members of the team. Naturally, therefore, he is qualified to take the lead in making contacts between the clinic and the public school system and is sometimes in a position, through offering valued technical help to the schools, to open the way for a wider range of service by the clinic. For the same reasons, the psychologist is the logical choice to carry the burden of treatment when the problem centers in learning processes or in school achievement. A number of psychologists serving the clinics have made themselves authorities in the field of reading and other special disabilities and are able to give and supervise special treatment of these problems as an important contribution to the child's adjustment (160, p. 120).

By 1938 the number of communities served by child-guidance clinics was approximately 650 in 34 different states. In May of that year the Commissioner of Education invited to Washington a group of 14 specialists active in clinical service for school children, to explore some of the major problems in child-guidance programs in school systems. A bulletin was published in 1939 describing the types of clinical organization for child guidance in communities and school systems of various sizes, the trends up to that time, and the direction which future development was likely to take (117).

THE GUIDANCE MOVEMENT

There may be some question as to whether guidance is a division of school psychology or school psychology a division of guidance. Witness Brewer's famous dictum, "education is guidance." Teachers College, Columbia University, offers its school-psychology program as an area in the Department of Guidance. Many school guidance counselors have little by little broadened their work and increased their training until they have become qualified school psychologists. The blurring of the boundary is natural. The good guidance counselor must be a specialist in the use of the results of tests which, even when they do not concern intelligence and personality, are modeled on the individual and group tests created by psychologists. He must be alert to the implications for mental health which are inherent in the correct choice of a vocation or an education. Students and parents who consult him are likely to ask questions about a wide variety of personal problems. Principals, deans, and teachers tend to send him students who are not adjusting well either to their courses or to their fellow students.

Vocational Guidance and the Public Schools (154), a federal pamphlet written in 1918 by W. Carson Ryan (now editor of *Understanding the Child*), and the report, published in 1932, of a subcommittee of the White House Conference on Child Health and Protection (183) describe the development and expansion of guidance. By quoting from the National Vocational Guidance Association, the White House Committee assigns a very broad field to guidance: "Problems of adjustment to health, religion, recreation, to family and friends, to school and to work, may be included under the general term 'guidance.' . . . it becomes evident that vocational guidance cannot be separated from educational guidance" (183, p. 4).

Testing has been recognized as a part of guidance, though not the most important part. In 1942 Brewer wrote:

Does testing come within the scope of vocational guidance? On the one hand "testing is here to stay" in any comprehensive plan of guidance; of that there can be no doubt. On the other hand the act of using a test, questionnaire, or blank does not of itself necessarily contribute to the education of the person filling it out. Therefore it may be argued that a separate agency—a school psychologist or psychometrist—should attend to the testing, furnishing the results (raw scores and comparative statistics) to the vocational counselor. Some students of guidance are strongly for the combination of these duties, stating that only the trained psychologist is competent to make the necessary interpretations of the data revealed by the test results.

Counselors, however, are concerned with many questions to which testing does not apply; moreover, so many counselors are needed that statistical training of all of them would be impossible.

If as seems likely there is to be a division of labor between testing and counseling, the issue will then remain: what relationship will subsist between the two groups? Will the psychologist and statistician serve the counselor, or will they control and direct his work? Or, will the two groups work together as independent experts, both under the general supervision of principals of schools and deans and presidents of colleges?

Experience and analogy would seem to indicate the propriety of a rather definite division of labor. Toolmakers are more expert than tool users, yet they serve the mechanics and do not do their work for them. Psychologists and statisticians will do well to perfect the tools and try these tools out in expert fashion, but they will hardly prescribe how and when these tools will be used, nor can they both make and use the tools as a steady professional task (**32**, pp. 284-285).

THE AIMS OF EDUCATION

The Conference summary of the discussion of the functions of the school psychologist starts: "Before describing the psychologist's role in the schools, we need to make clear our conception of the school's objectives. The major objective of the school is the optimal development of the individual child. This includes the child as a whole, his physical, intellectual, and social resources." The members felt that this volume should include a more detailed statement of the aims of education, both to show how the school psychologist can best cooperate in achieving these aims and to guide future development of the profession.

A large number of statements of the aims of education have been compiled and published by various organizations (**18, 59, 75, 103**). Two statements are quoted here: the goals of elementary education from *Education in the United States of America* issued by the Office of Education (**140**, pp. 15-16), and "The Ten Imperative Needs of Youth" from *Planning for American Youth,* published by the National Association of Secondary-School Principals (**130**, p. 9).

THE GOALS OF ELEMENTARY EDUCATION

American elementary schools are guided in their effort by certain specific objectives which every child is expected to attain in terms of his own abilities.

Every child should be helped to develop a healthy body and sound emotional attitudes.

Every child should become effective in the use of the tools of learning.

Every child should be able to identify and deal with his own personal and social problems.

Every child should develop worth-while recreational and creative interests and abilities.

Every child should have the opportunity to progress in terms of his own abilities.

Every child should be taught to understand the physical and social environment of which he is a part.

Every child should have the opportunity to grow in an understanding of the meaning of democracy as applied to all aspects of living.

THE TEN IMPERATIVE NEEDS OF YOUTH

All youth have certain educational needs in common. All parents can agree that the school should meet these needs, which become the modern goals of education.

1. All youth need to develop saleable skills and those understandings and attitudes that make the worker an intelligent and productive participant in economic life. To this end, most youth need supervised work experience as well as education in the skills and knowledge of their occupations.

2. All youth need to develop and maintain good health and physical fitness and mental health.

3. All youth need to understand the rights and duties of the citizen of a democratic society, and to be diligent and competent in the performance of their obligations as members of the community and citizens of the state and nation, and to have an understanding of the nations and peoples of the world.

4. All youth need to understand the significance of the family for the individual and society and the conditions conducive to successful family life.

5. All youth need to know how to purchase and use goods and services intelligently, understanding both the values received by the consumer and the economic consequences of their acts.

6. All youth need to understand the methods of science, the influence of science on human life, and the main scientific facts concerning the nature of the world and of man.

7. All youth need opportunities to develop their capacities to appreciate beauty, in literature, art, music, and nature.

8. All youth need to be able to use their leisure time well and to budget it wisely, balancing activities that yield satisfactions to the individual with those that are socially useful.

9. All youth need to develop respect for other persons, to grow in their insight into ethical values and principles, to be able to live and work co-operatively with others, and to grow in the moral and spiritual values of life.

10. All youth need to grow in their ability to think rationally, to express their thoughts clearly, and to read and listen with understanding.

THE ROLE OF THE SCHOOL PSYCHOLOGIST

The school psychologist can play a vital part through his own work and through cooperation with the teacher and other school personnel in furthering the achievement of these aims. His training should give him a special part in assisting in the development of mental health and sound emotional attitudes. He can help children solve personal and social problems and learn to live with others. He can discover whether a child is making effective use of the tools of learning and progressing satisfactorily in terms of his own abilities. He can suggest ways of bringing about more satisfactory progress. He can assist in discovering special interests and abilities. The ways in which the Conference felt he could best contribute appear in the next chapter.

IV.

The Functions of School Psychologists

THE summary of the Conference's discussion of the functions of school psychologists is given below. It is followed by excerpts from the materials prepared for the Conference, quotations from the literature, and by accounts of some of the more detailed discussions which preceded and followed the preparation of the summary. The Conference had no intention of bounding school psychology within the limits of present practice. On the contrary, diverse lists of duties found in the materials and sometimes conflicting opinions expressed by Conference members with varied training, experience, and background are offered here in the hope that individuals with differing interests will be attracted to the profession and lead it in a healthy expansion.

THE CONFERENCE SUMMARY

While only the psychologist can perform some of his functions, a large share of his contribution will be in the form of adding to the resources that other school personnel will use. His aim is neither to take over the functions of a classroom teacher nor to endeavor to have the teacher take over the unique functions of the psychologist.

Definition. The school psychologist is a psychologist with training and experience in education. He uses his specialized knowledge of assessment, learning, and interpersonal relationships to assist school personnel to enrich the experience and growth of all children, and to recognize and deal with exceptional children.

Functions. The school psychologist serves in an advisory capacity to school personnel and performs the following functions:

1. Measuring and interpreting the intellectual, social and emotional development of children.

2. Identifying exceptional children and collaborating in the planning of appropriate educational and social placements and programs.

3. Developing ways to facilitate the learning and adjustment of children.

4. Encouraging and initiating research, and helping to utilize research findings for the solution of school problems.

5. Diagnosing educational and personal disabilities, and collaborating in the planning of re-educational programs.

30

Levels.[1] Two levels of functioning and training are recommended. The position of *school psychologist* involves such broad comprehensive preparation at a high level that these responsibilities can be met only with doctoral training or its equivalent. This training should consist of four years of graduate study, one of which should be a year of internship. The position of *psychological examiner* is considered essential. The training for this position should be a two-year graduate program, of which one-half year should be an internship. Such training should equip the examiner to perform many psychological services.

THE DIFFICULTY IN SPECIFYING FUNCTIONS

The members of the Conference were keenly aware of how difficult it is to determine what the school psychologist's functions should be. There has been no substantial body of material to furnish a guide for the profession or the individual. In contrast, the classroom teacher has many aids to help him plan his work and to carry out his activities.

The services required of the school psychologist differ greatly from one community to another. The kind of population may require emphasis on one type of service. School administrators and teachers sometimes have different views of what they want. The services already provided by other staff members will affect what the school psychologist does. Parents and other community leaders will have an influence on what service is offered. The service may have been started at a particular stage of development in the field and be advanced or retarded because of that.

The qualifications and training of the persons employed for school psychological service will also influence the kind and amount of service offered. Some individuals will have a special interest in retarded children, others in gifted children, others in developing a good mental-hygiene point of view. Some will work better with children, others better with teachers. When there is so much work to be done, and so few to do it, the abilities and interests of the employee are sure to bring about emphasis on certain aspects of the work.

[1] Separate titles for the two positions are obviously necessary. There is general agreement that the title *school psychologist* should be used for the psychologist with the doctor's degree. No one title of the many proposed for the individual with more limited training has ever been generally accepted, nor was one discovered at the Conference. The title *psychological examiner* is found in the regulations of several states and was frequently used at the Conference. It is used in this report as a matter of convenience (see Chapter XIV).

THE CONFERENCE SURVEY OF FUNCTIONS

The Conference survey of functions of school psychologists presented an analysis based on reports which were received from 560 school psychologists, representing all sections of the United States and all sizes of districts, from 3 with an average daily attendance of less than 1,000 to 23 with 50,000 or more. Of the psychologists who replied, 453 were employed in 219 school districts in 29 states, 85 were employed by counties, and 8 were employed by 5 states. Fourteen were psychological personnel having supervisory positions in 4 states.

The questionnaire contained a list of functions and asked that each be ranked in order of importance as a present function and then reranked according to the individual's feeling of how the school psychologist should operate to make the greatest contribution to the schools. In all districts, "individual testing—mental, emotional, case studies" ranked first and "interviews—pupils, parents, school personnel, agencies" second in both the reports on present functions and the reports on desirable functions. In general, the reports on other present functions ranked in descending order as follows: "special education program"; "organizing, giving, interpreting group tests"; "clerical (case histories, compiling test data)"; "in-service training of school personnel"; "public relations—speeches, parent-education groups, professional organizations"; "administration and supervision"; "remedial work in basic skills and other areas"; "education programs—help develop curriculum, reports, records"; "research." Desired functions in general followed the same ranking except that "clerical" ranked lower and "education programs" higher. Forty-eight replies mentioned some form of therapy. Also mentioned were staff conferences, follow-up studies, test construction, teaching the mentally retarded, and supervising internes. Individual testing, interviews, special education, group testing, program development, in-service training, public relations, remedial work, and administration and supervision each received top ranking from some school psychologists. The replies from supervisors and from county and state personnel differed from those presented above as one might expect: administration, interviews, and research ranked higher; clerical work, lower.

When the rankings were arranged according to the size of the district in which the psychologist worked, the principal differences were that psychologists in the larger districts had less responsibility for special education and group testing, but spent more time in clerical activities (writing up case studies, compiling test data).

In ranking the functions the school psychologists considered desirable, there was a universal desire for more opportunity for in-service training of teachers and for participation in developing the educational program. There was a general desire to do less clerical work, and some wished to do less in the way of group testing, special education, and administration.

OTHER SURVEYS

Two earlier surveys are generally in line with the Conference survey. In 1950, 205 members of the Division of School Psychologists stated their major functions. Individual testing, conferences, and group testing ranked 1, 2, 3. Also in 1950, the school psychologists in California kept diaries of how their time was allotted (45). Individual testing, conferences, and preparing case histories ranked 1, 2, 3. These three duties accounted for about 70 per cent of all of these California psychologists' time.

PSYCHOLOGICAL WORK IN SAN MATEO COUNTY SCHOOLS

In 1952-53, the two psychologists in the San Mateo County Schools analyzed their work and noted the percentage of time devoted to each type of duty. These percentages appear in the parentheses. The report is given here because it fills in the detail necessarily omitted from the more general surveys.

Case Work. Involves individual psychometrics, classroom observation, child interviews, teacher interviews, parent interviews, conferences with administrators, conferences with other individuals connected with the case, conferences with other agencies such as social welfare, child guidance, probation department, and psychiatrists. We encounter wide extremes in the amount of time spent on cases. Some are referrals for psychometrics only and the minimum amount of time spent for such requests is approximately four hours. Some referrals require extended study of emotional disturbances ranging in severity from mild to extreme. The maximum amount of time spent per case is difficult to estimate but might be as high as twenty-five to thirty hours. Appointments scheduled for one to one and a half hours in length frequently extend to two or three hours in length. An adequate and complete psychological study demands flexibility of this type. In addition to the actual time spent in conferring or testing, the traveling time to and from the place of appointment must be considered.

Most of the psychological study is for the purpose of diagnosis and so recommendations are made for action both for the home and for the school. However, some therapeutic work and counseling is of necessity a part of this study. Also, writing of reports on each case for the referral agency constitutes a very important part of the work. (Dr. A., 60%; Miss B., 72%.)

Work with Programs for the Mentally Retarded. A large part of this program is case work and involves the screening of candidates for admission to special programs. The remainder of the time is spent conferring with the teachers, administrators, and parents, or in classroom observation with resultant reports and conferences. (Dr. A., 12%; Miss B., 12%.)

Professional Consultation. Conferences with other members of the staff concerning particular cases or policies, interviews with staff members of other agencies, talks with psychiatrists or other professional people. (Dr. A., 5%; Miss B., 5%.)

Total of areas involving *mainly* case work: Dr. A., 77%; Miss B., 89%.

Parent and Group Education. Speaking engagements for Parent-Teacher Associations, parent clubs, parent classes, special parent groups connected with specific organizations, discussion groups, AAUW, Mental Health Society, and other interested organizations make up a good part of the mental-hygiene program. (Dr. A., 7%; Miss B., 2%.)

Teacher and Administrator Training. Development of programs for teacher institutes, conferences with administrators on guidance procedures, individual conferences with teachers to discuss personal or classroom problems constitute another part of an over-all mental-hygiene program and/or in-service training. (Dr. A., 5%; Miss B., 1%.)

Professional Growth and/or Participation in Professional Groups. Attendance at such organizations as the Council of Social Agencies, the Committee on Guidance, a two-day conference of the California Association of School Psychologists and Psychometrists, observation of a special-education program in the San Francisco schools, participation in Business Education Day, research in areas pertinent to the profession. (Dr. A., 5%; Miss B., 5%.)

Administrative Work. Special administrative reports, staff meetings, correspondence, telephone conversations, supervision of the keeping of records, making reports for special research projects. (Dr. A., 1%; Miss B., 2%.)

Training of Field Workers in School Psychology. Four field workers have done psychometric work periodically throughout the year. Their work has been closely supervised. Supervision includes observation of test administration, discussion of cases, supervision of scoring procedures and report writing. (Dr. A., 5%; Miss B., 1%.)

Total: Dr. A., 100%; Miss B., 100%.

Functions Described in the Literature

Cornell analyzed the school psychologist's functions which she found described in the books listed in the Conference bibliography. This analysis presents the functions under nine headings, as follows:

A. Diagnostic study of individual children, psychological appraisement and assessment of individuals (integration of information, individual testing, interpretation, and recommendations)—25 references.
B. Special and remedial education—21 references.
C. General contributions to mental health of children and teachers (behavior problems, in-service training of teachers, school mental-health program)—18 references.
D. Classification of pupils, testing, and evaluation—18 references.
E. Therapeutic services to children—12 references.
F. General contribution to school policy (administrative and curriculum problems, teaching procedures)—10 references.
G. Community contacts—7 references.
H. Research—2 references.
I. Administrative duties—1 reference.

School Superintendents' Opinions

Before the Conference the members were asked to interview one or more school superintendents. Among the questions suggested were: What are the functions of the school psychologist as you see them? How do you think a school psychologist can contribute most to a school program? Of the 31 reports of such interviews, 29 were of the interviews with individual superintendents and 2 of interviews with groups of superintendents (one group with 15 in one state and the other with 11 in another state). Most of the superintendents individually interviewed had at least one psychologist on their staffs. Many of the members of the two groups also had psychologists on their staffs or had regular psychological service available. The reports came from areas extending from Connecticut to California and from Florida to Oregon. Twenty-one reports were from cities and 10 (including those from the two groups) were from rural or county school superintendents. There were no discernible differences between the opinions of superintendents from different sizes of communities or different areas. Every superintendent who was interviewed saw the need for school psychologists and was willing to express his views. One superintendent said he would rather have a school psychologist than an assistant superintendent.

The group of 15 consisted of administrative officers of rural schools who had met to consider mental-health problems. The report of their opinions states:

These superintendents all wanted *school* psychological service. Almost half had some psychological service in some of their schools. They all had access to child-guidance clinics conducted by the State Department of Mental Hygiene but found these clinics inadequate for two reasons: the lag between the time a pupil was referred and the time he was seen was too great, sometimes as much as six months; the clinic was not sufficiently related to the school. They wanted school psychologists to do two things: study individual children with emotional problems; help to make teachers more sensitive to the needs of such children in order that something can be done about such problems early.

Twenty-five of the individual reports included a statement to the effect that "the psychologist is a specialist who helps teachers and principals with the educational and adjustment problems of children." Actual work with teachers on individual problems and in-service training of teachers to understand children better and to promote mental hygiene were stressed. The consensus was that the psychologist is a consultant or staff officer, not a line officer.

Testing, including diagnosis and interpretation of test results, was mentioned in 22 reports. Study of the individual child was included by 8 more. Testing was also mentioned very often in answer to the question about how the psychologist could contribute most. One superintendent said: "As a result of his testing, the psychologist should be able to help the teacher see beyond the immediate performance of the child and show her how to interpret this performance in terms of the child's ability."

Some reservations were made about testing as a function. One superintendent said, "I've seen the school psychologist change from a tester of children for special classes to director of special-education services." Another says that the top-level psychologist should not be required to include testing among his duties. Two stated that the school psychologist should not give group tests. Only 4 failed to mention services other than testing which they expected from the school psychologist.

Therapy, treatment, and individual counseling were mentioned by 12, but one felt that the psychologist should do little direct therapy. That the psychologist often refers children to other agencies for treatment is shown by the fact that 9 superintendents say that one of his duties is to act as liaison officer with psychiatric and other services.

Of the superintendents, 14 thought a psychologist should consult on curriculum and instruction; 11 that he should give assistance to parents; 8 that he should advise on over-all policies; 2 that he should make recommendations to teachers for remedial work (but not do remedial teaching himself); 2 that he should engage in public-relations work; 2 that he should conduct research; and 1 that he should help in the selection and promotion of personnel.

The relies to the question about how the psychologist could contribute most to the school can be summarized in the words of one superintendent: "working cooperatively with other school personnel for the welfare of the children, with special emphasis on mental health." Another superintendent said, "Since the aims of mental health and education are practically identical, the school psychologist makes his most important contribution by 'selling' a mental-health point of view to the teacher."

A New York State report on psychological and psychiatric services in the schools includes these comments:

School superintendents are becoming increasingly aware of the part that psychological and psychiatric services can play in bringing about better adjustment in school and in the prevention of mental illness later on in life. Compared to the vast sums spent on the care of the mentally ill, the amount of money needed to provide a foundation level of psychological services in every school district of the state is a small price to pay.

The present study indicates that school superintendents today no longer consider the testing of intelligence and educational achievement to be the most pressing responsibility of the school psychologist. Our data show a growing awareness of the need for psychologists in individual work with pupils and parents. We also find a most encouraging recognition of the services a professionally qualified psychologist may render as a consultant to the entire teaching staff. But most heartening of all our findings is the almost universal recognition by our fellow superintendents of the vital role that the school psychologist can play in the prevention of serious mental illness in later life by promoting the personal, educational, and social adjustment of the children and youth in our schools. The single most important finding is that 90 per cent of our superintendents believe that our present provision for psychological services in our schools is inadequate. We are hardly beginning to meet the need for preventive mental-health work in our schools.

This broadening concept of the role of the school psychologist obviously demands increasingly thorough preparation. The data indicate a wide variation in the level of professional training of school psychologists. The specialized nature of the responsibilities involved call for a concomitant concern on the part of superintendents that psychological-service personnel possess the required technical competence (65).

TYPES OF CHILDREN SEEN

Luckey, in her 1950 presidential address to Division 16, classified the reasons for which Cleveland children were first referred for psychological service. In descending order of frequency these were: poor work (almost two-thirds of the cases), excellent work, behavior difficulties, requests from special agencies (e.g., the Family Service), group-test results, and physical handicaps. A breakdown of the referrals for poor work showed that the cases involve demotion (4.9 per cent of the total referrals for psychological service), placement (13.4 per cent), special-class placement (9.6 per cent), exclusion (5 per cent), passing or failing (15.5 per cent), failure in reading (8.8 per cent), failure in arithmetic (.35 per cent), kindergarten placement of six-year-olds (2 per cent), not living up to IQ (2.7 per cent), and disagreement between school and parent (.91 per cent). Of the children referred for behavior difficulties, Luckey said:

These pupils need more follow-up on the part of the psychologist. Conferences with teachers, principals, and parents are important. Helping the teacher establish a good mental-health situation will aid not only this particular pupil but others. The problem is not only one of treatment, but more important, one of prevention.

THE PSYCHOLOGIST IN A SMALL SCHOOL SYSTEM

When a city employs several psychologists, there is a natural tendency for each to specialize in those functions which are most in line with his training and interests. The functions of a school psychologist in a small community may, therefore, offer a truer all-round picture. The following analysis is based on the report prepared for the Conference by a member who is employed full-time in a system with under 2,000 students.

Testing. When I came, the teachers' particular interest was a comprehensive achievement-testing program, and their standing in regard to national norms. I felt I had a little more to offer than group-test results. But a psychologist has a duty to save his Board money by intelligent choice of tests and must have a knowledge of statistics and procedures to interpret results. The results often stir emotions and so afford a chance to help pupils, teachers, and administrators. Teachers need and welcome help in the construction of sound classroom tests.

Children coming from another district need to be tested for proper placement, as do children whom a teacher recommends for repeating or skipping grades.

Mentally Retarded and Handicapped. All such children are the responsibility of the psychologist. He must test them, recommend placement in the public school, private school, or institution. If the child is seriously handicapped, he must tell the parents, a task which is neither easy nor pleasant. If they remain in the system (which has no special class) they remain under his supervision.

Liaison with Other Agencies. When social workers or institutions have cases which involve questions of schooling, or when they need to know an individual's school background, they work through the psychologist. He works closely with local welfare and health agencies as well as the child-guidance clinic.

Personnel. Each May the psychologist confers with teachers and principals about the assignment of pupils to classes. He works with the principal to pick the teachers, "fitting" them to particular groups as much as possible.

Teaching Methods. When a teacher refers a child for poor reading she already knows he's a poor reader. She and the parents want constructive help as to what methods to try. I don't think my responsibility ends with simple diagnosis.

Parent Conferences. These take at least 10 per cent of my time. My training in what to expect of children is especially valuable here.

Clinical Psychology. I have less and less time to be a "clinical psychologist." So, I refer to the child-guidance clinic a case which needs a prolonged series of contacts. I limit myself to short-term sessions of a general counseling nature. I suppose one could define my function as one of group evaluation and individual diagnosis which is primarily concerned with education rather than "personality."

AN ANALYSIS FROM THE CONFERENCE

One of the groups of the Conference pointed out that the work of the school psychologist can be described in terms of the psychological knowledge which he applies. According to this analysis the school psychologist:

Applies *principles of learning* in:

a. Consulting with, organizing, or administering, special-education programs for the physically handicapped, the gifted, the retarded, and children with special learning disabilities.

b. Helping to adapt the curriculum to the child's particular background.

c. Consulting with teachers in order to help enrich the human-relations aspects of their program.

Applies concepts and techniques related to *individual differences* in:

a. Improving teacher selection.

b. Appraising readinesses for learning.

c. Evaluating the effects of learning experiences, including their effects on personality development.

d. Helping pupils identify their abilities and interests when choosing vocations.

e. In describing the particular children with whom individual teachers and particular schools deal.

Applies his knowledge of *child development* in:

a. Furthering the teacher's appreciation of behavior at various levels of development.

b. Furthering the teacher's knowledge of the effects of prior experiences upon school behavior.

c. Furthering the teacher's understanding of the range of individual differences in normal development.

Applies principles of *group organization and development* in:

a. Studying and understanding groups, gangs, and schoolroom classes.

b. Helping to develop classroom cohesiveness, morale, and school spirit.

c. Furthering the school's efforts to establish democratic controls.

d. Helping children to work with those who come from other social backgrounds.

e. Planning physical arrangements of schools in order to facilitate group activities.

Applies principles of *interpersonal relationships* in:

a. Furthering the teacher's effectiveness in consulting with children and parents.

b. Helping children understand themselves better when making vocational choices.

c. Helping children overcome the disabling effects of minor maladjustments.

Applies *physiological psychology* in:

a. Solving children's problems of learning which are related to perception.

b. Adapting the curriculum to children with sensory, neural, and motor anomalies.

Applies *research methodology* in:

a. Consulting on research planning and design.

b. Conducting research relevant to the aims of the school.

c. Stimulating a research attitude among colleagues and supervisors.

d. Identifying significant research problems of the schools which might be better pursued by other research psychologists.

Applies his *knowledge of community resources which pertain to the mental health and development of children* in:

a. Interpreting to school personnel the functions of community agencies.

b. Facilitating a team relationship with other workers within the school or from related agencies outside the school.

RESEARCH

The materials gathered for the Conference showed that school psychologists and their superintendents are frequently doubtful as to the extent to which research is to be counted among the functions of school psychologists. There might be less unfavorable responses to questions about research if people answering the questions stopped to consider its definition and to differentiate among its possible goals. Many think of research as a mere accumulation of materials instead of "careful or critical examination in seeking facts or principles." There is obviously much sympathy with the opinion of the school superintendent who said: "Most of what goes under the name of educational research is not worth the paper that it is written on. Studies on really significant problems would be all right if they did not interrupt teaching, and if the school psychologist had time and inclination to do them. But they are not what he is paid for." At any rate, "research" was generally ranked at the bottom of the eleven stated duties by the school psychologists who responded to the Conference questionnaire. When psychologists were asked to which duties they would most like to devote more time, research still ranked extremely low on the scale.

The school superintendents who were interviewed were asked these questions: Is it important for the school psychologist to be able to do research? If so, what problems would you like to see him work on? Does he have a consultative role in research?

Many of the superintendents stated that the school psychologist should be a person who can do research and understand and interpret it, but many doubted that he would have time to do much actual research. Only five stated that he should be expected to do research, and seven thought it should not be expected. Eight thought the school psychologist might be expected to make some practical follow-up evaluation or validation studies of surveys.

The five superintendents who thought the school psychologist should carry on research gave several reasons: the school psychologist is in a strategic position to promote and direct research; any program demands some research as part of the work; there is an obligation to education in general to study some problems in a school setting; research should contribute to the development of the school and to the growth of the school psychologist.

The problems which superintendents listed as desirable subjects for research show that local problems are uppermost in their minds. One said, "He will be used as a consultant on the study of local problems in which the staff are concerned. These will seldom be studies meeting all the criteria of university research, but many will be important to the school." The three types of problem most frequently mentioned were: evaluation (of materials and methods and of children's progress); studies of exceptional and non-conforming children (the mentally retarded, truants, delinquents, drop-outs); and methods of making psychological service more effective.

In general, then, school psychologists in service and school administrators agree with the conclusions which a group of Ohio psychologists reached in 1953:

Many schools maintain a continuing research program. Little if any of this is so-called fundamental research. Rather it is aimed at evaluating the current school program and developing programs which will meet immediate needs of day-to-day operation. The time of most school personnel is so well occupied by day-to-day duties that it is feasible to conduct research only on problems which have practical and relatively immediate significance.

The school psychologist should be encouraged, if not expected, to carry on research evaluating the effectiveness of his work in the schools. He should also do research which will improve the instruments with which he works and which will enable him to develop new, more useful techniques. Many of the techniques and instruments which the psychologist uses in his work with children were developed by organizations and institutions whose function it is to do research which is more basic and general in its nature. Within reasonable limits the psychologist should be encouraged to cooperate with universities and other organizations doing such research.

When other school personnel are doing research on various problems, much of it should be done in collaboration with the school psychologist. His training and experience should have required him to master many of the techniques of conducting research, and he is well equipped to act as a consultant to those doing research.

The Conclusions of the Conference about Research

The Conference unanimously approved the following statement: Every effort should be made to promote maximum research contributions of school psychologists and psychological examiners by:

1. Requiring adequate training in research (see Chapter XVI).

2. Clearly stating and demonstrating to school administrators that research by the school psychological worker can make a definite contribution to the solution of the school's problems and that through research the school psychological worker can best perform some of his functions e.g., in-service training of the school staff.

3. Encouraging the initiation of basic research in educational and psychological problems and cooperation with other research workers in planning such research.

The Conference's discussions about research centered around five topics: interpreting the findings of research, stimulating a research attitude among other school personnel, identifying significant problems for research, consulting on research planning and design, and conducting research.

Interpreting the findings of research. The school psychologist should continually study the results of research. He should understand the problem, what the investigator did, why he did it, and what results he got. He should evaluate the quality of the research; the significance of the problem, the adequacy of the research design, the appropriateness of the statistical treatment of the data, the validity of the conclusions, and the carefulness and completeness in reporting the study. He should consider whether the results are practical in the school situation. He should interpret the results of appropriate research for other school personnel or cooperate in such interpretation if other staff members are also qualified to do this. He should help in utilizing research findings in the solution of school problems. The job of applying research is primarily one of service.

Stimulating a research attitude among other school personnel. This applies not only to teachers but also and particularly to supervisors, members of departments of curriculum construction and of visual aids. In some school systems, the psychologist is in charge of a department of research and is often called the Director of Research. In other school systems the personnel in departments of research are not psychologists. The psychologist should always have close contact with such a department. The extent of his responsibility for carrying out research will depend somewhat on other personnel available on the staff.

Identifying significant problems for research. No alert professional psychologist will continue to face daily problems in his work without being aware of the fact that many of them can be investigated systematically. Even if the psychologist does not do the research himself, he should be able to point out to others what issues need to be investigated and what some of the initial approaches might be.

Consulting on research planning and design. In some communities, particularly where there are university departments of psychology and of education or testing bureaus, the school psychologist may have additional responsibility for planning research. He may be asked to assist the superintendent in determining what research will be valuable to the school or may be carried on without detriment to the children and school organization. He may be required to see that suitable arrangements are made for the organization of research activities.

Unless someone in the school system supervises these activities, they are likely to become so much of a nuisance that they are prohibited. Care in supervising them can help them to be very rewarding to every one. The projects must be of value to the school as well as to the investigator. They should be planned so as to spread the research over a number of parts of the school system or even over adjoining school systems. They must not exploit the children, in the first place because exploitation is unfair, and in the second place because the parents will protest. They must be planned so as to inconvenience the teacher as little as possible. They must not make unreasonable demands upon the teacher. Projects must be interpreted to the school personnel and often to parents, so that they will see the value of the research. Probably a project which cannot be so explained should not be undertaken. The school psychologist is often the person best qualified to do this. He appreciates the value of the children's time in school and all they are expected to do. He appreciates the load the teachers and principals carry. He is attuned to community feeling and parental interest. He should be known to the organizations carrying out the research.

The Conference discussion indicated that relationships between the school and those carrying on research are not always harmonious and that the best results are not always obtained. There was evidence of difficulty on both sides. "The schools make it hard for us to get a child or children to do research." "The parents don't want to let students use their child as a subject."

Two suggestions were made. It was hoped that universities might be encouraged to consider the school psychologist as a member of the team for cooperative planning of research in schools. It was also suggested that Division 16 might study the problem and suggest ways in which research could be made mutually valuable to the schools and the investigator.

Research conducted by the school psychologist. Some of the school psychologists differed somewhat from other members of the Conference as to how much original research the school psychologist could carry on. The school psychologists appreciated the need for research but also saw the overwhelming need for direct service, which tends to absorb all of the available time. Many doubted that their school systems would permit them to take from other duties the time which research entails, and most of the interviews with the superintendents bear them out. It was, however, suggested that the annual reports which most systems require from the school psychologist give him a chance to gather and study facts and arrive at principles which would be of value to the system and of interest to the school superintendent.

Certainly it is a fact that many school psychologists have made original contributions to the field. In general these are the result of overtime and vacation work, but psychologists have often had the voluntary collaboration of teachers and parents in providing materials. More individual work would be carried on if private sources, including the foundations and government agencies, contributed some financial encouragement. Small grants that enabled psychologists to take some time off or even to secure clerical assistance might work wonders.

The Conference saw clearly the need and the opportunity for the study of normal development and of mental health. Many members felt that such studies might become a major function of the school psychologist. Furthermore, they said, research promotes the school psychologist's professional development and advancement. If the school psychologist recognizes that "research" and "service" are often synonymous, if he realizes that the critical examination of the information on which he bases his recommendations actually constitutes research, he might change his own attitude and that of his employers. An awareness of the importance of research on the part of both school administrators and school psychologists may make possible the employment of sufficient personnel and an allotment of duties which will encourage more practical and fruitful research than is now possible.

THERAPY

At a post-Conference meeting of school psychologists of one state, those present were asked to write three questions they would like answered about the recommendations of the Thayer Conference. The question asked most frequently was, "Should the school psychologist carry on therapy?"

The members of any profession are naturally concerned with the limitations of their field, and of their own positions in the field. The conscientious individual with special training does not wish to handle problems beyond his competency nor yet to waste on minor or unrelated problems time which might better be devoted to his specialty. Equally, he resents having a less-well-qualified person intrude on his specialty, both because such intrusion deprives the specialist of another opportunity to exercise his skill, and because the less-well-qualified person may bungle the job. But it must be admitted that specialists in overlapping fields often compete with each other.

The history of school psychology and the analysis of the functions of school psychologists today both show that the psychologist is inevitably dealing with problems of adjustment, and very often of maladjustment. In particular he is called upon to help in cases where a child's behavior seriously disturbs the work of the school, whether or not the behavior in itself is evidence of basic maladjustment. Under any given set of circumstances the psychologist, like any other specialist, must decide both whether or not he is the best available person to handle the problem and what steps he should take. He is concerned with what he should do when he sees a teacher, parent, or doctor following procedures which are psychologically inadvisable. If he is called upon to act, he is concerned lest he take steps which trespass on the provinces of teachers, parents, clergymen, doctors, or psychiatrists. Sometimes his course of action is clear, but very often it is in doubt. Human behavior, particularly human "misbehavior," is so complicated and the profession of psychology so new, that the school psychologist can be forgiven if he often wonders just where he stands.

OPINIONS OF SCHOOL PSYCHOLOGISTS

The Conference survey of school psychologists did not list therapy as one of the functions which was to be ranked. But under the item "other," 48 mentioned psychotherapy, and, in a later section of the survey, 109 of the responses to the questionnaire listed psychotherapy as a course essential for the school psychologist. This ranked fifth in the list of essential courses.

The report of one meeting of the school psychologists and psychometrists has a section on therapy (44 II). The group indicated that one of the greatest problems in working with emotionally disturbed children was facing frustrations as a result of lack of facilities for study and treatment. One of the speakers suggested that psychologists might consider doing less testing and administration so that they would have more time for adjustment work, such as careful follow-up with individual children, individual counseling, play therapy, and group therapy. Several questions were raised. What kind of treatment do teachers and administrators expect of the school psychologist? If therapy, which is very time-consuming, is undertaken, who would do the testing which the psychologist now does? Are most psychologists actually prepared to do therapy?

Throughout the discussion, the members of the group showed great insecurity. The point was brought out that many psychologists have more training in testing and diagnostic work than in therapy and that they were not prepared to do this type of individual work. They felt that if school psychologists are to do more therapy, there will be a great need for in-service education.

THE ADMINISTRATOR'S OPINION

The outline which was used in the interviews with school superintendents did not include any question about therapy. But fifteen of the twenty-nine individually interviewed volunteered some opinion on the subject, but without stating whether or not they were referring to intensive therapy. Three said the psychologist should not do therapy. "The psychologist is limited to diagnosis only. Two municipal guidance clinics serve as treatment or therapy centers."

Twelve superintendents described some form of direct treatment as a function of the psychologist. While the superintendent's concept of therapy may be quite different from the psychologist's, these data suggest that a number of superintendents do expect some activity in this area. Of the twelve superintendents, five said the school psychologist works directly with the pupils; one added, "i.e. psychotherapy." Three said the school psychologist served as counselor. "The psychologist will work with children, the parents, the teachers concerned and administrators, and relevant agencies in collection of information, diagnosis, counseling, and further referral if necessary." Four superintendents mentioned therapy or intensive work with children. "The school psychologist has an important role to play in counseling and therapy with problem children and their parents." There were two qualifying statements: "if sufficient psychological service is available," and, "if the psychologist has sufficient training and skill."

One superintendent spoke of the school psychologist's going beyond his training and capabilities. This superintendent recommended as a safeguard a standing board of one or two outstanding teachers and two or three capable administrators to help "in an on-going analysis of the functions and goals of the position of school psychologist particularly in the therapy area."

THE CONFERENCE'S OPINION

The summary of the discussion of the functions of school psychologists concluded with the following statement:

The extent to which psychotherapy can be regarded as a proper function of the school psychologist has not been agreed upon. While it was accepted without question that the school psychologist can and should carry on, or consult with respect to others carrying on, those counseling activities which can be regarded as psychotherapeutic measures appropriate to moderately emotionally maladjusted children, the division of opinion was most sharp with respect to the utilization of psychotherapeutic procedures by even the higher-level person with children where intensive psychotherapy appears to be indicated.

On the one hand, it was contended by those who favor including psychotherapy with relatively severely maladjusted children that:

a. Other sources of adequate or nearly adequate services of this sort are extremely limited, if not totally lacking.

b. In many instances where such facilities are nominally available, the quality of such service is no better than that which can be provided by the school psychologist.

c. The practice of psychotherapy by the school psychologist is or can be a legitimate way of demonstrating the desirability of and the need for the community's providing more adequate facilities.

Those opposing the exercise of an intensive psychotherapeutic function by the school psychologist held that:

a. His services can be more beneficial to the school system if he engages in activities other than time-consuming intensive therapy.

b. Clinical psychologists are regarded as having only limited competence in psychotherapy at the end of their doctoral training program.[2] School psychologists, in order to attain psychotherapeutic competence comparable to that of the clinical psychologist, will need a training program even greater than that of the clinical psychologist, since orientations other than clinical are required of the school psychologist.

c. The school psychologist can make a more fundamental contribution to the school community by helping work toward the establishment of community mental-health clinics where intensive psychotherapy can be provided, than by endeavoring to provide, even though he might be well qualified, such psychotherapy to a necessarily small number of cases.

As the Conference progressed it became evident that there was not as deep disagreement as the discussions of the first day indicated. The members saw that the apparent disagreement was partly one of terminology. They recognized that the therapy which any psychologist attempts is largely dependent on the situation in which he finds himself, the time which he has available, and the amount and kind of training he has had (see Chapters V, XV, and XVI). They were emphatic that no individual should undertake work for which he was not qualified (see Chapter VIII). They felt that the greatest emphasis should be placed on the influence which a school psychologist can exercise in the schools and in the community in promoting general mental health.

THE QUESTION OF TERIMINOLOGY

Many members of the Conference pointed out that part of the school psychologist's doubts about his function might be a matter of terminology. "Clinical" and "therapy" are essentially medical terms. "Psychotherapy" was originally associated with psychiatry," which is a branch of medicine. And there is some confusion, in the public

---

[2] Some of the clinical psychologists themselves are often in doubt about "psychotherapy." After the Boulder Conference, one remarked, "I am afraid that in spite of our efforts we have left therapy as an undefined technique which is applied to unspecified problems with unpredictable outcome. For this technique we recommend rigorous training" (110).

mind at least, between "psychotherapy" and "psychoanalysis," a technique which the school psychologist is not expected to master.

If the school psychologist used the word "re-education" or "counseling" instead of "therapy," he might feel more comfortable and less open to criticism. After all, there is a sound psychological theory that behavior is learned. Teaching new ways of behaving might well be considered within the sphere of the school psychologist. Similarly, the school psychologist might speak of "counseling" or "guiding," rather than "treating," and certainly a "child" or "parent," rather than a "patient."

COMMON-SENSE PROCEDURE

A member of the Conference remarked that the school psychologist who is faced with an urgent problem has no time to worry over what he ought to do. The demand for immediate action is so insistent that he must pitch in and help, even when this means putting in overtime to meet his other obligations, including those involving the general welfare of all the children in the schools. If, for example, a 13-year-old girl who has been dismissed from two private schools is reported during her first day in public school as overturning bookcases, kicking teachers and principal, jumping feet first on the backs of unsuspecting first-graders, and generally making life miserable for everyone, he has to see what he can do. Careful review of actual cases suggests that the school psychologist's procedure in such cases will be something as follows:

1. The school psychologist receives and studies the referral, which comes from the teacher or principal. In most cases additional information will be necessary.

2. He obtains information from school personnel such as teachers, principals, nurses, school social workers, attendance officers. He follows the routines in his school system; he observes protocol.

3. He gathers information from social agencies, the pastor, and from the parents directly if this is necessary and desirable.

4. He discusses the problem with the teacher and gets additional sidelights.

5. He suggests that the teacher start keeping a diary to give a better picture of the child's behavior. He asks the teacher to include observations of the child on the playground and notes on the reactions of other children.

6. He gathers information from the child in interviews and from appropriate tests.

7. He requests a physical examination from the school physician or family doctor. If there has been a recent examination, he requests a report. He talks the situation over with the physician. If either of them can think of further medical information that would be helpful, he tries to see that further, specialized, medical examinations are given and that he receives reports and recommendations.

8. The psychologist correlates all the information that has been obtained and formulates a plan.

9. He writes a detailed report for his files and an appropriate report for the school with pertinent observations and recommendations. He gives some idea about what outcome to expect. He may talk this over with the teacher.

10. He makes suggestions about other school procedures which he and the teacher consider desirable, i.e., remedial teaching, special program, changes of classes.

11. He talks with the child and parents at intervals to gain further insight into the problems and the progress that is being made, and tries to interpret to them what he has learned in such terms that relationships between them are improved.

12. He refers the child to any other community agencies that can be helpful, i.e., family-welfare, recreational, and religious organizations.

13. He gets all the psychiatric aid he can and as soon as he can.

14. Referring a child to a psychiatrist does not end his obligations. He may need to interpret the psychiatrist's recommendations to the teacher. He may request further psychiatric service if it is available and needed.

15. He takes part in any staff conferences about the child.

16. He continues to see or telephone the teacher frequently if this is desirable, and he makes further suggestions as indicated. He stands by the teacher and offers all the encouragement he can.

17. In certain cases of seriously maladjusted children, he may arrange for the child to attend school on a part-time basis for a short period, to see if less than a whole day can be tolerated.

18. In cases of severely retarded children, if special classes for such children are available he helps the parents understand the need for placing the child in a special class. If exclusion is necessary, he

makes sure that any authorities who can offer further service or protection are notified. He helps the family to understand the child's limitations and to make appropriate plans.

PROMOTING GENERAL MENTAL HEALTH

The summary of the Conference discussion about psychotherapy quoted earlier refers to the contribution which a school psychologist can make by helping work toward the establishment of community mental-health clinics. The school psychologist, because of his training and because of the number of contacts which he has with maladjusted children and their parents, is especially aware both of the service which clinics can offer and of the degree to which his community needs such service. His contacts with public officials and with welfare agencies give him a chance to suggest the establishment of a clinic. He should know the possible sources of help, e.g., the state department of mental health, and the steps which other communities have followed in setting up successful clinics. His contacts with parents as individuals and with the public, for example through speeches which he may be asked to make at meetings of service clubs or PTA groups, allow a certain amount of special pleading. He can point out how the well-managed clinic serves not only the more-or-less-seriously maladjusted individual but also the cause of general mental health.

The school psychologist who is aware of the extent to which teachers and school administrators are interested in mental hygiene will be alert to capitalize on this interest. How sincere and broad is this interest is shown by the fact that recent yearbooks of the American Association of School Administrators and the Association for Supervision and Curriculum Development have been devoted to mental health (1, 17, 19, 20). Books on mental health and hygiene written for teachers had a wide sale (28, 67, 69, 79, 111, 150, 155, 162, 176). Mental-hygiene courses conducted by psychologists, psychiatrists, and teams are a usual part of in-service training programs for teachers (78; see also Chapter VII). The school psychologist who is called upon to advise with a teacher in the case of a child who is having difficulties of any kind has a golden opportunity to help the teacher generalize the principles of mental health.

One member of the Conference summed up this situation as follows:

The school psychologist, through his work with teachers, influences their development in understanding child behavior and in developing their daily procedures to take account of the personality development of the whole class. He also influences the development of the curriculum so that it gradually includes more content designed to help the child gain an appreciation of the dynamics of his social environment and thus facilitates his adjustment to it. In this way the mental health of all children is fundamentally enhanced.

The Conference was unanimous in the opinion that the major goal of the school psychologist was to help promote the best possible mental health of all children. How the school psychologist who works with maladjusted children, their teachers, and their parents serves this end is more fully implemented in the next chapter, "Potential Impact of the Public-School Psychologist on Community Mental Health."

V.

Potential Impact of the Public-School Psychologist on Community Mental Health

Commissioner, Department of Mental Health, Massachusetts;
Clinical Professor of Psychiatry, Harvard Medical School

THIS discussion is by a public administrator who by law is required to organize and operate a mental-health program for one state and to concern himself with all things in the state that affect the mental health of its citizens. My concept of a mental-health program is a broad one. It means organization of the cultural assets of the community so that each individual may, as nearly as possible, find in his world those elements he needs to satisfy his basic impulses in a way that is acceptable to his fellows, or failing this, find a suitable sublimation for them. If the program succeeds, people who find the community unsatisfactory in some features will take constructive steps to bring about changes desired. We attempt to develop a kind of resilience of character so that the person can adapt himself to the vicissitudes of fortune, bouncing back to find new ways of satisfaction or sublimation after defeat, and, in the process, leading a reasonably happy and productive life.

FOUNDATIONS OF A PROGRAM

It is my belief that so many cultural forces bear on a citizen that the mental-health program cannot be artificially grafted on the community, but it must develop as a part of daily living. Such a program must have many facets. Basically we attempt to develop within the homes of the community an understanding of human needs, and the essential dignity of man, so that the interpersonal relations within the family lend support and guidance to the individual. We hope that schools and churches of the community will lend additional support and offer ways of acting out or sublimation for shortcomings of the home. (This is the basic constituent of a mental-health program.)

The next level of function is organizing service for detecting areas of personal stress or potential stress, and the early recognition, diagnosis, and prompt treatment of mental disturbance before it becomes fully developed. This service is usually called a community mental-health, behavior, or child-guidance clinic. We also rely heavily upon the pediatricians trained in child psychiatry and upon the private practitioners who are qualified.

Another facet is to provide proper institutional or hospital care for patients in all categories; that is, those requiring acute treatment facilities, such as would be found in a general or a psychiatric hospital; facilities for those requiring more prolonged care; and special facilities for those who are retarded, have organic brain disturbances, or who suffer from the aging process. An essential feature of the hospital program is a rehabilitation service so that persons recovering from their illness at any of the above levels may be placed back in their homes in an orderly, intelligent, and effective way.

It is obvious that a program as broad as this requires the participation and cooperation of all citizens in the community.

THE ROLE OF THE SCHOOL PSYCHOLOGIST

The impact of the school psychologist on this community health program will be for good or for evil, depending upon the role he plays in relation to his own resources, training, abilities, and opportunity. Therefore, the bulk of this discussion will center around the role of the school psychologist in a community mental-health program. We will assume a knowledge of the theories and familiarity with the pertinent literature and approach this problem from the orientation of a public administrator of a mental-health program in a particular state. I believe the school psychologist is an essential person in a complete mental-health program, and I will outline what we expect him to be able to do and what we think he should do in sample situations that bear on mental health.

The public-school psychologist should be competent to give mental tests of all types, not only intelligence tests appropriate to the individual's chronological age, but tests for aptitude, specific abilities, and the commonly used projective tests. In my opinion he should have had enough clinical experience to be able to recognize the early symptoms of emotional distress or mental disease in both children and faculty members. He should be able to distinguish between the symptoms due to educational problems and those due to serious neurotic disturbances. He must know how to manage educational problems through manipulation of the learning situation, and how to manipulate dynamic situations involving other children, teachers, or parents. In my opinion he should be sufficiently impressed with the importance of his own profession to have no ambitions to become a social-service worker, a psychiatrist, a school principal, or a school nurse. Such a person will probably have a Ph.D. degree, and while I doubt it practical to make this a requirement at this time, it seems desirable to work towards this goal.

THE SCHOOL AND THE HOME

The basic aim in any mental-health program is to promote healthy emotional ties within the home. They are the most important elements in determining the mental health of a child. The school system, second in importance to the home in the over-all community mental-health picture, is important for a variety of reasons. In the first place, a child spends the major portion of his time away from home in the school. Furthermore, it is the principal source, other than the home, for guidance and for forming identifications with persons who will play meaningful roles in the life of the child.

Through the medium of the school nurse and the visiting teacher, one also has ready access to homes that would not otherwise be opened to persons like welfare workers, psychologists, or physicians who have not been called. Situations of stress in the home with which the child is having difficulty often manifest themselves in behavior observable in the school. It is in this very important area that the school psychologist, if competent, can play a key role in the total mental-health picture of a community.

RETARDED CHILDREN

Certainly the school psychologist plays a critical role in the mental-health picture of the particular child. He may play his role in this area in a variety of guises. If the child's basic difficulty is in reading or some facet of the learning process, the school psychologist may, through his function as a skilled tester, make the diagnosis of this type of learning disturbance, and, depending on its type, decide whether it is due to a basic retardation and faulty placement in school, or whether it is psychogenically determined. Whichever it is, and certainly it is of the essence that this be a skillful determination, the psychologist must now broaden his approach from the child to an appraisal of the school situation and the home situation. For example, if it is one of retardation, the facilities of the school for handling problems of a special education must be surveyed and the child appropriately placed. Depending on the resources of the school system and somewhat upon the size and location of the community, and certainly upon its geographic location in the world, the resources available will vary. Whatever they are, the psychologist must be aware of them, and if resources are lacking, he must then be prepared to improvise.

Not only must the psychologist be aware of the available resources, but he must be prepared to interpret the need for using them to the parent and to the child. The anxieties, uncertainties, and hostilities, often engendered by such interpretation and special placements, must be handled by the school psychologist. Whether they are handled in a constructive and effective way, or whether they are handled in a destructive way that will complicate rather than clarify the situation, rests entirely upon the training and abilities of this one person. He must also be sure enough of his own key role to accept the help of another profession in the interpretative phase of this problem. The trained social worker who is skillful in handling family and interpersonal relations of an environmentally originating sort, can be of tremendous help in explanation and interpretation to the family, and in bringing about the placement necessary if it happens to be outside the school system. In large communities such a trained worker may be available as part of the school system, as part of a local child-guidance clinic, or in other towns in the public-welfare or private family-agency programs. In some of the smaller communities where all of these are lacking, the county nurse or the school nurse can frequently be of great help. The good school psychologist will not only be aware of resources of this type available in the community, but will have worked out a liaison with them.

If the placement of the child is in special classes in the same school system, further checks of the child's progress, interpretation of his progress, and redefinition of his program as progress or deterioration appears, will be obvious roles in which the school psychologist will function.

A READING DISABILITY

To explore further the key role our psychologist plays in the program, let us assume that our mythical child is not mentally retarded, but is one of those children showing a reading disability, thought to be psychogenically determined. The next step is to determine the source and if possible the nature of the disturbing elements. Clues may have been obtained during interviews with the child, before, during, or following the testing procedures. The psychologist may find that the disturbance in the school situation is due to difficulties with a specific teacher, membership in a minority group, some physical defect, or he may find it originates outside the school. In many children the cause of tension will be found in disturbances in the home.

A knowledge of the educational procedures and a general knowledge of the schools in which he is working, will usually help the well-trained psychologist to determine what role the school situation is playing in the development of the disturbances in a particular child. He will also know what suggestions to make to the teacher or the recreational directors in the schools, in terms of class assignments, class placements, and perhaps even administrative suggestions for rearrangement of curriculum. Specific instruction of a specialized sort that will remedy the particular symptom defect the child is showing are, of course, to be included in such a program.

COLLABORATION WITH OTHER SPECIALISTS

If the school situation in its broad sense is found to be not particularly informative in explaining the child's difficulties, the attention should shift to the outside environment, particularly the home. The psychologist will now need assistance from some of his professional colleagues. The psychiatric social worker, the school visiting teacher, or the school nurse would be the next persons to whom the school psychologist would turn. These persons now become collaborators in managing the case. Depending on the circumstances or causes of the child's illness, the role of the school psychologist will vary somewhat. If it is found that the home situation is a very bad one due to ill health, poor living conditions, or other situations amenable to environmental manipulation, the social worker will handle most of the therapeutic aspects of the case, and the psychologist will content himself with desensitizing the child and giving him specific remedial instruction in his reading. He must know how to handle the positive transference that will develop during these remedial sessions, and also how to handle the so-called negative transference or outbursts of hostility which he will receive during this period. He should, however, be secure enough within himself and in the purpose of his efforts to avoid delving into what at this time may be extraneous issues. He will also need to instruct the teachers handling the bulk of the child's educational program, in ways of helping the child to adapt to his disability during the period of therapy, and assist the teachers in making the classroom exercises sufficiently rewarding, so that the temporary handicap will not cause the child to reject the total learning process.

The teaching situation may be used by the child as a source of stimulus, and a way of acting out some of the difficulties originating at home. The psychologist must be able to instruct the teachers and guide them in providing a firm hand or a permissive, loving approach to children as the case demands. He must be able to consult with the teacher and support him if he is made anxious by hostility or by overtures of affection by the child. He should instruct the teachers in ways that such affection can be accepted and reciprocated within the general framework of class teaching. This phase of his operation is one of the most important in promoting the mental health of the children.

WORKING ALONE

In some schools, particularly if the communities are small or the schools are poorly organized and staffed, the psychologist may find that he does not have the collaboration of professional colleagues because there are none. In this situation it may be necessary for him to make a home visit or call the parents in to interview them and explain the situation in his own office. It may be necessary for him to assume the major role in providing the child with substitute emotional outlets. While this can be successfully done during remedial instruction, for example in reading, it is unfortunate that in schools where it will be necessary for the psychologist to assume this variety of roles, he would probably also be the only school psychologist and there will be so many demands upon his time that the extra time necessary for these things will not be available. These are merely the realities of the situation and there is no magic to overcoming the lack of facilities, resources, or time. One can only advise a person to do the best he can.

A Severe Neurosis

To explore a different role for the psychologist, let us assume that a hypothetical child is, on investigation, found, in addition to having a reading disability, to be developing a severe neurosis due to rejection by one or both parents and that the home situation superficially seems ideal. In this event it is necessary for the child to be referred to some type of psychiatric care, preferably one of the well-equipped psychiatric clinics, or a physician in private practice of psychiatry who is skilled in handling the psychogenic disturbances in children and who has available resources for manipulating the social forces. For purpose of our illustration we will assume that in collaboration with the school in which this child and the school psychologist are found, there is available in the community a well-equipped child psychiatric or so-called child-guidance clinic. Here the school psychologist again plays a complicated but key role in the management of the child. We will assume the child is placed in psychotherapy with a child psychiatrist. We will assume that the parent is intelligent and cooperative, and is placed in therapy with another psychiatrist or perhaps the same one. In selected cases the therapy, under the guidance of the psychiatrist, may be by a properly trained social worker or by a clinical psychologist in the child-guidance clinic.

The addition of these professional colleagues to the picture complicates rather than simplifies the matter for the school psychologist. To dabble in the field of his colleagues complicates and confuses the picture. If, however, he decides he is outnumbered and withdraws from the case entirely, it handicaps all of his colleagues and more importantly the child. The matters of remedial education still must be handled because, even though the cause is removed, the basic fact will remain that the child has not learned to read and must be taught by special methods.

If the psychologist withdrew, the role of the general classroom exercises would be left unsolved. Here, again, the psychologist of the school must be skillful in working with the teachers and enabling them to make the classroom experience so rewarding for the child that it would be a help rather than a hindrance to the general management of the case. In the instance of a child under treatment for neurosis, these classroom setups will be somewhat different than in a simple reading difficulty, but of equal importance. The psychologist must counsel and support the teacher so he may be tolerant of the acting out that the child will inevitably do during the course of treatment. The teacher may also be the recipient of verbal blasts or other manifestations of hostility from the parents as they act out during the course of their treatment, and the psychologist must help the teacher handle them.

Children who are treated effectively, reasonably rapidly, and on a more or less complete basis, must have the collaboration of all of the above groups. It is obvious that if the school psychologist deserts his key role and begins to participate in the field of his colleagues, his own role will suffer. It is perhaps true that his own role is so subtle and complex that it is somewhat like playing on a harp, and it is perhaps understandable that he wishes to desert this role by busying himself with other activities.

If one assumes that the community is poorly equipped, and lacks some or all of the above-mentioned resources, the school psychologist is in an extremely complicated situation. His first temptation may be to ignore the problem entirely, or refer it to the family physician, or to one of the local ministers who likes to dabble in psychiatry, and busy himself with the all-too-pressing problems of other types that will occur in such a situation. The alternative may be to attempt to undertake detailed and intensive therapy with the child in question. If the psychologist has been trained in therapy, the particular child may benefit, but the time spent in intensive therapy will handicap the management of this child in that the key roles of the school psychologist will therefore be neglected, and of course, the teacher, the children, and the other elements in the school program will suffer from the disproportionate amount of time spent with the one child. Thus, the over-all effect on the mental health of the community and school will not be good. If he is not trained in therapy, the situation is not too much more complicated because it merely means that the child as well as all the other factors mentioned will be improperly managed.

SUPPORTING THE TEACHER

In the above hypothetical situations, that can be very real in daily practice, we have repeatedly referred to the support and guidance that the psychologist must render the teacher. This work with the teachers may be the most productive insofar as the over-all mental health of an area is concerned. The psychologist should be aware of the peculiarities in some teachers. He should know that most teachers are in education for the very healthy reasons of wanting to earn a living, and preferring to earn it by teaching children that they like and want to aid in development. He should also recognize that others are teaching for reasons that might be called neurotic, and some of this group may be quite hostile to children. The psychologist, by recognizing emotional problems in the teacher, supporting and counseling him as he studies his reactions to his colleagues and his reaction to individual children in the school system and their reaction to him, may change a teacher's entire approach to the problem of education and to the emotional interplay between him and the students. These slowly developing insights acquired through working with a school psychologist, a community mental-health consultant, or other personnel from a child-guidance clinic, give a teacher much deeper insight into general mental-health problems than could ever be acquired through reading pamphlets or taking courses in mental hygiene in the process of his teacher training. If the school psychologist is properly trained and qualified, group discussions with small groups of teachers can also help them understand their reaction to their colleagues and students.

In certain areas in Massachusetts we are now placing in our mental-health clinics an additional person who is called an area mental-health consultant. His principal duty will be to work with teachers, with the school psychologists, and with the parents in developing this feeling for, and skill in handling, the emotional interplay between children, between children and the teachers, and among the school faculty. As mothers learn of these things through discussing the problems of their own child, as teachers learn through handling the problems of their students, there is gradually built into the community a general use of mental-health principles that are part of daily living. Then, and only then, in my opinion, will we have an effective type of mental-health program, sometimes referred to as a "preventive program." It is obvious that the school psychologist can be a key person in this operation, but he will be effective only if he understands clearly his own role and plays it well.

WARNING TO THE SCHOOL PSYCHOLOGIST

At this time I wish to digress from the central theme and issue a note of warning to school psychologists. A professional person confronted with a situation that is frustrating or impossible, tends to

retreat within his office, confine himself to testing, "research," placement, and to making speeches before the local Rotary, PTA., or
similar groups. By preoccupation with scoring and charting results,
and by telling people what a fine program one would have except for
the lack of resources, and by going to professional meetings, it is easy
to imagine the best job possible is being done. This is a form of sublimation or escape from an impossible situation into artificially created
activity that diverts one's attention from the real failure. From an
administrator's point of view this is one of the most difficult problems
to cope with at all levels of human activity, and I am thoroughly
convinced that a great many of the forms, charts, etc., that we so
copiously accumulate, have been created by people who were frustrated in their regular activity and devised these things as a form of
escape, and they are perpetuated by other people, likewise needing to
keep their attention diverted from the urgencies of the real problem
with which they are supposed to deal.

RESEARCH

Another possible role of the school psychologist is in the field of
research. There is a great need for assessing the value of harm done
by so-called mental-health education. Making people health-conscious
no doubt brings more of them to our screening and diagnostic studies,
but we really have no knowledge as to whether it is beneficial or harmful insofar as a total mental-health picture is concerned. The psychologists, basically trained in research techniques, can and should play the
leading role in these studies. Many of us spend time attempting to
teach people good mental-health principles. This material is based on
facts gained from treating sick people. The impact of such facts on a
healthy population is not nearly so well known. For example, we know
that children who are loved by their parents tend to do well from a
psychological point of view. We know that if the child is rejected by
one or both parents, or if one or both parents are missing from the
home, the child must compensate for this lack by some type of sublimation. If the resources in the community are such that he finds
ways of sublimating, or if the resources within himself are unusual,
he adjusts in almost any community and everything is fine. If sufficient resources within the community or within the child are lacking,
symptom formation of some sort results to compensate. These are
well-known and easily substantiated facts. These facts have become

generally known to the better-educated segment of our population. They are popularized in various magazines and a variety of books. We have little knowledge, however, of what effect this information has on the mothers and fathers who love their children.

For example, a mother caring for a child whom she loves dearly is made aware of the fact that she should love the child, and that if she doesn't love the child, it will result in some type of difficulty. If in considering the child she now thinks, "Do I love this child as I think, or is this a form of compensation for unconscious hostility?" does such contemplation introduce into the mother-child relationship an artificial action which, in spite of the fact that the mother may recognize it as being artificial, so interferes with the spontaneous flow of affection between the two that the child senses that something is wrong? If this happens, does this have an adverse effect on the child's development? If it does have an adverse effect, would the child have been better off standing his chances with parents who did not know that they were supposed to love him, but just "did what comes naturally?" When I ask these questions in most quarters, the first response, usually by a well-trained social scientist or psychologist, is that such a project would be easy. When asked to elaborate or outline one, however, none has offered a satisfactory plan. The more one studies it the more complicated it becomes.

ADMINISTRATIVE ORGANIZATION

One other relevant phase of the problem I have not mentioned is the place of the school psychologist in the administrative hierarchy of the school system. At the moment, in our state, there is some discussion between my department and the Department of Education as to whether these persons should work for the school system, for the central Department of Education, or for the Department of Mental Health. By history and tradition in Massachusetts, the Mental Health Clinics and the so-called Traveling School Clinics furnish the basic psychological service to school health services and are part of the State Department of Mental Health. In my opinion the school psychologist should serve on the staff of the local school administration. Freed of administrative responsibilities, he would play a role like that of the school nurse and school physician. We have been attempting to withdraw the activities supplied by the Department of Mental Health in the field of school psychology. In the large cities this was accepted many years ago, and some of them have well-organized and functioning departments, sometimes called guidance departments, sometimes called counseling bureaus, and sometimes called guidance bureaus, but in most instances they are well-organized school psychology services. The smaller communities, and some of the larger ones that have excellent psychological services, object to withdrawing of the Department of Mental Health functions in the field of examination and testing of the children. We have expanded the child-guidance clinics to handle clinical problems, but it is my belief that a competent psychological service for each school should be provided. We are now working on a plan with the State Department of Education and the local school committees to supervise this service but to have the person work for the school administration.

SUMMARY

There are many other facets of my assignment that might be discussed, but I think we have gone into sufficient detail to indicate that from an administrator's point of view one of the key persons in the mental health of a community is the school psychologist. If competent and well-trained, he is the one who may first see the disturbed child and who first consults with the teacher in the management of the problem. Improving the education and skill of the teachers in handling these particular problems, increasing the ability of the parents in the community to handle problems of emotional stress, will depend in large measure on the efforts of the school psychologist. His own professional skill and his ability to integrate his activities with those of other colleagues in the community are of primary importance in developing an effective program. The competent school psychologist will have alternate methods of management if optimum resources are lacking, and he will refer some cases to other communities having proper facilities. He plays a key role, and he will do this effectively only if he is properly trained and competent to handle his role, and if he is sufficiently convinced of the importance of his role, so that he is willing to play it effectively and not attempt to assume the role of his professional colleagues.

VI.

Relationships with Administrators and Classroom Teachers

THE extent to which school psychology comes to be accepted and the speed with which it grows depend very largely on the personal relationships which individual school psychologists establish with their employers and their colleagues. Psychological knowledge and devotion to service are not enough if superintendents and classroom teachers feel that psychologists are interfering and critical.

A superintendent who adds a psychologist to his staff will quickly abolish the position if he thinks the morale of the teachers in the system suffers. Moreover, he will discourage other superintendents from making the experiment. A classroom teacher who dislikes the psychologist or resents his recommendations will generally fail to carry them out, and he and his colleagues will be wary about calling for help in the future. It is essential therefore that every effort be made to select for training as school psychologists only people who are good in human relations, and to train them to understand both the teacher's point of view and the organizational framework within which the psychologist must work. Ways of accomplishing these objects are discussed in later chapters.

This chapter is background material. It describes the usual public-school line of authority, the mistakes which superintendents report that psychologists make, and the approach which the regular school personnel prefer. Definite ways of satisfying these preferences are suggested. The material presented here will seem self-evident to the experienced public-school teacher or official, but discussions in the early days of the Conference indicated that some of the members of the Conference were basing their recommendations for the training of school psychologists on a misconception of the practical situation. The give-and-take of discussion frequently resulted in broader concepts.

THE LINE OF AUTHORITY

The superintendent of schools is the executive officer of the board of education and its responsible advisor in all professional matters.

The board is supposed to set policies and to reflect public opinion. The superintendent takes the actions necessary to carry out policies approved by the board.

The establishment of the position of school psychologist in a city school system normally and almost invariably comes about as follows. The superintendent, because he is faced with problems which he recognizes can best be solved by a trained school psychologist, e.g., the inauguration of a testing program, the prevention of truancy, or the training of classroom teachers to handle emotionally disturbed children, explains the situation to his board and asks them to create the position of school psychologist. (The title may be any one of seventy-five or more which he thinks will impress the members of the board most or antagonize them least.) The board will discuss the need, the probable cost, how this can be met within the budget, and the possible public reactions to the type of service and the additional expense. If similar service has been offered in the past and not met with acceptance by parents or teachers or both, or if there is criticism of similar service in a neighboring community, at least one of the board members inevitably knows the facts and has strong opinions on the subject. Poor service and disliked personnel deter expansion even more than does the prevalent shortage of money. If the position is approved, the requisite qualifications and the salary to be offered are determined by the board on the recommendation of the superintendent and in line with state and local regulations (see Chapters X and XI).

The actual nomination of the candidate is, by state law, entirely the responsibility of the superintendent. The board can veto his recommendation or refuse to fill a position, but no member can make a formal nomination. In some cities local candidates who meet all the requirements are given preference, and in a few cities there are civil-service examinations, but legally the primary responsibility rests with the superintendent. There is a similar situation when it comes to dismissal. The superintendent recommends, the board votes. But it must be recognized that disgruntled parents (and even teachers) are quick to speak directly to a board member whom they know, and he is no less quick to repeat the criticism. The public identifies the superintendent with the system. They blame him for all the shortcomings, real and fancied, of the personnel under his direction, and for anything which smacks of extravagance. His professional life is a precarious one and he is understandably reluctant to add to the risks.

THE SCHOOL PRINCIPAL

The principal of a building is legally and actually responsible, under the general direction of the superintendent, for seeing that the policies of the board and the laws of the state are carried out in his building. He is supposed to supervise the teachers and *all other school personnel* when they are in his building. The principal sets the tone of a school. His influence with children, teachers, and parents is tremendous. Wise superintendents listen to his advice and yield to his judgment. The school psychologist works with the children and teachers in a given building only through and with the cooperation of the principal.

THE CLASSROOM TEACHER

The classroom teacher is the person who is legally in charge of the children in his room. The ancient common law says the teacher stands *in loco parentis.* The courts have held that when he is in his class-room he is vested with all the powers and duties which a parent has in the home: to direct, to exact obedience, to punish disobedience, and to protect. The teacher, in other words, is the responsible adult, and the child, because he is legally not responsible, is subject to the teacher. And psychologists should be the first to recognize that the child is to some extent dependent on the teacher—or, if you prefer, that he takes the teacher as a model. The relationship is subtle, but it is not one to be disturbed lightly. Especially serious is any action or criticism which lowers the teacher in the estimation of children or parents or makes the teacher think he is so lowered.

The teacher is at all times responsible for the group. He must be conscious of the entire group and in control of it while he is working with an individual child. He has a difficult and sometimes nerve-wracking task. The psychologist must be realistic about the classroom situation. He should be able, when necessary, to help the teacher in the development of pupil morale and a wholesome classroom atmosphere free of tension and conducive to effective learning for all pupils. Recommendations which appear to the teacher to require an impos-sible amount of attention to one child will be rejected.

CRITICISMS FROM SCHOOL SUPERINTENDENTS

The school superintendents who were interviewed by members of the Conference were asked, "Where is the school psychologist most likely to make mistakes, to be less useful than he might be, or to fail?"

They expressed themselves directly or indirectly, and often very emphatically, in relation to these questions. There is more than a little danger that the school psychologist who reads their opinions will misunderstand them and be resentful. It must be remembered that the superintendents had been asked what was wrong, and were saying just that. Equally, they had good things to say about school psychologists, and the fact that they are continuing school psychological services in their systems shows that their over-all reaction is favorable. In other words, these criticisms must be taken as coming from friends who would like to see faults eliminated. This is one reason that the criticisms cannot be taken lightly. Another reason is that these superintendents represent many varied types of United States communities. The number is small, but when almost half agree on a given point, school psychologists must take stock. The following analysis presents the main categories into which the criticisms fall. The number in parentheses indicates how many of the 31 reports included criticisms like those quoted.

The feeling that the school psychologist tends to be a law unto himself is common to many of the criticisms. Either because of ignorance of regulations and customs or because of a tendency to consider only the individual children with whom they are working, some psychologists have "failed in cooperation." They do not keep the superintendent informed of even the broader aspects of their work. They do not notify principals when they enter a building, though all peripatetic personnel, including the superintendent, generally observe this courtesy. They give orders to the principal as if they outranked him and could carry out the threat, "Do this, or else—." They expect classroom teachers to interrupt their work and violate schedules in order to hold conferences at a time convenient for the psychologist. They ignore matters like recess and lunch hour when talking with children—and the child complains bitterly, and legitimately, to his parents. (13 criticisms.)

Poor human relations is another fault laid at the psychologist's door. "Too many psychologists do not have the ability to work with people. A school psychologist's work is with parents, teachers, children. He must work as a member of a team composed of teacher, visiting teacher, school nurse, and school physician. He cannot go it alone." Some superintendents speak of failure to earn the liking and confidence of principals, lack of tact, superior attitude, and an aloofness from the community. (13 criticisms.)

Unfortunate personal characteristics antagonize teachers. Superintendents speak of psychologists who "lack adaptability, are too rigid and compulsive," of those who "try to be spectacular in dress, manner, and conduct. The school has no place for eccentrics, freaks, or crackpots." "The psychologist must be satisfied to do a solid, modest, quiet job." (4 criticisms.)

Failure to understand the practical problems of the classroom is mentioned directly and by implication. In particular the superintendents felt that "the psychologists do not understand that they are recommending on the basis of the individual child, whereas the teacher has to interpret the recommendations in terms of a group." (11 criticisms.)

Failure to communicate, to make the teacher understand what the cause of a difficulty is and what the recommendations mean, is a common fault. The remarks vary from, "recommendations should be communicated so as not to engender misunderstanding," to "gibberish." (9 criticisms.)

Recommendations are often inadequate. "The teachers say the psychologist merely says back in his report what the teacher has already told him about the child." "The teacher already knows Johnny is a slow reader." "They fail to give sufficient data and suggestions to those working directly with the children." "The school does not want flash-in-the-pan recommendations but wisely thought-out courses of action." (9 criticisms.)

Inadequately trained psychologists may fail to recognize their own limitations. "The greatest mistake is made when the psychologist does not realize his own limitations and tries to foist false notions on the rest of the staff." "He may limit his service to his own specialty or, on the other hand, try to make it too inclusive." (9 criticisms.)

Poor community relations result in lack of public understanding of the psychologist's work. "Part of the job in any new position is to see that interested members of the community understand it. PTA meetings, service-club meetings, and friends chosen from the community itself are all important." (5 criticisms.)

WHAT THE CLASSROOM TEACHER WANTS

Some of the criticisms of the superintendents are repeated in remarks of classroom teachers. Six superintendents spoke about delays —delay in answering a call for help, delay in arranging tests, and delay in reporting results. A classroom teacher at the Conference gave a clear picture of the teacher's point of view and her hopes :

What do I want of a school psychologist?

I want a person to help me in the classroom in problems where I'll need help.

I want one to help me with a solution to my problem rather than give me a *diagnosis* of my problem.

I want one to *help me* solve my problems *within* my classroom setting (as much as possible) rather than to take my problem *from* my class-room.

I want one to give me advice on my relations with my fellow staff-members if I need it.

I want one who may give me ideas on new techniques of teaching, but not one who would do them for me.

I want one who would be a member of my staff, rather than an *assistant* in the administrative office.

I want one who would be a member of the *team*.

I want one whose personality traits would be outstanding.

In teaching, we start with the child—we get back to the child. *We are all in this together.*

PROFESSIONAL COLLEAGUES

No criticism is more devastating than the one which says psychologists look down on teachers. Failure to recognize teachers' competencies in education and their primary responsibilities is partly the cause of this difficulty. The wise, experienced school psychologist—and there are many!—has quite a different attitude. He looks on the teacher as a professional colleague. He knows that the good teacher is a highly-trained specialist in education. He recognizes that the teacher is not only responsible for each child in the classroom but that only the teacher can give the child who is in difficulty the minute-by-minute and day-by-day help which re-education entails. The Conference recognized this in agreeing that the psychologist's position was "staff not line," in other words that the psychologist is an advisor and not an executive.

The good classroom teacher is respected by parents, by the school nurse and doctor, and by the representatives of the community agencies which work with school children. He can be invaluable in assisting the psychologist to mobilize all of these people when and as their help is needed.

Witmer credited to a classroom teacher the stimulation which resulted in the first psychological clinic. The classroom teacher of today is in a position to promote the growth of school psychology and the wide application of good principles of mental hygiene. If, like Witmer's teacher, he receives the help he knows the psychologist should be able to give, he will demand more and more of it.

The criticisms voiced by the superintendents and the statement of what the classroom teacher wants not only reflect shortcomings in psychological service but also point the way to correction. The psychologist may do too little too late, or too much for too few. Both failures are to some extent the result of there being too few psychologists and too much for them to do. But correct organization cooperatively designed by teachers, principals, superintendents, and psychologists to meet given situations, and thoroughly understood by all concerned, can do much to correct faults and to promote good will.

PROCEDURES

Many school systems or groups of school psychologists have issued handbooks to post personnel on the procedures followed by the psychologists working in the schools (16). The subject has also been covered in articles in professional magazines (47, 187), books (69), and a Division 16 newsletter. Flexibility is of course advisable not only in adapting a set of regulations to a system but also in carrying them out once they have been adopted. Good will on all sides produces an informality that can be extraordinarily efficient.

The following brief survey of the principal points of procedure in the contacts of psychologists with individual children is based on practical experience. It is not meant as a test for psychologists or superintendents, but as a reminder to all concerned, and especially to those who may be responsible for training school psychologists, that though there are difficulties these can be minimized or avoided.

Referral procedure. The school principal is the key. The teacher requests the principal to call the psychologist. If another person, e.g., a parent, the school doctor, or an agency worker, requests the psychologist's help with a child, the psychologist should always talk with the principal.

Referral blanks. A simple blank to be filled in by the teacher makes a convenient means of referral and facilitates the psychologist's organization of his time. Complicated blanks which take much of the teacher's already overcrowded day may prevent requests for help, particularly when service is new and the teachers have not learned that the psychologist may actually save them time and trouble.

First contacts. The sooner the psychologist can establish contact with the teacher who has asked for service the better. Everyone's convenience should be consulted. This sometimes seems a problem for an electronic calculator. The psychologist must not waste unnecessary time driving from one school to another and back. The teacher must not be asked to sacrifice time with the group for the sake of one child. The child should not be kept in from recess, or be made to think that seeing the psychologist is a punishment. But, in practice, teacher and psychologist quickly learn each other's routines and adapt themselves.

Conference rooms. Every effort should be made to place a bright, attractive, private room at the disposal of the psychologist, especially for conferences with a child or a parent. A chair behind a screen in the hall is not a desirable meeting place!

Preliminary report. An oral or written report of progress should be made as soon as possible. This should be free of what the superintendent quoted above called gibberish. The psychologist should know from previous contact which technical terms he can use without explanation, which he should explain, and which omit. The preliminary report should suggest a tentative schedule for any conferences that may be necessary, should state what agency or other personnel are involved, who may visit the school, and should indicate what the future course of events is likely to be. The teacher should be encouraged to express opinions, make suggestions, and ask questions. The more informal and reciprocal such contacts are, the better. Re-educating a child or a group is a democratic process.

Recommendations. Frequently the psychological examination suggests the desirability of a change in school placement or some other administrative or classroom action. The psychologist usually can do nothing more than make a recommendation to the school officer concerned. He should be careful in his conference with parent or child not to promise what may not occur or otherwise to assume the prerogative of the school officer.

Successful communication is essential in making recommendations, and care in the use of terms is a part of the process. The recommendations should be as brief as is consistent with making clear what the child needs. (The psychologist will have a more detailed report prepared for his file.) In general they should be practical, which means they should consider the time, equipment, and skills of the specific teacher in charge of a child. They should not involve taking undue time from other children for the sake of one child. It is good to point out briefly what ideally might be done (e.g., to place a child in a psychiatrist's care), provided the actual situation is recognized (e.g., no psychiatrist available) and the concrete steps which are within the teacher's power to take are pointed out. The teacher should never be blamed; on the contrary, the psychologist should take every opportunity to praise the teacher sincerely. If such praise is included in the written recommendations it is particularly effective. The recommendation should outline the probable course of change in behavior and the limitations inherent in the child or the situation. Psychology has been oversold to public and teachers. This is no fault of the psychologists, but they will suffer when anyone expects a miracle which fails to come to pass.

THE SOCIAL SIDE

The school psychologist's social relations with teachers, principals, parents, and the local community at large can forward his work and make his life more pleasant. He should be open-minded about accepting invitations to join formal or informal groups: the principals' club, a service club, a church social group. He should welcome chances to explain his work at meetings of all kinds, but always remember the superintendent's advice about being content to do "a solid, modest quiet job."

A famous university president once said that more good was accomplished by members of different departments happening to lunch together than by all the faculty meetings ever held. More than one school psychologist has found his first acceptance at a teachers' picnic.

VII.

Organization of School Psychological Services

WHEN a school superintendent is picking a psychologist to fill a position, he obviously has to consider just what duties he wishes to have performed. What these duties will be, at least in the beginning, depends upon a variety of circumstances: how large the school system is; whether the psychologist is to serve one school or several and, in either case, the grades included in these schools; whether or not there are other psychologists employed and, if there are, the special qualifications and interests of each; what clinical services are available in the school system or in the community; and the departmental organization, if any, of specialized personnel.

A psychologist who is offered a position must consider all of these matters and decide how well qualified he is to fill the needs of a particular situation and whether or not there is a good chance that the situation will give him an opportunity to develop along the lines of his special interests. And he must consider whether the over all organization of the system establishes what his responsibility and authority will be. Luckily, the present demand for psychological service is such that he can afford to be sure that the people with whom he is to work are pleasant and cooperative.

RESPONSIBILITY

When a psychologist works in only one school, he is normally and properly a member of the principal's staff (see Chapter VI). Whatever the scope of his duties, he must remember that the principal is in charge. When the psychologist is consulted about a decision, whether it be one concerning placement or one affecting curriculum, methods, or policy, the power to decide rests with the principal. In practice the teacher, the psychologist, and the principal work together. Agreement is usually unanimous, though it may involve some compromise and time and good will to work out changed attitudes.

When a psychologist is assigned to more than one school, he may be directly responsible to the superintendent or, in large systems, to the assistant superintendent in charge of a group of schools, or to the director of a staff department. This does not relieve the psychologist of the obligation to work under the principal of a school in matters pertaining to that school, even when the psychologist's official ranking and salary exceed those of the principal. But being responsible to the superintendent helps solve many problems, which range from the minor, but ever-pressing one of how to allocate time, to major ones of policy, e.g., the type of work on which the psychologist is expected to concentrate. When any ethical problem involving personnel occurs, the psychologist needs direct access to the highest authority (see Chapter VIII).

In rural areas, psychological services are sometimes provided by a centralized authority serving more than one school system. In such cases, the psychologist's responsibility may be divided and he must exercise unusual tact and caution. He may be called upon to deal with problems which from his point of view are essentially the same but which may have to be treated differently under different local authorities.

ALTERNATIVE FORMS OF ORGANIZATION

There are four common types of staff organization in which school psychologists work. Three of these are largely confined to cities, namely, departments of special education, of psychological services, and of pupil personnel services. In some states, psychological service to the schools, even in the cities, is a function of the state department of mental health or the state department of education (see Chapter V).

A DEPARTMENT OF SPECIAL EDUCATION

Psychologists are frequently assigned to a department of special education. Historically the primary concern of such a department is the education of mentally retarded children, usually in special classes. Currently, departments of special education provide for a wide range of types of exceptional children, including not only the mentally retarded but also gifted children, the deaf, the blind, the crippled, the anemic, the epileptic, the truant, the delinquent, the recent immigrant, and others. Special services in speech therapy and home and hospital instruction are usually assigned to these departments.

The school psychologist studies the children referred to him and makes recommendations for their placement and treatment. He does not himself usually have authority to place or transfer a child. The final decision on placement depends on administrative considerations as well as on the needs of the child. The school psychologist should no more overstep his function as an advisor and consultant in special education than he would in other areas of the school system. But the school psychologist, especially in a small community, may be assigned more responsibility about special-class placement. The principal may request his assistance with parents, especially when they are uncooperative or irate. The relationship of the school psychologist to the special-education program should be specifically and clearly understood both in the local school system and in the local community.

The school psychologist may actually have started work as the teacher of a special class. He sometimes becomes the head of such a department, with full administrative authority, including responsibility for the choice of teachers, for supervising them, and for in-service training. If the psychologist is to supervise special-class teachers, he should have teaching experience in the field, or at least enough experience in such a department to understand the teacher's difficulties. Some states require the head of a department of special education to qualify for a supervisor's certificate. At the same time, the school psychologist in a system where the department of special education is the sole current consumer of his psychological services should be aware of opportunities for expanding his service to other fields. The members of the Conference agreed that it is essential for school psychologists to work toward a program of mental health for all pupils rather than to let themselves be confined to the relatively narrow field of special education.

A DEPARTMENT OF PSYCHOLOGICAL SERVICES

Some cities have a department of psychological services. This may include one or all of the functions usually assigned to psychologists, from testing for special-class placement to the re-education of maladjusted children, liaison with child-guidance clinics, planning research, and supervising research projects carried on in the schools by outside agencies.

The head of a department of psychological services is usually a psychologist. Dr. Margaret E. Hall found, in response to a questionnaire sent to the largest cities, that three-quarters of the eighty-eight cities employing psychologists reported that they had a chief or supervising psychologist. The titles for these positions were varied. In very few does the word "psychologist" or "psychological" appear. Typical titles are Director of Child Study, of Special Education, of Psychological Services, of Research, of Tests and Measurements, or of Guidance (87).

The duties of the head of a department of psychological services are supervisory as well as advisory. He selects or assists in selecting the psychological personnel in his department, assigns and supervises their work, provides for in-service training, and makes sure the psychological services are well integrated into the school system and coordinated with the work of social agencies.

Pre-Conference questions show that problems can arise here. "Does one psychologist have the prerogative of interpreting the test results of others. How much credit can a 'director' take for the work of others? This is often done by affixing the signature of the director to all reports regardless of the worker who does the testing." Another psychological examiner complains, "The school psychologist goes over all my reports and changes them without consulting me. My name is still signed to the report. When I get to the school, the principal shows me the report. Often it is not what the situation indicates at all." There are enough of these statements to suggest that the school psychologist in a position of administrative responsibility should apply his special knowledge of leadership to his own supervisory activities.

When the school psychologist is responsible for deciding which children shall be referred for psychiatric assistance, the small amount of psychiatric service usually available places a particular responsibility on him. Service must be allocated to those children from several schools who are judged to need it most. The administration of such referrals must be done with care, whether the psychiatric help is a voluntary contribution to the work of the school from a free child-guidance clinic or whether the school pays for the service.

A DEPARTMENT OF PUPIL PERSONNEL SERVICES

A modern trend is the creation of a department of pupil personnel services. Such a department often includes persons working in school psychology, school social work, school health services, guidance counseling, child accounting and attendance, home instruction, remedial teaching, particularly in reading, speech and hearing, and special education for exceptional children of all types. Authorities in school administration frequently recommend this type of organization and may recommend that it be placed under the direction of an administrator with training and experience as a psychologist. For example, a survey of one medium-sized city noted that a program of special services had grown up with very little direction or unity of purpose. The survey recommended that existing services should be reorganized into a more functional program in one division under a director "who must qualify as a trained clinical psychologist and as a counselor as well as administrator" (134).

Dr. William J. Nolan polled 110 of the large cities in the country (137). Twenty-eight of the 47 replies he received indicated that there were coordinating units for special services. The director's specialization was given for 24 of the units as psychology in 12, educational administration in 6, psychiatry in 3, social work in 2, and guidance in 1.

SCHOOL PSYCHOLOGICAL SERVICES FROM STATE DEPARTMENTS

State departments of education, of health, of mental health, and of public welfare sometimes provide psychological services either directly to the schools or through clinics to which the schools or other agencies may refer children. The training of the psychologists who are employed and the services which they render vary from state to state. A well-rounded program provided by a state department of mental health was described in Chapter V.

The development of such programs within state departments of education is an outgrowth of the special-education movement (see Chapter III). Psychologists originally employed by states to make recommendations about the admission of children to special classes have had to examine children with very complex problems and advise with teachers as to how the emotional adjustment of these children can be improved. They have been influential in the establishment of psycho-educational clinics. They have added psychological examiners to their staffs and supervised their work. They have had an impact on guidance programs, on the curriculum, on school administration, on pupil-enumeration procedures, and on many other matters in which policies impinge on mental health. They supervise research workers and conduct independent research.

A REASONABLE CASE LOAD

Whatever the organizational framework within which he works, the psychologist is likely to carry a heavy load. It is hard to say how heavy this ought to be. The Advisory Pupil Personnel Committee in Connecticut suggested one psychologist or examiner for each 2,000 enrolled students (55). A report of a survey of the New York City Bureau of Child Guidance includes the following recommendation:

For school psychological and social-work service, over and above child-guidance clinical service, there should be a team of one psychologist and one social worker to not more than 2,500 students. This comes to 370 psychologists needed for 925,000 public-school students, and 130 psychologists for 300,000 parochial-school children in New York City, making a total of 500 psychologists for 1,250,000 public and parochial children.[3]

The consensus of the Conference was expressed as follows:

There is no question of the need for school psychology. It has been estimated that fifteen to twenty per cent of school children can use some form of special individual help. While the psychologist is one of several professional workers sharing in responsibility for this group, he can and should contribute to the welfare of all children. Thus, he should not be thought of in terms of the exceptional child alone, though this group may constitute one important area of his work. He should seldom if ever confine this work to any one class of deviate.

Because school districts vary so much in area, in population, and in resources and needs, it is not possible to fix an optimum numerical relationhip between psychologists and pupils. We believe that a school population of 800 or 1,000 can profitably use the services of a full-time school psychologist. This figure may be considerably modified in terms of other specialists' services which may be available. Nor do we believe it wise at present to state a desirable case load for those working individually with children.

THE PSYCHOLOGIST AS A MEMBER OF A TEAM

Even in a school system where there is only one psychologist, he should not think of himself as working alone but rather as a member of a team. The team concept is historically associated with the guidance clinic, where psychiatrist, psychologist, and psychiatric social worker combine their specialties for the benefit of a patient. Very

[3] Morris Krugman, personal communication, September 24, 1954.

few school systems employ all of these specialists, though there are some where the school psychologist, in his capacity as liaison between school and clinic, is, in effect, an important member of the clinic team. More often the school psychologist's fellow team members are the school doctor, the school nurse, and the school social worker or the attendance officer—and always the teacher and the principal. Which of the specialists plays a part at any given moment will vary from case to case, according to the child's needs and the situation. But the team concept is essentially sound and should always be borne in mind.

Theory and experience agree that several purposes can be accomplished by working as a team:

1. The group can solve many problems where the specialist or the teacher each working by himself could not have been successful.

2. The team concept serves to emphasize the teacher as the key person, with the specialists, psychologists, counselors, and psychiatrists working with him (21).

3. The other team members may prevent the school psychologist from making mistakes, particularly those arising from failure to consider the total school situation.

4. The team concept gives school personnel a stake in the progress of school psychological work and helps them to see beneficial results with the children (152).

5. It helps the psychologist to observe and develop proper relationships within the school system, and to keep him from becoming involved in jurisdictional disputes.

6. The other team members give the school psychologist needed support because they share weighty matters involving the mental health of children. This helps prevent his overstepping the limitations of his knowledge and competence.

7. The team concept helps stimulate community concern for promoting mental health and developing adequate clinical facilities (108, 185).

INTRAPROFESSIONAL RELATIONSHIPS

The 1951 APA Committee on Intraprofessional Relationships found considerable overlapping in the functions of clinical psychologists, psychological counselors, and school psychologists. This committee recommended that the doctoral-level training in school psychology and counseling and guidance be evaluated along with clinical training programs (4). Several other reports have dealt with one phase or another of the subject (9, 29, 53, 55, 86, 102, 114, 165).

THE CLINICAL PSYCHOLOGIST

Although there is divided opinion among clinical psychologists as to what their duties are, these occur in four general areas: diagnosis or assessment of personality, treatment, research, and teaching or training. One group of clinical psychologists is primarily concerned with diagnostic work in mental hospitals, using the whole range of instruments intended primarily for adults. Outside of mental hospitals, many clinical psychologists are employed in clinics where they must be familiar with diagnostic procedures for individuals of all ages from infancy through adulthood. These psychologists frequently engage in educational assessment and diagnosis of school children. In child-guidance clinics, the psychologist's role is often defined as that of educational and vocational diagnosis and counseling. It is usual practice to employ clinical psychologists in diagnostic work with mental defectives and physically handicapped children who are not attending school.

The school psychologist differs from the clinical psychologist by his emphasis on the diagnosis and treatment of children rather than an understanding of all ages. He is a specialist in child development. He usually has more knowledge and skill in educational diagnosis and educational disabilities. He has more practice in the diagnosis of exceptional children and making recommendations about school procedures. Because he works in a school rather than a mental hospital, university, or clinic, he must have greater knowledge and understanding of school organization and procedures. Usually the school psychologist has neither the time nor the training for intensive psychotherapy that the clinical psychologist has. The contacts of the clinical psychologist with the school psychologist in research projects were discussed in Chapter IV.

Many clinical psychologists are teaching in colleges and universities and supervising and training interns. Those in community clinics frequently contribute to the in-service training of teachers by working with them in case conferences. Even more often, one of the major functions of the school psychologist is in-service training of teachers. It must be noted, however, that responses to the Conference survey included so many titles of college classes taught by school psychologists that they were not listed.

The Counselor and the Counselor-Psychologist

Originally the guidance worker or counselor was concerned with vocational guidance only (see Chapter III). As counseling developed, educational guidance became part of the work of the counselor. This led to concern with exceptional children, emotional problems, psychological testing (at least group testing), child growth and development, mental hygiene, and other areas commonly associated with the functions of the school psychologist. All of these functions are prominent in the currently developing field of guidance in the elementary school. There, major emphasis is placed on the personal, social, and emotional adjustment of young children, rather than on educational and vocational guidance (114).

More and more counselors are receiving training at the doctoral level and becoming counselor-psychologists. Conferences on the training of counselor-psychologists were held at Ann Arbor, Michigan, in 1949 and in 1950. The report shows that the counselor-psychologist with doctoral training may be competent to undertake most of the functions of a school psychologist (29). The Thayer Conference recognized this fact. Some members thought that, at the secondary level at least, it might be desirable to combine the functions of these specialists. This is not to say that the school psychologist should be restricted to the elementary school. On the contrary, the Conference deplored any tendency in this direction.

The Conference did, however, raise the question of the training of the lower-level guidance worker. There was a feeling that unqualified school personnel might attempt to use the techniques of the psychologist without having either the training or the experience to warrant it. All workers at all levels should have training adequate to their responsibilities. For example, the Conference pointed out that the functions of the psychological examiner, with his limited training, are much more circumscribed than those of the school psychologist who has doctoral training. By the same token, the guidance worker with limited training should not attempt tasks out of line with his qualifications.

There is more than enough demand for the services of both psychologists and guidance workers in the schools. It seems necessary for their respective professional organizations to explore the problems in overlapping functions and training and to clarify issues so that competitive situations will be minimized and collaborative relationships increased.

THE SCHOOL SOCIAL WORKER

In one of the interviews a superintendent said:

There is some overlapping in functions between the psychological services and those of the social worker. . . . They both handle the problem of the child who is emotionally upset, but the psychologist is the greater specialist in diagnosis. He should be able to diagnose educational disabilities and to diagnose problems of exceptional children.

A committee studying pupil personnel services had this to say about the distinctive emphases of the school social worker and the school psychologist.

The social worker has emphasized work with pupils who have, or appear likely to have, serious problems of school adjustment which also involve aspects of social adjustment. These problems often can be more successfully solved if home or other community forces are utilized to help. The social worker often turns to the psychologist for clinical diagnosis and to the school counselor for information about many of the pupil's characteristics as seen in the school situation. A carefully planned program of adjustive help is a basic part of social work. Attention is also being given to consultative services to help teachers adapt classroom work to children with special emotional needs.

The psychologist has emphasized work with pupils who have serious learning or behavior difficulties due to mental, physical, or emotional handicaps and for whom an intensive clinical psychological diagnosis is sought by the school. Although many psychologists outside of education specialize in adjustive techniques, there is as yet no generally accepted practice in school psychology except that the psychologist always includes recommendations in his report to the school. He may secure additional data helpful in diagnosis from the social worker or the counselor and, in turn, gives to each of them a picture of the child which will enable them and the school to work more effectively with him. The psychologist also serves as a consultant to the school staff on the application of principles of educational psychology and mental hygiene (55).

School psychologists have found many informal ways of developing good relationships with social workers in their communities. They frequently belong to social workers' clubs and serve in various capacities in the Council of Social Agencies. Often they serve as board members. They frequently take part in community-chest drives. These activities build a feeling of unity and cooperation which make daily contacts pleasant and fruitful. A school social worker attended the Thayer Conference.

THE SCHOOL NURSE

The school psychologist finds a good friend in the school nurse. She often knows more about the children than any other person in the school. Especially in small communities, she is likely to deal with problems that would tax the skills of all professions where such services are available. The contributions of the school nurse to the work of the school psychologist are varied and significant. She helps in identifying exceptional children. She is highly conversant with extra-school facilities that can be brought to contribute to the well-being of children. She is in a strategic position to work with the parents, and help them understand the efforts of the school to help the child.

THE SCHOOL PHYSICIAN

The school psychologist usually finds the school physician cooperative and invaluable. A good medical examination is essential in dealing with children with problems. The school physician is on hand to give it and to advise the psychologist and the school about the best medical attention. Both physician and psychologist have important services to render to children. They are cooperating, not competitive, personnel. The psychologist and the school physician from University City, Missouri, attended the Conference. They furnished a good example of cooperation between the two professions. The doctor said many of their cases were overlapping. Who was called first depended on the teacher and principal. The case was referred to the other if that was needed. There was no conflict over who got the credit. They were only concerned with what they accomplished for the child.

THE PSYCHIATRIST

The psychiatrist at the Thayer Conference expressed appreciation of psychologists and said he became interested in psychiatry through Dr. Raymond Dodge at Wesleyan, Healy and Bronner in New Haven, and Dr. David Shakow in Worcester. He also said he learned more from the teachers than they learned from him. Teachers have had courses with credit toward a master's degree in connection with his clinic. He does not want to draw them away from teaching but to make better teachers of them. The aim is to spread mental hygiene.

Conflicts between school psychologists and psychiatrists do not seem to have arisen as they have between clinical psychologists and psychiatrists. This may very well be because the school psychologist working in an educational setting is making recommendations in his area of employment and because very few school psychologists have the time, training, or inclination to engage in intensive psychotherapy, even when it is called re-education. Such differences as exist in point of view are reconciled as work progresses, and cooperation rather than antagonism is the rule rather than the exception.

THE CONFERENCE SUMMARY

The summary of the Conference's discussions on the organization of psychological services reads:

The school psychologist will take his place in the school organization in terms of his particular competencies, personal as well as professional. Problems arising from overlapping concerns and interests of workers from several professional persuasions will require work at several levels—discussions by appropriate liaison committees at top levels of professional organizations, close attention in recruitment and in training to the professional competencies set forth elsewhere in this report, and the application of good judgment in local situations by individual school psychologists as professional persons.

We look forward to the establishment of liaison committees representing school psychology to the professional organizations of superintendents, classroom teachers, social workers, nurses, counselors, and other professional specialties in education.

While the team concept as developed in the clinical field may not be applicable directly in the school setting, the concept of professional collaboration on a footing of mutual respect is certainly sound. The school psychologist who has not had experience on a clinical team should recognize the desirability of initiating working relationships with such other members of the mental-health team as may be available in the community. When dealing with mental-health problems, he should learn to recognize his limitations and to use channels of referral to other resources. School psychologists should also recognize an opportunity and responsibility to stimulate community concern for promoting mental health and developing adequate clinical facilities.

VIII.

Ethics

THE school psychologist, like all human beings, needs a clear statement of moral principles to guide him in his tasks. Good will and common sense are valuable, but they are not enough. There are always situations where the proper course is doubtful. And no situation presents greater problems than one in which each of two courses has claims to being the loyal, responsible, correct course. For example, a school psychologist must often decide whether or not his first obligation is to an individual child or to the school as an organization.

Luckily there are two excellent codes of ethics which help school psychologists determine what they should do in common situations. As a psychologist, he has the APA *Ethical Standards of Psychologists* (77). As an educator he has the *Code of Ethics of the National Education Association of the United States* (52). The codes reinforce and supplement each other in a way which proves the philosophers' claim that all ethics are in fact natural rules for living. Certainly every school psychologist should own copies of the codes and be familiar with them.

This chapter stresses the codes' points of view toward the specific problems which, in the experience of the members of the Conference, are most likely to cause difficulty for school psychological workers. It concludes with some recommendations as to how the codes can be vitalized for workers in the field and in training institutions. It is not a summary, a substitute, or even an implementation, but it does show that many of the conclusions of the Conference are in line with those of other psychologists and educators who have dealt with similar questions.

PRIMARY PURPOSES

Both codes stress the individual's duty to be a good citizen and to serve society. This entails not only the ordinary obligations of laymen but also special obligations due to special training. It is not enough for a school psychologist to be a loyal observer of law and custom. He has an obligation to do what he can to improve the general welfare. He must set a good example. He must strive to improve his own knowledge and to pass this on. The APA says he "is committed to increasing man's understanding of man." The NEA says he should "seek to make professional growth continuous by such procedures as study, research, travel, conferences, and attendance at professional meetings." The members of the Conference were concerned with the duty of school psychological workers to conduct research. Nowhere is there greater need or greater opportunity, or therefore, a greater moral obligation.

PERSONAL LIMITATIONS

Again and again in this report emphasis is placed on the individual psychological worker's obligations to be aware of his own limitations and not to undertake duties for which he is not qualified. The APA devotes several sections of its code to a consideration of one or another aspect of this rule. The NEA speaks of applying for employment "on the basis of competence only."

The Conference was particularly concerned with this rule because of its recommendation for two levels of position. Of course no amount of training guarantees that an individual will be competent to undertake all kinds of duties. But it is especially important for an individual with limited training to be aware of the gaps in his knowledge and the boundaries of his competence. Furthermore, school administrators should take care not to assign duties out of line with an individual's training.

The Conference fully realized the difficulties which the school psychological worker of any level faces in these respects. Few states have established regulations which define the duties of psychologists or correlate duties with training and experience. In many communities a relatively untrained psychological worker may have more pertinent knowledge than anyone else readily available. Psychology is a magic word to many parents and teachers. They continually request and expect service which individuals, regardless of their level of position, are unqualified to render. The psychological worker who yields to pressures of this type may do great harm to the person whom he mistakenly tries to help. Less important, but still vital, he may endanger his own position. Certainly he does no good to the cause of psychology. The Conference specifically recommended that training institutions take pains to make their students aware of this situation.

Referrals to Specialists: Teamwork

The APA says a psychologist "must refer his client to an appropriate specialist when there is evidence of a difficulty with which the psychologist is not competent to deal." But he must normally follow up the case until he is sure someone else has accepted responsibility. In therapy (or re-education) the psychologist is "obligated to make adequate provision for the diagnosis and treatment of medical problems arising in his work." This report has emphasized the fact that the school psychological worker must keep posted on the special services which are available in the school system, the community, and the state and must cooperate with them. He must remember the ideal of the team. And he must remember that teachers and principals are specialists in their own right.

In school psychology, where the pupil and his parents have seldom initiated the request for psychological service, the task of persuading them to accept needed help from community clinics and other sources is very great. The parent must be stimulated to overcome his inertia and his fears and make the suggested contact. The psychologist shares responsibility with the teacher and principal for this type of follow-through.

Safeguarding Individuals: Professional Confidences

No rule is more firmly established, more widely discussed, better understood, or more often broken by careless, thoughtless, or too human members of all professions than that which forbids gossip. A school psychologist who betrays a professional confidence ruins his usefulness. Unfortunately there have been egregious examples of such betrayal. Talk about a child's IQ to curious neighbors is a notorious error. Another is for a psychologist who has been consulted by another psychologist or another member of the team to relay the information when that is not his responsibility.

The ethical problem is when and with whom information received in confidence must be shared. The NEA Code says: "Respect the right of every student to have confidential information about himself withheld except when its release is to authorized agencies or is requested by law." But there are times when silence might be dangerous. According to the APA, "When information received in confidence reveals clear and imminent danger that the client may do serious harm to himself or others, intervention by the psychologist may be required." The APA suggests that such decisions can often be avoided by skillful handling of the individual. There is, however, no limitation on sharing responsibility with the team. "Information obtained in clinical or consulting relationships should be discussed only in professional settings and with professional persons clearly concerned with the case."

Extreme examples are easy to handle. A psychologist who has examined a child for special-class placement will obviously discuss test results and their implications with the teachers concerned, and perhaps with the child's parents. But the psychologist who in the course of an interview learns that a child is illegitimate will not pass this information on to the teacher if it will not clearly help the teacher to help the child, and even then only after securing the permission of the parent or guardian. Borderline decisions are best discussed in professional settings and with professional persons clearly concerned with the case.

Not seldom a psychologist will realize that there is a conflict of personalities or some more serious emotional difficulty which is adversely affecting a child, a whole classroom, or a whole school. A group at the Conference dealt with this problem as follows:

> We have frequently affirmed the school psychologist's general responsibility to advise on matters pertaining to the psychological or mental-health climate of the school. This responsibility will quite generally take the form of a constructive program as well as treatment services to particular children. In all phases of his work the school psychologist must weigh the welfare of children, the welfare of staff members, and the welfare of the school as an educational organization, keeping the welfare of children central in his consideration. He must avoid getting himself into situations which involve betraying a child (or staff member) on the one hand and disloyalty to the school on the other. Weighty matters involving the mental health of children can often be shared by consultation with appropriate, related professional persons such as the school psychiatrist, physician, nurse, or social worker.
>
> When the psychologist detects some feature of the school which in his opinion is inimical to healthy development and learning, he will seek to correct the condition by constructive, advisory means. If he cannot bring alleviation, it is his duty to report the fact to the proper administrative authority, and tactfully and to the best of his ability follow through to see that the situation is corrected as adequately as may be. He must exercise great care not to jeopardize

his advisory relationship with any person or group in the school family, it being better to indicate the circumstance to be investigated, not to bring the charges.

PUBLICITY

Psychologists have the duty of promoting their profession, but the APA emphasizes that they should be careful not to make undue claims. They should also be careful not to publicize case materials where there is even a remote chance that the individuals concerned could be recognized.

FEES

Both the APA and the NEA make clear statements on the subject of fees. "A psychologist should not accept a private fee, or any other form of renumeration, for professional work with a person who is entitled to his services through an institution or agency." "Accept no renumeration for tutoring except in accordance with approved policies of the governing board." A school psychologist would do well not to accept fees for examining a public-school child without first consulting the superintendent, even if the child's parents offer to pay for a special examination.

TESTING

The school psychologist should study with extraordinary care the APA discussion of the ethics involved in testing. The codes take up questions like who should know test results, the responsibility for testing programs (including testing, supervising, or sponsoring testing, and teaching courses in testing), the use in private research of test results obtained in school or through colleagues in school, the supervision of testing done by psychologists in training, the discussion of test results with the person tested when the tests are given for practice, and securing individuals to act as subjects for practice testing.

The Conference was particularly concerned with possible violation of ethics by students who are practicing testing or engaged in other "laboratory" exercises. One member of the Conference remarked on "the enormous value and usefulness of people who submit themselves to us for training purposes. If this were pointed out, I think instructors and other people would find it easier to deal with it. . . . A child who allows himself to be tested is really contributing very much." In discussing this subject during the summary sessions, the Conference unanimously approved this statement:

It is the first responsibility of the institution providing training to ensure a level of ethics within its staff which guarantees respect for, and the safeguarding of, basic human rights of individuals to whom it renders service, and from whom it receives help in supplying training material for the preparation of future professional workers.

Special attention should be paid to the ethics of training students in laboratory courses, with reference to the current practice of testing intimate friends, spouses, fellow students, children of friends, or any unsupervised testing of any individual. Such practices have serious social and emotional implications and effects. Admittedly, the problem of obtaining subjects for Binet, WISC, Rorschach, and other tests, is taxing to the ingenuity and patience of a course instructor as well as to students. However, in the current stage of social sophistication, practice such as is entailed in assessment courses can be done ethically only where the course instructor has sufficient personal supervision to prevent serious emotional repercussions, or in the event that this cannot be assured, at least to deal with them professionally when they occur.

SUPERVISION

According to the APA code, "the professional psychologist has an obligation to intervene in situations where a professional confidence is obviously being violated with possible harm to an individual." Many school psychologists are responsible for supervising other school psychological workers. They should give serious thought to the ethics of professional consultation, not only by their subordinates but by themselves. It is worse, if that is possible, for a supervisor to gossip about a case which a subordinate has referred to him, than for the subordinate to talk too freely. But examples of such failure are not lacking.

Another rule which supervisors have been known to break involves the handling of reports made by subordinates (see Chapter VII). No amount of superior training or knowledge can justify a supervisor's changing a psychological examiner's reports without consulting him. Some supervisors have been known to submit to superintendents and school boards, or even to publish as papers, reports that are in all essentials the work of subordinates, but to give the subordinates no credit. "Credit," says the APA code, "should be assigned to all those who have contributed—e.g., research design, collection of data, writing." And the NEA code says the teacher should "deal with other members of the profession in the same manner as he himself wishes to be treated."

Developing Ethical Codes

Ethics become real to individuals only when they apply them personally. Hobbs, the chairman of the APA committee which prepared and published *Ethical Standards of Psychologists* wrote: "I have a very strong conviction that if school psychologists actively work on their ethical problems, provision should be made for widespread participation in the process. I think little is gained by having a committee study the problem, since the process of examining ethical principles seems to be more important than the product of such an examination."

This APA committee has requested that school psychologists send them proposed principles and illustrative incidents and the Conference endorsed this request.

The Conference made this recommendation:

In future revisions of the Codes of Ethics, the Division of School Psychologists together with the Ethics Committees of the APA and the NEA should work toward a clear statement of general principles that apply in school psychological work. These should be supported by pertinent illustrations.

There is no school psychologist on the APA committee at the present time, and the Conference felt that Division 16 should request representation.

In the meantime and all the time local organizations of school psychologists and classes in training institutions should actively apply themselves to a consideration of ethical problems. Only then will they be prepared to choose the right course in time of doubt or emergency.

IX.

Professional Status and Problems

IN THE Conference's discussion of professional development and recognition, it was pointed out that school psychology is such a rapidly developing field that continuous study is necessary. Although members of the Conference considered doctoral training important, it was emphasized many times that no program is terminal, that good work depends on a continuous growth and development. The well-trained psychologist will always feel the need to branch out, to deepen his skills and understanding in specific areas. Moreover, part of the schoool psychologist's duty is to provide in-service training for teachers. The one who teaches or supervises others needs to be continually learning in order to enrich his background for the task.

In-Service Training

Many individuals now working in school psychology do not have the training required of those newly entering the profession. As one psychologist said, "I worked into school psychology by slow stages." Even in recent years training facilities have been extremely limited and opportunities for adequate training were just not available at all or difficult to obtain. In many localities this is still true. Two psychometrists in California are cited who drive two hundred miles twice a week to take courses toward their school psychologist's credential. In-service training for those with the more limited training is especially important. Schools using the services of these psychological workers have a special responsibility to assist them to find opportunities for professional growth.

Actual training courses offered by colleges and universities in out-of-school hours and in summer vacations might be the first thought for in-service training. At the present time such courses are difficult to find. One group of school psychologists canvassed the region for some one within traveling distance to provide a training course in the use of projective techniques with children. A year's search finally achieved success, but it was the result of much correspondence beyond

94

the area and frequent conferences within an area of one hundred miles. They had previously taken all the local courses available and useful to them.

Even when a psychological examiner is able to take a year's leave of absence, he may find it difficult to secure valuable training. In spite of the Conference's emphasis on doctoral training for the school psychologist, there are few institutions which offer graduate work organized with a view to helping the worker in service secure such training. Gathering a group of the best psychological examiners together in one institution and letting them be the guinea pigs for evolving a truly functional program would be a practical approach to the problem. As in any teaching, the faculty at the training institution would learn as much as the students. The communities who lost the services of the psychological examiners during the training program would probably be the ones to suffer. They might suffer doubly because at the end of the training period their psychologists would probably be offered employment as supervisors of psychological work in other communities.

INFORMAL TRAINING

Members of the Conference mentioned several ways in which school psychologists are now increasing their competence and other ways that might be developed. In-service training in Los Angeles County is a primary responsibility of the Office of the County Superintendent of Schools, Division of Research and Guidance Consultants. The office functions through:

(a) consultation service and/or special testing when needed on specific district problems, working with and through the district school psychological workers; (b) monthly full-day or half-day meetings with the school psychological workers in the districts served by the same consultant; (c) such other special meetings as may be necessary to develop inter-district cooperation in building educational programs for the physically handicapped; (d) county-wide meetings of school psychological personnel based on the assumption that district size tends to vary the type of functioning and interest of psychological personnel; (e) state-wide meetings annually or semiannually to give familiarity with state-wide problems and methods; (f) representative attendance at national organizations, whose findings are reported back at the district level.[4]

[4] Beatrice Lantz, personal communication, November 16, 1954.

Books and magazines are an important means of keeping up-to-date and of increasing knowledge. Books are expensive and the school budget should provide for a good professional library that will help the school's employees maintain their efficiency. But, even in communities where there are several school psychological workers, the specialized literature required by the psychologist is not usually to be found in public or school libraries. Many groups of psychological workers have formed clubs which purchase books and magazines and circulate them among the members. One group established the practice in their training period and has continued it over the years. For the members of the APA and the Division of School Psychologists, newsletters are a help, especially the bibliographies of current articles of central concern to school psychologists.

Visiting days, which are part of many school programs, afford an opportunity to visit school psychologists in nearby communities or to visit clinics and other agencies with which the psychologist works. Sometimes visiting days can be arranged in such a way that visits may be made at greater distances. Sabbatical leaves have been suggested. These are valuable, but infrequent at best, and constant contact with developments is necessary. Some teachers are obtaining grants which permit them to take a year off for study and visitation. The possibility of this for school psychologists should be explored.

Close working relationships should be maintained with other professional groups, such as social workers, family-welfare organizations, guidance groups, public-health associations, and mental-health organizations. Psychological groups should arrange joint meetings with these organizations. School psychologists should welcome every invitation to participate in programs and other meetings of physicians, social workers, and related professions. Teachers' conventions often furnish an opportunity for meetings. Attendance at local, regional, state, and national meetings, both psychological and educational, allows the psychologist to meet others doing similar work and to hear speakers and participate in discussions which help keep him up-to-date. These meetings are an important responsibility for such organizations. Workshops for school psychologists held by the International Council for Exceptional Children are good examples.

National organizations, perhaps the APA itself, might retain consultants to help promote in-service training of school psychologists. Such a consultant might actually give courses in different centers over a wide area. He could be sure that the meetings of professional organizations in his area provided worthwhile activities for school psychologists. He could show college and university departments the need and the opportunity for offering both in-service and full-time training for school psychologists.

Possibilities for the planning and support of meetings, institutes, and workshops should be explored. These possible resources were suggested: the National Institute of Mental Health for regional conferences crossing state lines, the state mental-health authority responsible for the administration of National Institute of Mental Health funds within the state, the National Office of Vocational Rehabilitation, state health and education departments, the Council of Parents of Retarded Children, or similar local organizations, the polio foundation, and private foundations.

One member of the Conference belonged to 17 professional organizations and paid $113 in dues each year. The school psychologist finds his professional growth expensive both in money and time. Belonging to two fields, he pays dues to educational organizations and to psychological organizations. He attends meetings of both groups and their allied professional meetings. He reads the literature in both fields. He maintains friendships in both. There were statements at the Conference about psychology as a home base for the school psychologist. He must, however, have two home bases. He cannot work in the school satisfactorily as a "stranger." He must actually feel for himself, and have others feel toward him, that he is a "member of the family" in both camps. This requires careful selection of his voluntary activities and expenditure of funds.

THE APA

The summary of the Conference's discussion of professional development and recognition states:

School psychologists should be encouraged by those who train them and by those who supervise them on the job to join and take active part in the major educational and psychological professional organizations on the national level (NEA and APA), the state level, and the local level. In addition, they should be urged to take part in specialized organizations, in particular those which are interdisciplinary (ICEC, AAMD, and AOA). Provision for taking part in conventions and other professional meetings should be made. The sensitivity of the school psychologist to the need for his own professional development through such membership and participation, can best be initiated by example and precept during training. Further professionalization with respect to sensitivity and other considerations certainly presumes the need for a close relationship to a national professional organization. In psychology this function is now served by the Division of School Psychologists, and it should continue to serve this function, however the over-all divisional structure of the APA may be modified in the future.

It would seem axiomatic that a school psychologist or psychological examiner who is eligible for the APA should be a member of the general organization and of Division 16. A strong professional organization is one of the principal means of securing leadership. But, as was pointed out in Chapter I, though there are well over 1,000 active workers in the field of school psychology, Division 16 had only 314 members in 1954. The Division membership requirements for an associate are an M.A. in psychology and two years' work in the field. That these requirements are not the main reason that school psychological workers do not join the APA is shown by two local surveys.

In Milwaukee County, Wisconsin, 213 persons who were doing psychological work were identified. Of this number 54, or 25 per cent, were APA members. There were 44 psychological workers in the schools, of whom 9, or 20 per cent, were APA members. Of the 35 nonmembers working in the schools, 1 held a doctor's degree 29 held a master's degree, and 5 a bachelor's degree (49, pp. 23-24). Unless they had served less than two years or the master's degree was not devoted to the study of psychology, 30 psychological workers in the schools were eligible for membership but were not members. In Providence, Rhode Island, 77 persons were identified who were doing psychological work. Of those 32, or 42 per cent, were members of the APA. There were 16 psychological workers in the schools, of whom 3 were APA members. Of the 13 who were not members of the APA, none had a doctor's degree, 7 had a master's, 5 a bachelor's, and 1 less than a bachelor's (50, pp. 22-23). Presumably 7 of the 13 were eligible for membership.

Membership in the APA is important for independent psychologists working with school children. Frequently a psychologist not connected with the schools will be consulted by parents. When reports are sent to the school, inquiries are made by school officials. A school principal recently called a school psychologist about recommendations made by an independent psychologist. They seemed to show an ignorance of school conditions. The independent psychologist was unknown to the APA member and he was not listed in the APA directory. This fact raised further doubt in the principal's mind about the value of the report.

AMERICAN BOARD OF EXAMINERS IN PROFESSIONAL PSYCHOLOGY

The APA was reorganized in 1945 to include all psychologists, and concerned for their professional responsibilities as well as their scientific contributions. Because standards of membership in the APA are based primarily on academic and scientific considerations, there was a need for standards of training and competence for psychologists engaged in rendering professional service. As one step in this process, the American Board of Examiners in Professional Psychology was formed in 1947 and charged with the national certification of advanced specialists in professional psychology. The ABEPP is an independent corporation but its membership is controlled by the APA. Psychologists who apply for this certification and who meet the requirements are awarded a diploma. Diplomate status is recognized as a distinction within the profession and it serves to identify those who are advanced specialists in a field of professional psychology. Up to 1953, diplomas had been awarded to 707 psychologists in clinical psychology, 233 in counseling and guidance, and 155 in industrial psychology. From the membership list of Division 16 and the 1953 list of the ABEPP, it was found that 101 members were diplomates, 75 in clinical psychology, 24 in counseling and guidance, and 2 in industrial psychology.[5]

If the ABEPP were to establish a diploma in school psychology it would strengthen the position of school psychology as a field and serve as a recognition of competence. The diploma would also be a safeguard and a standard for prospective employers of school psychologists, particularly in those states where certification requirements are still lax or nonexistent.

One of the issues discussed at the Conference was: Should there be a certificate (ABEPP diploma) independent of credentials which may develop in state departments? There was some initial disagreement as to whether there should be a diplomate designation distinct from the one in clinical or in counseling psychology or whether the

[5] Milton Saffir, personal communication, November 29, 1954.

similarities in the requirements for the different fields (especially school and counseling psychology) were great enough so that a separate diploma was not required.

It was felt that the school psychologist whose qualifications and training approximate the recommendations made at the Conference will be a specialist comparable to those already recognized by the ABEPP. There was consensus that some form of diplomate status should be established as soon as possible and that the policies and procedures for awarding the diploma include a "grandfather provision" such as was used in the three specialties already established. This formal statement was adopted after the discussions:

There is agreement that there are two types of individual certification. It is suggested that the ABEPP should make provision for individual certification in the form of a diploma. Action by the ABEPP should be initiated at the request of Division 16 as soon as possible (See Chapter X).

LOCAL ORGANIZATIONS

A promising professional development is the establishment of state and regional associations of school psychologists. Thirteen such organizations have been reported: California Association of School Psychologists and Psychometrists; Connecticut Association of School Psychological Personnel; School Psychology Section, Illinois Psychological Association; Michigan Diagnosticians; Minnesota Association of School Psychologists; Essex County (New Jersey) School Psychologists Association; Association of School Psychologists of New York City; School Psychologists Committee, Nassau County (New York) Psychological Association; Westchester County (New York) Association of School Psychologists; School Psychologists of Upstate New York; School Psychologists of Ohio; Division of School Psychologists, Pennsylvania Psychological Association; and Wisconsin Association of School Psychologists.[6] Such organizations are particularly valuable because the members can meet frequently and study problems of immediate concern to them. Surveys and reports have been made, and handbooks issued. Reports of the activities of some of these associations were available for the use of the Conference members.

[6] Doris Miller, chairman, committee on relations with local groups, Division 16, personal communication, March 13, 1955.

The values of in-service training and professional activities promoted by local organizations are clear from two examples. The California Association of School Psychologists and Psychometrists conducts annual conferences (44). The attendance averages about 250. The sessions in a recent year were devoted to the subject of case-study practices with children. Mimeographed summaries, which included an excellent bibliography, were later distributed. The Connecticut Association of School of Psychological Personnel was organized in 1950. It has been successful in securing a revision of certification procedures and has taken active part in planning improved legislation.

PUBLICITY

The school psychologist seeks ways of making the value of his work known to psychologists, educators, and students about to start psychological training. Of course the best way of doing this is by good daily work. But even a strong light can be hid under a bushel. A certain amount of publicity is both ethical and desirable. The studies and reports made by local organizations serve this purpose.

Members of the Conference felt that the psychologist was wise to describe his service qualitatively rather than to rely on figures of case loads. There should be a carefully planned and versatile program to educate the school personnel and the public on how they can use the services of the school psychologist.

The superintendent of schools uses his annual and interim reports to the board of education to give information which will secure support for the program of the schools. He may include in his reports those of various subordinates. So materials which the school psychologist prepares for the superintendent may become effective public-relations documents. Sometimes a piece of local research has dramatic possibilities, for example the disclosure of the number of children with behavior problems who live in slum districts. The local newspapers may reprint all or part of what the psychologist has written. This does much to awaken public interest.

Because psychological work is a recent addition to the public-school service, parents and public-spirited citizens are asking questions about it. The school psychologist finds himself in demand as a speaker at PTA meetings, service clubs, women's organizations, workshop sessions, and conventions of regional or state organizations. He will be called upon from time to time to report on his work to the community and to his colleagues. All of this consumes time and energy, but the school psychologist must be prepared to do this, or his own work will not prosper and will not spread in his own or surrounding communities. Ewing, in his address to the Conference on "The Public School's Expectation of the School Psychologist," emphasized the importance of this duty, saying, "Since the work of the school psychologist is a special service, the community must be sold upon the results of this service in order to secure adequate funds for its continued operation." But, in the interviews with superintendents, five said the school psychologist made the mistake of not keeping his community informed.

PUBLICATION

One Conference summary stated that the present psychological journals seem adequate for the publication of research and professional articles in school psychology. More attention, however, needs to be given to the writing and publishing of informative articles in the journals used by teachers, administrators, and others in related fields, such as state educational journals, *Personnel and Guidance Journal, NEA Journal, Parents' Magazine,* and *The National Parent-Teacher.* The preparation and submission of such articles should be encouraged by the profession.

The school psychologist in his writing should first determine the public he wishes to reach. This determination made before the preparation of manuscripts will assist him to select the appropriate journal. It will also increase the probability of acceptance of articles for publication, since they will be prepared in a manner which fits the policies and objectives of the journals to which they are submitted.

Some of the professional organizations might devote an issue of their yearbook to school psychology. The yearbook of the National Society for the Study of Education was suggested as a possibility. Such an issue would make a good companion volume to the forty-ninth yearbook on *The Education of Exceptional Children* (**132**). The yearbook of the American Association of School Administrators was suggested as another possibility.

WORKING CONDITIONS

The school psychologist has a real task to see that an adequate place is provided wherever he is to meet children. To insure conditions which will enable the psychologist to carry on his work most advantageously, some room must be provided where he can have privacy. This room should have good acoustics. Outside noises should be excluded; it should have sound-absorbent walls and ceilings. It should be comfortable, with adequate ventilation and temperature control. It should have furniture of appropriate size and be pleasantly decorated. The difficulty of securing such accommodations is well known to the present generation of psychological workers.

Suggestions were made at the Conference that the school psychologist might well work, through his superintendent, with the architect when buildings are being remodeled or new buildings constructed. More-appropriate quarters are likely to be provided if the school psychologist will explain what activities he expects to carry on with children. The large number of new school buildings which must be built in the next few years offers a great opportunity for securing accommodations specially designed for the work of the school psychologist.

Except when he is assigned to a single building, the psychological worker needs some central office space. This should have auditory and visual privacy. He will have many conferences confidential in nature with teachers and administrators, and often with parents. He needs a central place to keep supplies and to file his own records. There should be space for clerical and stenographic service.

Probably no school psychologist thinks he has enough secretarial help. The writing or dictating of reports, and their preparation for circulation to the schools and social agencies requiring them, is a substantial part of any school psychologist's job (see Chapter IV). The work of the school psychologist is largely ineffective if this process of reporting and keeping records is not carried out.

SALARIES

There is very little current comparison of the salaries earned by school psychologists with those earned by psychologists in other fields. In 1948 Wolfle surveyed a sample of APA members and reported that the poorest-paying positions, on the average, were in state and city governments. The median of the total sample was $4,850; of the state and city employees, $4,250 (186).

But school salaries have risen very rapidly in the last five years. A great shortage of teachers and rapidly increasing enrollments have forced school systems to compete. And the public at long last seems to have awakened to the need for paying salaries which will keep teachers and other school employees from shifting occupations and will attract able young people into school work. In any event, salaries are still rising, and figures computed in 1953 and 1954 are already out-of-date. Even so they afford some evidence that the school psychologist is now at least as well paid as his colleagues in other fields.

Public-school employees are almost always paid on the basis of established salary schedules. These vary enormously in different areas of the country and even within the same state. In general, large cities pay better than small cities, though certain suburbs rank very high. Rural towns do not pay as well as cities. A state government generally pays about what the larger cities in the area do. Many schedules still provide a higher pay scale for men than for women, though there is a strong trend toward a single schedule.

Schedules generally provide separate scales for teachers, principals, supervisors, assistant superintendents, and superintendent. Psychologists and other special-service personnel may be placed on separate scales or on that for teachers, principals, supervisors, or assistant superintendents. In any case, most employees, including psychologists, are given credit for each higher degree (in some cases for each advanced course) which they take. Up to stated maximums, each employee is given an annual increment for each year of service. Of course, a psychologist who becomes an administrator of any rank is paid according to the scale for those with that rank.

Information about salaries was gathered from twenty-nine superintendents interviewed in preparation for the Conference. All but one said that psychological workers were paid according to established schedules. In one system the psychologist with a Ph.D. is on the assistant superintendents' scale; in two, those with the Ph.D. are on a scale higher than the supervisors'; in six, regardless of the Ph.D., on the supervisors' scale; in five, on a combined supervisors'-principals' scale; in three, on the principals' scale; in ten on the teachers' scale (in seven of these there is an additional credit of $200-$600 for the M.A. or the Ph.D. degree); and in one (outside the United States) on the nurses' scale.

Several superintendents commented on their reasons for placing psychological workers on a scale higher than the teachers. Three mentioned a longer school year, one stating the psychologist worked eleven and one-half months. Several superintendents said that the school psychologist was a consultant to the staff and on the level of supervisor, that he should be on the administrative level because he should rank with others who direct specific phases in the school, that the administrative level was appropriate to the level of competence and responsibilities. The salary should indicate his importance and add dignity to the job. His salary level gains the respect of the teachers. It emphasizes that his major contribution is in working with the staff, although perhaps the major part of his time is spent with individual pupils. He should be an integral part of the staff, not an outside consultant or part-time employee.

The superintendents reported psychologists' salaries ranging from $3,000 to $15,000. The minimum or starting salary ranged from $3,000 to $4,600, the maximum (with all credits for degrees and service) from $3,600 to $15,000. Most of them mentioned annual increments and fringe benefits, such as sick-leave and retirement provisions. Two of them indicated that there was an allowance for transportation.

The two studies of psychological workers mentioned earlier in this chapter present information about salaries. In Milwaukee County in 1953, the median salary for all of the 213 psychologists and for the 44 school psychologists was in the $5,000 to $7,000 range. Twenty-five per cent of the total group and 11 per cent of the school group had the doctor's degree. In the school group, 19 had salaries less than $5,000, and 23 in the range from $5,000 to $7,500. One was on a schedule providing a salary from $7,500 to $10,000, and one from $10,000 to $15,000 (49, p. 26).

In Providence, Rhode Island, in 1953-1954, the median for all of the 77 psychologists and for the 16 school psychologists was in the group with salaries below $5,000. In the schools, where 1 has a doctor's degree, 9 have salaries less than $5,000, and 7 in the range from $5,000 to $7,500. There are no salaries beyond this level (50, p. 25).

In Pennsylvania, the county supervisors of special education, who function as rural-area school psychologists, have a legal minimum of $7,000, with an allowance for travel. There is no legal maximum, but some salaries reach $9,500. In Illinois, qualified psychological examiners have a minimum of $5,000 to $5,500. In neither Pennsylvania nor Illinois is the doctoral degree required.

State psychological associations can be of assistance where salaries for psychological workers are out of line with other scheduled salaries.

In one state the psychologists in state service, especially in state institutions, were not placed on a step in the salary schedule appropriate to their training and duties. When their protests were ignored, they enlisted the aid of the state psychological association. Representatives of the association worked with the psychologists to determine what would be fair salaries and then, working with proper state authorities, saw that changes were made. Later, a professional survey of the salary schedule by outside consultants again made an unfair placement on the schedule. The state association was able to see that this was corrected a second time.

Organizations of school psychologists might investigate the possibility of seeing that consulting firms studying salary schedules are familiar with the training and duties required of school psychologists. It is important that the ratings on the salary schedule should be appropriate beyond the need of the individual psychologist to support himself adequately. Salaries for school psychologists, like those for other school personnel, are published in booklets for school use and often in the newspapers. The prestige of the position and relationships with other personnel are dependent on the recognition which the salary schedule affords. And if able young people are to be attracted into the field of school psychology and spend the years necessary to secure the best training, they must know that they can eventually command salaries which will repay them for their investment.

PROMOTION

The opportunities which a profession offers for advancement in salary and responsibility have an important influence on the professional choices of young people and on the efforts for self-improvement of those in service.

There are four ways (in addition to automatic annual increments) by which the school psychological worker can advance. He may go up the ladder of jobs in the field if he demonstrates all-round ability and has or acquires the necessary degrees. In other words, the psychological examiner becomes a school psychologist, then a supervisor of psychological services or pupil personnel services. He may, at any level, change to a school system which pays higher salaries or gives him responsibilities in line with his particular interests. He may shift to administration and become a school principal or a superintendent, if he can meet the legal requirements for these positions. He may seek employment as a psychologist in some other field, e.g., in industry or in private practice.

One of the principal reasons for making school psychological work satisfying to persons of the highest caliber is to avoid defection to either administration or private endeavor. No one can blame a school psychologist who leaves the field to accept a much higher salary. But there are too many cases of psychologists regretfully becoming principals or making other changes simply because they cannot afford not to accept a higher salary. High salaries, good working conditions, professional recognition, including the chance to be a diplomate, and pleasant professional relations are all necessary if the profession is to rank among the best and fulfill its opportunities.

X.

Certification

THE Conference, in discussing professional development, recognition, and accreditation, took up the problem of certification by state boards of education. Such certification makes it possible to ensure that only qualified psychological workers are employed by the schools. Good certification requirements kept up-to-date are an effective means of elevating the level of the profession. When school psychological workers, teachers, and administrators work together on certification requirements, they increase their own and others' understanding of school psychological work.

THE NEWLAND SURVEY

Although several surveys of the certification of school psychologists had been made in previous years (**51, 61, 68, 87, 96, 121**), it was obviously desirable for the Conference to have up-to-date materials. The task of securing these was undertaken by Newland and this chapter is based upon his findings. The survey will be published in *The American Psychologist*. Newland says:

> Copies of school laws, state-board-of-education statements of policy, and other formalized special-education provisions were solicited from all state departments of education and from the District of Columbia. The provisions in these formal statements were combined into a summary report, which then was sent to each state and the District of Columbia in order that the accuracy of the meaning could be checked. The final report incorporated suggestions for changes in so far as they applied to formally issued statements of current practice.

In twenty states and the District of Columbia, either the school laws or the regulations of the state boards of education certificate school psychologists. These states are Arizona, Arkansas, California, Colorado, Connecticut, Delaware, Florida, Illinois, Indiana, Iowa, Michigan, Mississippi, Missouri, New Jersey, New York, Ohio, Oregon, Pennsylvania, South Carolina, and Wisconsin.

There is very little agreement between what is required by any two states. The psychologist who is looking for employment must make a special check on the legal requirements of each position for which he applies to be sure he qualifies. And he would do well to make a second check to be sure that no change in the rules and regulations is likely to occur before the date when he would start work. Nationally, the situation is—in one word—chaotic.

LEVELS OF SERVICE

Thirteen states and the District of Columbia certificate psychologists at only one level; the terms used by all of these states vary so greatly, as does the preparation required or suggested, that the "one level" is rather misleading. Six states define services on two levels. The lower level is designated by words like "psychological examiner," "psychometrist," "tester," "diagnostician," and "assistant." The upper level is called "school psychologist," "clinical psychologist," "staff psychologist," "counselor," "director of special education," or "psychologist" without any qualifying term. Indiana has three levels: technician, examiner, and psychologist. When there are two or more levels there is a difference in requirements for certification, but what qualifies a candidate for the lower level in one state may more than meet the requirement for the higher level in another.

CERTIFICATION AND DEGREES

The degrees required for certification run all the way from a B.A. or a B.A. with a major in psychology, to the doctoral degree and APA membership. Thirteen states require the M.A. degree for one or another level of certificate, and three require the doctoral degree. In several instances the requirements are listed not in terms of degrees, but in hours of graduate study of psychology. Twelve states specify the B.A. or the B.A. plus some number of credit hours, among the requirements for at least one level of service. This is misleading because of the number of hours required. At least six states place the number of hours required at an equivalent of that usually required for the M.A., and at least four states at a higher point. Two approximate the number of hours usually required for the doctorate.

The amazing fact is that in more than half of the forty-eight states there is no statement of the training (as evidenced by degrees) required of a person who may serve as a school psychologist or psychological examiner. One state in 1951 passed a school law providing for the examination of handicapped children by a "medical person" or by a "public-school psychologist or psychological examiner" approved by the state board of education. In 1953 this law was changed. The reference to psychologists was eliminated and the responsibility delegated to a "competent physician." The remedies for the situation include not only the education of the members of state boards of education and state legislatures to the need for setting standards but also a very great increase in the number of qualified school psychologists. In the meantime it would be at least unrealistic to say that every school psychological worker should have the doctoral degree. The numbers now employed who have qualified for the M.A. indicate that this requirement would be entirely feasible (see Chapter XII).

EXPERIENCE

In thirteen instances, certification as a teacher is specifically made a prerequisite to certification as a school psychologist. In seven of these, teaching experience is also required. In one state, the top level psychologist is required to hold a supervisor's certificate, but no mention is made of teaching experience as such. Three states permit more-or-less-well-defined "clinical experience" to substitute for requirements covering preparation for teaching or teaching experience.

Seven states require practical experience in psychology, in addition to credit requirements, for certification at one or another level. One state requires the equivalent of 8 semester hours, another 350 clock hours. One requires two years of full-time experience of at least 25 hours a week, and another two years of experience, of which one must be internship or clinical experience with children.

Several states provide for "successful experience," presumably as a certified school psychologist working in a school situation, for the renewal of a certificate or for advancing to a higher grade or a permanent certificate.

RECOMMENDATIONS FROM THE CONFERENCE

In one of the summary sessions of the Conference it was unanimously recommended that:

The legally constituted state authority, such as the state board of education, should be encouraged to provide certification for one or more levels of psychological service. It is suggested that the Division of School Psychologists request cooperation of the Conference of State Psychological Associations in interesting its member associations in securing action in this regard within their states.

Certification standards influence the training of school psychologists, which in turn determines to some extent the quality of school psychologists available to the school system. Therefore the members of the Conference emphasized the need for continuing study of certification. Division 16 has worked over problems of certification for several years. Surveys have pointed out the chaotic situation. The variations have increased as a greater number of states have required certification. The APA as an organization and its members as individuals should be encouraged to interest themselves in certification of school psychologists. Members of Division 16 should continue and intensify their efforts through committees of the Division, committees within the states, and as individuals. State psychological associations can be very influential in promoting high standards for school psychologists. Members of these organizations should stand ready to give their services to state boards of education in the formulation of new certification standards and the improvement of present standards.

Recommendations were made about specific aspects of certification. The establishment or revision of certification requirements for school psychologists should be independent of the certification or licensing of psychologists in other branches of psychology, for several reasons. The precedent for certification through the state boards of education is already established. The American school system is organized on the basis of certification by the education authority for all professional school personnel. The certification of school psychologists does not involve certain problems, such as fees for services to individuals, inherent in the certification or licensing of some other psychologists.

In state certification procedures and standards, regulations should not be retroactive. Certification regulations are not retroactive for teachers and should not be for other school personnel. It is highly important that this be made clear and that a "grandfather clause" be included in new regulations as they are adopted. Certification of the psychological examiner should be renewed periodically on presentation of evidence of professional progress in the field. Certification of school psychologists should be permanent. Reciprocity of certification should be considered. The New England states, New York, and New Jersey have an agreement by which a person holding a certificate valid in one of these states may exchange it for a similar certificate in any other of the states named, upon meeting prescribed requirements. This plan was adopted in 1949 and outlines basic provisions for reciprocity (58).

The Conference also recommended that the E & T Board of the APA, in consultation with Division 16, study the problem of state certification and develop model standards and procedures which may serve as guides in various states. It is important that representatives from state boards of education, certification departments, and superintendents of schools work with these psychological committees. Representatives from organizations that have had many years of experience in the certification of school psychological workers could furnish valuable suggestions about how to set up a model plan.

XI.

Personal Characteristics and Recruitment

THE Conference, as part of the discussion of the selection, training, and experience of school psychologists, took up the question of what sort of person a school psychologist should be and how individuals with the desired characteristics could be encouraged to enter the profession. It was agreed that some of the qualities desired, or not desired, are easily determined, but that there is no easy method for discovering whether or not any given individual has or can develop these qualities.

DESIRABLE CHARACTERISTICS

It was said at the Conference that the school psychologist should have the best qualities of the best workers in his two fields, education and psychology. A summary of investigations of the efficiency of teachers lists the qualities of the good teacher under the following fourteen headings: teaching aptitude, resourcefulness, intelligence, emotional stability, considerateness, buoyancy, objectivity, drive, dominance, attractiveness, refinement, cooperativeness, reliability, general personality (26). The Committee on Training in Clinical Psychology presented the following list of characteristics which experienced observers believe the clinical psychologist should have: superior intellectual ability and judgment; originality, resourcefulness, and versatility; fresh and insatiable curiosity; interest in persons as individuals rather than as material for manipulation; insight into his own personality characteristics and a sense of humor; sensitivity to the complexities of motivation; tolerance and "unarrogance"; ability to adopt a therapeutic attitude, and ability to establish warm and effective relationships with others; industry, methodical work habits, and ability to tolerate pressure; acceptance of responsibility; tact and cooperativeness; integrity, self-control, and stability; discriminating sense of ethical values; breadth of cultural background; deep interest in psychology, especially in its clinical aspects (5).

Individual members of the Conference, in talking about the characteristics a school psychologist should have, stressed those which would

113

promote good relations with children, teachers, and parents. It was said that fundamentally he should like children. He should have high intelligence, be wholesome, attractive, emotionally mature, socially minded, outgoing. He should be humble and have a sense of his own limitations. He should be secure, even-tempered, have a sense of humor, and be able to tolerate frustration when working with critical and antagonistic children and adults. He should have a considerable understanding of himself and his own feelings and be able to handle his conflicts in a socially acceptable manner. He should have, by intuition and training, an insight that lets him understand individual children, groups of children, and classroom situations. He should be able to establish a confident relationship with individuals and groups of all kinds, a close sympathetic rapport.

One psychologist, after reading this list, remarked, "All we want to be is George Washington, Abraham Lincoln, and Albert Einstein made into one—only we wish Einstein had been a kindergarten teacher."

THE RESPONSIBILITY OF ADVISORS AND TRAINING INSTITUTIONS

A committee of psychologists working on the problem of teacher selection and promotion in New York City has concluded that at present the best method of judging personality traits and the probable course of an individual's personality development is for a team of skilled observers to observe the person at work (81). Everyone who is concerned with an individual's taking up school psychology as a career should give careful thought to whether the candidate's behavior indicates that he has the proper personality, or, if there are defects, whether he is likely to overcome these. Training institutions have a heavy responsibility because they can observe the individual over a considerable period. They should select their student groups with care, observe them closely in situations which simulate actual conditions in the field, and work to help them develop good qualities and overcome faults. Special attention is called to the section of the APA code of ethics which stresses the obligation of giving prospective employers honest information about all candidates for positions.

THE NEED FOR RECRUITMENT

The shortage of trained psychological workers suggests that those already in the field should do what they can to recruit desirable candidates for the profession. Occasionally the question is raised as to whether higher standards will not result in cutting down the number of candidates. This has not been the effect in the case of other professions. On the contrary, the rule seems to be that higher requirements for admission increase the respect in which a profession is held and so attract more and abler people. This has been the history in the case of law, dentistry, and medicine. Despite the current shortage of teachers, there is some evidence that the relatively recent requirement of a bachelor's degree has been a favorable factor in recruiting teachers.

MAJOR SOURCES

The Conference survey of school psychologists showed that 356, or 71 per cent, of the 501 who gave information about their careers, entered school psychology from the field of teaching, while 145, or 29 per cent, came direct from the study of psychology or from psychological work in child-guidance or mental-hygiene clinics, or from the Veterans' Administration or an institution. Teaching experience ranged from one semester to 40 years and clinical experience from one semester to 28 years.

Both women and men are making successful careers in school psychology. The Conference survey indicates that 59 per cent of those in service are women and 41 per cent are men. The percentages vary in different areas and governmental divisions; in large cities and among supervisors, 70 per cent are women, and in state departments of education 88 per cent are men.

TEACHERS

Regardless of whether or not teaching experience should be a prerequisite for certification as a school psychological worker (see Chapter X), teachers in service are obviously the principal present source of school psychologists. There is every reason for the profession of school psychology to do what it can to point out to teachers who have the desired characteristics the possibility of developing into psychologists.

From a teacher's standpoint there is the obvious advantage that psychologists generally receive higher salaries than classroom teachers (see Chapter IX). Moreover, the teacher is familiar enough with the services which psychologists render to judge whether or not the work would have a special interest for him. For example, many teachers have professional interests, like remedial work or the emotional adjustment of children, which they might develop more fully by working as psychologists. Often a teacher may secure a promise of employment as a psychologist which will make it safe for him to undertake advanced study. Superintendents at present clearly prefer psychologists who have had teaching experience (see Chapter XIII), and naturally encourage teachers whom they already know and like to prepare for positions which they expect to have open.

From the standpoint of the profession, the good teacher is a desirable recruit. He has given proof of his interest in children and of his ability to work with them and with parents. He has a thorough knowledge of school practices, teaching methods, and curriculum problems. He is familiar with the psychological aspects of education. The teacher considering such a change, however, must be helped to understand the extent and variety of the training which he must undertake. Any belief that the change of profession can be effected by a few scattered courses obtained in odd moments must be dispelled. The profession and those responsible for employing school psychologists should, of course, be wary of the teacher who is changing his field because he has failed in the classroom, or doesn't like children en masse, or is merely looking for prestige or an increase in salary.

School psychologists who conduct courses for teachers might well discuss with their best students the possibility of becoming psychological workers. Psychologists who write articles for teachers' journals can describe their work and call attention to the number of openings. Speeches at teachers' conventions offer similar chances.

Psychologists in Other Fields

Another major source of school psychologists is found in people who are already qualified psychologists. There is evidence that psychologists working in other fields (and students starting the graduate study of psychology) are often ignorant of the opportunities in school psychology. The salaries of school psychologists and the chances for promotion seem to be high enough to attract even the best-qualified young people. The chances for service are appealing. The opportunities for original, important research are endless. Of course, the psychologist or student of psychology who thinks of becoming a school psychologist should have a thorough understanding of the work. He should also have the desirable qualities which were listed earlier in this chapter. He should know that in many states teaching experience is a prerequisite for a certificate. He should really want to work with children.

Just as a poor teacher sometimes thinks he can escape into psychology, there have been examples of poor psychologists trying to work in the schools when they had failed elsewhere. One school superintendent reports having candidates who had been trained as clinical psychologists referred to him in the spring. They scorned the salary which he could offer so he didn't investigate them further. By fall, having failed to find employment elsewhere, they were begging him for jobs. When he investigated, he found that he didn't want them either. School psychology is in no sense a poor relation.

An examination of the APA Employment Bulletin shows that very few school systems are using it in their efforts to find candidates for unfilled positions. During six months of 1954 there were only nine requests for school psychologists, but 21 applications for work as school psychologists. It is more than probable that many school superintendents are not familiar with the APA Employment Bulletin. Division 16 might well send sample copies of the Bulletin to all members of the American Association of School Administrators. An increase in requests in the Bulletin for school psychologists would certainly stimulate professional interest in the field. And it might result in more school psychological workers joining the APA.

The more direct approach is for teachers of psychology and employers of psychologists to tell practicing psychologists and teachers who might become psychologists of the openings which school psychology affords.

STIMULATING UNDERGRADUATE INTEREST

In addition to teachers and psychologists already in service, another source of school psychologists should be young people who have not yet selected their profession. Some of these may choose their courses with a view to entering the field as soon as they can secure the proper training. The availability of training programs and their specific listing in college catalogues will help.

One pioneer in the field of school psychology read an article in the old *Youth's Companion* about psychological tests that were being developed, and from that day had a clear ambition. The bright child who early determines on a career has an enormous head start in life (70). Many of the most important advances in a variety of fields have been made by relatively young geniuses who did their basic reading in their teens or earlier. The APA has from time to time urged its members to interpret psychology to the public. School psychologists are well equipped to write for young people and they are strategically placed for marketing articles in appropriate magazines.

Psychology is among the sciences discussed in junior-high-school guidance courses. Division 16 should be sure that pamphlets suitable for such courses and for the use of high-school guidance counselors are available (74, 156). Writers of textbooks could well include school psychology in the chapter on psychology as a profession, as Hilgard does (92). School psychologists, particularly in secondary schools, might be interested in sponsoring Future-Psychologists associations, similar to the Future Teachers of America.

But the main source of starting able young people along the path to becoming school psychologists may well be the admiration they feel for some school psychologist they know. If school psychologists are the type of people they should be and fulfill the opportunities of service they have, they will never lack successors.

XII

Pre-Conference Studies of Training

CONFERENCE studies of the professional and preprofessional backgrounds of school psychologists in service illuminate the problem of recruitment and training. And psychologists' opinions of what is desirable in the way of training are one of the major means of determining standards. Another is the opinion of potential employers, that is, in the case of school psychologists, school superintendents.

Degrees

Newland reports: "A small but random sample of 20 pages in the APA directory for 1951 revealed that 13 of the 20 persons listed as holding public-school positions as their primary responsibility held subdoctoral degrees. Five of the seven holding doctoral degrees were in large school systems. The subdoctoral persons tended to be pretty much 'on their own.'"

Reports from five separate localities give percentages for degrees which vary as follows: Ph.D. or Ed.D., from 6 per cent to 26 per cent; M.A., from 56 per cent to 88 per cent; B.A., from 6 per cent to 31 per cent.

The Conference survey of school psychologists presented facts about the 468 individuals who supplied information about their education. All of them had the B.A. degree. No more than 46 had this degree only. Four hundred and twenty-two (90 per cent) had an M.A. degree. There were 119, or 25 per cent of the 468, with doctoral degrees (91 Ph.D., 28 Ed.D.). An additional 85, or 18 per cent, are working toward a doctoral degree (73 Ph.D., 12 Ed.D.).

Only a few psychological workers answered the survey's question about which degree should be required at different levels of positions. With one exception, those who did respond indicated that the psychological examiner should have at least an M.A. in psychology or educational psychology. Of the 65 who indicated the degree or amount of graduate study required for the position of school psychologist, 27 thought that the Ph.D. in psychology or educational psychology should be required, and 6 of these thought a year of internship should be added. Thirty-eight thought two years of graduate study in psychology or educational psychology should be required, and most of these mentioned some kind of supervised experience.

The reports of school superintendents who were interviewed expressed varying opinions about degrees. Nine did not consider a graduate degree a requirement. One of this nine said he "was more concerned with the background and content of training than with a degree." Eighteen superintendents thought psychological workers should have an M.A. degree. Nine of these said that the M.A. was a minimum and that the worker should have extra training in a specialized area and continue his training in service. Four of the 18 considered a doctor's degree desirable. It was considered necessary for the school psychologist in four reports. The reasons given include the prestige of the degree and the length and breadth of training for which it stands, but one group of superintendents who said they saw the value of the degree feared the use of the title might alienate the teachers who particularly needed the psychologist's help.

FIELDS OF CONCENTRATION

The great multiplication of courses and course titles within a given field makes it difficult to analyze reports on training. Moreover, students who are concentrating in the field of education certainly take many courses with contents very similar to the contents of courses taken by students who are concentrating in psychology, and vice versa. The holder of an Ed.D. has not necessarily had more or less training pertinent to the field of school psychology than the holder of a Ph.D. in psychology. Nonetheless, it seems safe to assume some differences between the individual who reports a major in education and the one who reports a major in psychology.

The Conference survey of school psychologists secured information about fields of concentration. Of the 426 who reported on their studies for the B.A., 184 had majored in psychology, 108 in education, 44 in English, 21 in mathematics, 16 in history, 14 in sociology, and 39 in other subjects. These figures probably reflect the large number who enter school psychology from the field of teaching. At least it is interesting to note that less than half (43 per cent) had an undergraduate major in psychology, and that almost one-third (31 per cent) majored in some subject other than either psychology or education. Of the 378 who reported on their studies for the M.A., 247 concentrated in psychology, 62 in education, 50 in educational psychology, and 19 in guidance and counseling. Of the 91 who had taken the Ph.D., 78 had concentrated in psychology, 7 in guidance, 3 in education, 2 in educational psychology, and 1 in English. All of the 73 who were still studying for the Ph.D. degree said they were concentrating in psychology. Of the 28 who had taken the Ed.D., 16 had concentrated in education, 4 in educational psychology, 3 in guidance, 4 in school psychology, and 1 in child welfare. Of the 12 still studying for the Ed.D., 8 were concentrating in guidance, 3 in educational psychology, and 1 in education.

The figures show that as training progresses psychology tends to dominate. Of the M.A.'s, 65 per cent had concentrated in psychology. Of those who either had a doctor's degree or were studying for the doctor's degree, 74 per cent reported psychology as the field of concentration. The remaining 26 per cent reported fields of concentration that obviously included many courses that were mainly psychological in content.

In answer to the request that courses be listed which were felt to be essential, the responses to the Conference survey mentioned 168 course titles. These can be condensed to some 52 titles, 29 in psychology, 15 in education, and 8 miscellaneous. These listings rival the variety found in certification requirements. Each of the following was listed by more than 100 persons as essential: child psychology, tests and measurements, individual mental testing, clinical psychology, and psychotherapy.

EXPERIENCE IN PSYCHOLOGICAL CLINICS

In response to the Conference survey, 176 of the school psychological workers reported experience in psychological clinics other than in schools. Of these, 145 entered school work with a background of training in psychology only, and 31 with both teaching and clinical experience.

THE CONFERENCE SURVEY OF CURRENT TRAINING PROGRAMS

The survey of universities and colleges made by Moore in preparation for the Conference was reported in Chapter I. Several institutions said that the program was just being worked out, and some invited suggestions. It seems that this is a strategic time at which to have thought given to the problem and make suggestions' available.

For admission to the graduate programs in the 18 institutions reporting a program for school psychological workers, the required work in psychology varies from 6 to 45 semester hours, with 12 semester hours as a mode. Teaching experience or the training necessary for a teacher's certificate is required by 10 and preferred by 2 additional institutions. Course requirements in the program vary widely, but all require work in both education and psychology. Most of the courses in psychology are essentially courses in techniques or applied courses, with little emphasis on a basic program in psychology. Thirteen of the 18 institutions require practicum or internship, at least part of which must be in school situations. Seven of the 10 institutions granting the doctor's degree require a thesis or dissertation. The institutions which reported that they offered doctoral training are located in eight states: California, Indiana, Illinois, Michigan, Nebraska, New Jersey, New York, and Pennsylvania. The subdoctoral training mentioned may also be found in Colorado, Kansas, Massachusetts, Minnesota, and Ohio.

People who are studying training programs may be interested in knowing which universities sent in materials describing specific training programs. These are: Teachers College of Columbia University, University of Illinois, University of Pittsburgh (starting 1954-55), Purdue University, University of Michigan (two-year training program in operation), Ohio State University (approximately two-year program).

TRAINING IN CALIFORNIA

Dr. Louis Levine, of the San Francisco State College, made a survey of school-psychologist training programs in California for the Conference. Information was supplied by 12 institutions, only 2 of which were included in the Moore survey described above. Each institution indicated that the training which was offered met the California education-code requirements for the school-psychologist credential. This is a teaching credential, plus one year of successful teaching experience and a master's degree in psychology or educational psychology. An applicant may be considered to have the equivalent of this degree when he has completed 36 semester hours of training, distributed among 5 specified areas of training, as part of his undergraduate or graduate program. Therefore many school psychologists may never have been enrolled in specific training programs for the credential. Although all of the 12 institutions provide training which will meet the state requirements, there are varying prerequisites, and selection and internship procedures. At several institutions admission depends on successful work as a school psychometrist. There is great variation in the amount and type of field work. In some cases this is obtained as the student takes specific courses in diagnostic and intelligence testing. Seven departments have specific field work requirements ranging from part-time for one semester to full-time for two semesters. In some of the institutions the school-psychologist program consists of a number of courses possibly given in several different departments. In these cases there may be little integration between courses, and the courses may bear only an indirect relationship to the work of the school psychologist.

The California report comments on the fact that, during the revision of the state code, psychologists had given much more attention to the certification and licensing of clinical psychologists than they had to standards required of school psychologists:

The least involved, the least informed, and the least interested in the identification and character of school psychologists have been the professional psychologists themselves. . . . For the last several years the Western Psychological Association has scheduled meetings on the master's degree in psychology. At the Seattle meeting a serious discussion was centered on whether applied programs such as the school-psychologists program were rightly within the province of psychology. The group at that meeting comfortingly came to the affirmative conclusion—a conclusion, in the case of school psychology, apparently arrived at by the public somewhat ahead of the profession itself.

The point with reference to the training of school psychologists is obvious. The profession of psychology must exercise its concern, its interest, and its responsibility in the specification of the practice of psychology in public schools.

In 1952, the State Committee on Credentials for Pupil Personnel Services in California recommended the following training:

For the school psychometrist: Possession of a general teaching credential or a four-year college course with the B.A. and a major in psychology. Specific requirements:

1. An understanding of child and adolescent development, with directed observation of children of varying age levels, and with emphasis on individual differences in social, emotional, and intellectual development.

2. Understanding of the general field of educational psychology including problems of the education of exceptional children, educational measurement, and statistical method.

3. Training in individual and group mental tests including field work.

For the school psychologist: Possession of the M.A. in psychology granted by an institution of higher learning approved by the State Department of Education. Specific requirements:

[1, 2, and 3, as above, plus]

4. Remedial instruction, psychology of learning.

5. A broad understanding of the fields of clinical psychology, mental hygiene, and personality development.

6. Proficiency in the following clinical methods and procedures, developed through courses and supervised field and laboratory work:

a. Individual diagnostic procedures.

b. Group testing.

c. Counseling procedures, including interviewing.

d. Case-study techniques.

e. Remedial instruction.

f. Individual and group therapy (**46**, pp. 53-55).

THE PROVIDENCE SURVEY

The Providence survey gives an illustration of training which may be obtained by taking certain courses. In the Psychology Department of Brown University, emphasis is on research in experimental and physiological psychology. Courses are also offered in clinical and applied psychology. Two psychologists employed in clinical work in the community teach courses at Brown in mental testing and child psychology. Courses in testing and educational psychology are also given in the education department (**50**, p. 13).

THE CONNECTICUT STATEMENT OF REQUIREMENTS

The Connecticut Association of School Psychological Personnel has drawn up a statement of the training which should be required.

General Psychology. This includes basic psychological theories and principles of behavior, such as intelligence, feelings and emotions, motivation and learning, racial and cultural differences, perception and thinking.

Human Behavior and Development. Courses in this area treat the behavior and psychological development of humans from birth to maturity, the influence of heredity and environment, the psychology of deviates, mental health, etc. Emphasis is given to childhood and adolescence.

Diagnostic Skills. This includes training in clinical methods and techniques for appraising individual functioning and behavior, as well as in group testing techniques applicable to the school situation.

Educational Principles and Methods. This seeks to increase the psychologist's understanding of the pupil in the school situation, and his ability to improve the school situation for the pupil.

Counseling Skills. This includes training in principles and procedures in counseling, necessary in the readjustment of individual pupils.

Research Skills. Courses in this area include scientific methods of psychological and educational research. Statistical techniques are, of course, part of this area.

Orientation to Problems and Resources of Family and Community. This fosters an awareness of the forces that are at work and the resources that are available in the family and in the community.

Practicum. This refers to supervised practice in the diagnosis and correction of learning and behavior difficulties, with participation in case studies. It is a type of internship taken in a school or other clinic dealing with school age children (55, pp. 14-15).

PREVIOUS STUDY OF TRAINING BY THE DIVISION OF SCHOOL PSYCHOLOGISTS

Committees of Division 16 have studied the problem of the training of all levels of school psychological workers. The committee studying training in 1950 presented a report which outlined a program beginning with introduction to psychology in the sophomore year and continuing through a first year of graduate work. The report included a statement about the differences of opinion about a requirement of at least one year's experience as a regular classroom teacher.

The recommendation was made that since adequate training for carrying out the functions of the school psychologist was the equivalent of that required for a doctoral degree, this degree should be expected of all who intend to become psychologists. The report stated that this recommendation did not imply that workers such as psychometrists, counselors, remedial teachers, or play therapists should be required to have a doctoral degree before appointment. It was felt unrealistic to expect all specialized personnel in the educational field to obtain doctor's degrees, and that it is probably unnecessary or possibly even undesirable that they do so. However, the recommendation was made that individuals should not be listed as school psychologists unless they have doctoral degrees or the equivalent. Division 16 took no action on this report because of divided opinion on the issues raised.

The report of the committee on certification standards, July, 1952, included the following recommendations about background training:

The psychological background: should assure knowledge of psychological theory, experimental psychology, child and adolescent psychology, psychology of exceptional children, psychology of learning, clinical and abnormal psychology, mental hygiene, personality dynamics, and statistical techniques. It should assure efficiencies in individual clinical diagnoses, case-study procedures, case-conference techniques, and an acquaintance with individual and group therapies. It should include field work in school psychology.

The educational background: should assure knowledge of educational philosophies, methods, and techniques, including remedial techniques, and administrative insights, as well as a practical knowledge of classroom procedures. It should assure skill in educational psychology, and in the critical analysis and use of group measurement techniques which serve as guides to understanding child growth and adjustment to the curriculum.

Socio-anthropological background: should assure a knowledge of the socio-economic factors which influence child behavior and learning, and insight into the satisfactory adjustment patterns of other cultures.

Desirable additional backgrounds include: an understanding of the dynamic interrelationships between home-child-teacher-administrator, together with the ability to manipulate these; acquaintance with group dynamics, with ability to assume leadership in the development of sound learning, adjustment, and mental-health concepts within the school and the community; a knowledge of the possible contributions of community resources toward the solution of individual problems, and the development of wholesome school-community relationships; and a creative inquisitiveness that promotes research in the many uncharted areas of human learning and human relationships in education.

This committee recommended that the school psychologist should have as a minimum an M.A. in psychology or educational psychology, and a minimum of two years of experience in school psychology. One year of internship in a psychological clinic which serves a large school population and works with the schools might be substituted for one year of experience in school psychology. Teaching experience would not be considered in place of experience in school psychology.

This report was adopted in September, 1952, as a progress report, with a recommendation for further study. Division 16 thus expressed more agreement with this report than with previous reports, but was still so divided in the opinions of individual members as to teaching experience and the doctoral degree that it was unwilling to give unqualified approval.

Basic Areas in the Training of Clinical Psychologists

The Boulder Conference report presented a list of the basic areas in clinical psychology which one group agreed should be included in a core curriculum. This list, included here because many members of the Thayer Conference would like to see the preparation of the school psychologist include all the requirements for the clinical psychologist, follows: human physiology, personality theory, developmental psychology, social relations, psychopathology, personality appraisal, clinical medicine and clinical psychiatry, psychotherapy and remedial procedures, clinical-research methodology, professional and interprofessional relationships, community resources and organization, practicum and internship experiences (149, pp. 69-70).

The APA Committee on Counselor Training

The APA committee on the training of counseling psychologists at the doctoral level proposed the following areas of training and tentative time allotments. The ranges of time are suggested for a four-year program including one year of internship. Proportions of one year's study in the various areas of training (total of 4 years = 400) are as follows: basic concepts, tools, and techniques common to all psychologists, 65-70; personality organization and development, 20-30; knowledge of social environment, 15-20; appraisal of the individual, 35-45; counseling, 20-30; diversification, 30-50; professional orientation, 10-20; practical field work and internship, 120-135; and research, 45-50 (9, p. 180).

The APA Committee on Intraprofessional Relationships in Psychology

Recommendations about training were made in 1951 by an APA committee. It was assumed that the Ph.D. degree is required for full responsibility in professional psychology, but the committee recognized that many persons (school psychological examiners among them) will be performing psychological functions in an effective manner at a lower level. Such people will not need full psychological training, but what training they have should be correlated with their responsibilities. They will need some basic courses in psychology and the training necessary for carrying out their duties. The graduate programs may be one or two years and should be recognized by an appropriate degree or other credential. A partial Ph.D. program is not suitable training. The committee found that a common core of theory, concepts, and research design and methods has become a part of the basic training of graduate students in psychology at the Ph.D. level in many universities. This trend is likely to continue and should be encouraged. Specialized courses, supervised internships, and post-doctoral training may meet the needs in specialized areas (4, p. 93).

XIII.

The School in School Psychology

THE Conference had no doubt that the school psychologist needs an intimate and thorough understanding of the processes of education. The disagreement over whether or not he had to have classroom teaching experience was largely about the most efficient method of acquiring the knowledge necessary and only partly about how much knowledge was needed. In fact, there was general agreement that sometime, somewhere, the school psychologist should acquire: (a) basic knowledge of education, including its history and philosophy, curriculum construction, methods and materials, remedial methods, test construction, exceptional children; (b) skill in educational diagnosis along with his other assessment skills; (c) practical knowledge of the classroom and the school, the roles and responsibilities of the teachers, principals, supervisors, and other specialized services, the necessary rules and courtesies for work in the schools, including a respect for what other school workers do, the practical limitations of the school situation, the school hierarchy, and the relations of the school to the various forces in the community.

How necessary such knowledge is, is shown by the statement of one member of the Conference, a clinical psychologist who is working in schools. He says:

I feel inadequate about teaching methods. If a child is referred to me as a reading problem, for example, his teacher already knows he can't read. Simply to test the child and tell her he is low in specific areas is not enough. I should be able to delve into the particular methods used up to this point and then on the basis of my interview with the teacher, child, and sometimes the parent I should be able to lay out a specific program of attack to be followed. I am unable to perform this service adequately and it is an extremely important one, especially in a system where there is no special remedial-reading person. A school psychologist should have a sound background in the theory and methods of teaching reading. I might add that the techniques of teaching *any* subject should be thoroughly understood. I don't think my responsibility ends with a simple diagnosis of the trouble.

Many clinical psychologists and psychiatrists who have conducted

129

discussion groups with teachers or taught courses for teachers have been temporarily frustrated by failure to understand the teacher's point of view. An account of the Rochester Plan for Mental Health describes what often happens. The clinical team lost sight of the teacher as a leader of groups. Their misconceptions brought about changes in the teacher's activities so that children acted in a most disturbing fashion. The team reported: "In essence we were forced to shift from an approach rooted in case-work orientation to one that had its base in attempts *to help teachers deal with emotional problems from the standpoint of sound instructional techniques. . . . Mental hygiene's contribution is to help teachers become more effective teachers, not part-time therapists"* (78, p. 378).

THE PRESENT SITUATION

Twenty states and the District of Columbia certificate school psychological workers. Twelve of these states and the District of Columbia require a teacher's certificate as well as specific training in psychology (see Chapter X), and seven of that twelve (California, Colorado, Florida, Indiana, Michigan, Ohio, and Wisconsin) also require from one to three years of teaching. The eight other states which certificate school psychologists do not require a teacher's certificate or teaching experience. This divergence of state practice sharpened the controversy in the Conference. Should the states which do not now issue certificates be encouraged to include a teaching requirement when the hoped-for time of universal certification arrives? Should those states which do not now require teaching be asked to change their regulations? Or, on both questions, vice versa?

The Conference survey of the 501 school psychologists who reported their teaching and clinical experience showed that 356, or 71 per cent, had taught from one semester to forty years. Of these, 51 per cent had taught two years or more. The average number of years of teaching experience was eight years. But 145, or 29 per cent of those reporting, entered school psychological work without having taught. Should a psychologist who is thinking of transferring to school psychology be told that teaching experience is a practical necessity even when the state in which he expects to work has no regulation about it?

PRIOR EXPRESSION OF OPINION

These questions are not new, and groups discussing them have been known to generate considerable heat.

A California committee studying the duties of school psychologists and the training required, sent a questionnaire to school psychological workers and to administrators employing them. The questionnaire included various suggestions for changing certification requirements. The year of teaching experience which is required in California provoked the most comment. The psychologists were divided on this question. Of the 64 administrators polled, 56 said they believed teaching experience was necessary for successful work as a school psychologist (46, p. 51).

A conference on the role and training of the school psychologist, held at Pullman, Washington, in May, 1954, discussed the necessity of a teacher's certificate and teaching experience. A professor of psychology and a professor of education each thought the school psychologist should have a teacher's certificate. The latter said he should have a year's teaching experience before going into the field of school psychology. One administrator said he thought that when a psychologist tended to act too much like an expert in talking with the teacher and to make suggestions that were too perfunctory, this was due not so much to lack of teaching experience, as to inadequate psychological training and general emotional immaturity. If the psychologist is not a mature and adequate person, the teacher will be critical and may blame the psychologist's lack of teaching experience. The professional preparation of the school psychologist should develop genuine insights about the school program and curriculum and about problems met by the teacher in the classroom. This administrator had once felt that only classroom experience gave such insight, but said he now felt it could be acquired without taking the time for actual classroom teaching.

WHAT SCHOOL SUPERINTENDENTS SAY

The opinion of school superintendents on any issue involving training is vital. If most of them are inclined to feel one way, candidates for positions will have to conform until the superintendents change their collective mind.

The pre-Conference interviews with the 29 superintendents individually interviewed showed that 14 definitely did not wish to employ a school psychologist who had not had teaching experience. The majority of each of the two groups interviewed felt the same way. Of the 15 other individual superintendents, 11 thought teaching experience desirable but not absolutely necessary, though two of this 11 said they would generally give preference to a candidate who had taught. Of the other four, two said that the school psychologist needed an understanding of schools but that teaching was not necessary, and two said definitely that teaching experience should not be required.

The superintendents recommended periods of teaching varying from the practice teaching required for a teacher's certificate to four or five years. One said:

> Four and better five years of practical experience over several levels are needed before entering upon the position of school psychologist. This time, spent at different levels, is required in order for the psychologist to get the "feel of" and to know the school situations under which children live and learn. Such prior experience is more likely to guarantee rapport with classroom teachers, who otherwise may take the attitude that the psychologist does not really understand their problems.

One Conference member reported working for two years with a group which included two school psychologists, two social workers, and eighteen superintendents. This was in a state where a school psychologist must have a teacher's certificate and one year of teaching experience. At the end of the committee work, the superintendents agreed to the idea that education and psychology are equal partners. The superintendents agreed to work with the psychologists to plan an acceptable alternative for the actual classroom experience. (So group opinions can be changed!)

THE CONFERENCE DEBATE: AFFIRMATIVE

The members of the Conference who continued to insist that actual teaching experience should be a prerequisite to work as a school psychologist were convinced that, practically speaking, such experience was the only way to acquire the necessary knowledge. An examination of the Conference's statement of the things a school psychologist should know about education shows that few teachers have more specialized training in education. The pro-experience group felt that many of the mistakes which school superintendents say psychologists make (see Chapter VI) would be avoided by psychologists who had first-hand experience with being responsible for the progress of a whole classroom of children. And this general progress is, after all, the basis of the development of general mental health, the goal toward which the Conference thought all school psychologists should work.

Establishing the rapport between teacher and psychologist, which all agree is essential, is a two-way process. Nothing can convince a teacher that a psychologist sympathizes with his problems as much as the knowledge that the psychologist has had personal experience with them. The modern teacher has formal training in psychology. If the psychologist has a similar training in teaching, the two are more likely to understand each other and work well together.

The Conference Debate: Negative

The extreme opponents of requiring teaching experience went as far as to claim that such experience might even make an individual less competent as a psychologist. They thought that the person whose background differed from the teacher's looked at problems from a different standpoint and so saw facts and possibilities that a teacher didn't see. This fresh approach might be valuable in working on matters like the school curriculum as well as in promoting the mental health of a child or group of children. Few of the members adhered to this extreme. In fact, there was general agreement that the good classroom teacher could become a good school psychologist.

However, the opponents of the teaching requirement continued to feel that it was neither necessary nor desirable for an individual starting out to be a school psychologist to sacrifice the time it takes to qualify for a teaching certificate, plus the year, more or less, given to work in a classroom. They reasoned that the essential knowledge of education and of school procedure could be acquired in other ways and much more quickly. (These are discussed below.) They felt that the school psychologist needs so much training in psychology, distinct from education, that he cannot afford to take time to become a specialist in both fields.

The opponents feared that if teaching were a prerequisite, school psychology would not recruit many graduate students of psychology or psychologists in other fields. They felt that this would be a grave loss, both quantitatively and qualitatively, and in particular that many men who are becoming psychologists might be unwilling to delay their full employment. They said that a teaching requirement in effect limits recruitment to individuals who have meant to be teachers, and so largely to women.

One member of the Conference, a psychiatrist, pointed out that the medical profession has not found double certification desirable. Psychiatrists, pediatricians, surgeons, and orthopedists are all certified as M.D.'s.

Another member of the Conference, who has had practical experience with this problem, made the following statement:

I believe (a) that psychology and education working together can provide training that will furnish the necessary skills, information, and understanding without requiring actual classroom experience; (b) that superintendents will accept and employ these psychologists; (c) that it is not necessary to decide whether those coming from teaching are more or less competent than those coming from psychology. Each group has distinct competencies, and a well-organized staff in school psychological service needs the contribution of both groups. Some of the positions for psychological examiners working more or less independently in smaller districts can best be filled by persons with teaching backgrounds and others by persons whose training is largely that of the clinical psychologist.

THE VOTE

The members of the Conference discussed three methods by which a psychologist in training might acquire practical familiarity with education. All of the methods presume a basic background in education, obtained through well-designed courses. In addition, the first method would require a teacher's certificate and successful teaching experience of at least one year. The second method would require practice teaching and a teacher's certificate, but no responsible teaching experience. The third method would require neither practice teaching nor a teacher's certificate. It would consist of a nine-months' (one school year) internship, mainly in a school setting.

Many members of the Conference were emphatic that the second alternative, which includes practice teaching as the only teaching experience, was not satisfactory. In the final vote that possibility was eliminated. Though many still felt that teaching experience was essential, in the final Conference vote, 34 out of 41 members present voted that they thought there might be some route to the profession of school psychologist other than that of classroom teaching.

Suggestions from the Conference

There was general agreement from both sides that the study of education and the gaining of practical knowledge of school procedures should not consume more than one year of a four-year graduate training program in school psychology. A committee of the Conference suggested the following substitute for actual teaching experience:

a. Observation at several grade levels in various types of schools.

b. Work with individual children, including exceptional children, in such activities as play therapy, tutoring, and remedial instruction.

c. Work with small groups of children in such activities as speech and dramatics, or on playgrounds.

d. Regular classroom work assisting the teacher or acting as a substitute teacher.

e. Observation and participation in school-community relationships and parent-teacher programs.

f. Attendance at lectures by colleagues and conferences with various administrators and supervisors of the school.

Many members of the Conference felt that this is not a satisfactory substitute for teaching experience and that much experimentation is needed.

The present shortage of teachers has brought about several emergency or intensive training programs for liberal-arts-college graduates which may offer some suggestions. One such program provides study and observation during a summer session. The following year the student becomes a classroom teacher under the supervision of the teacher-training institution. Thereafter this beginning teacher teaches full-time and studies part-time until 30 semester hours of work in education have been completed. This arrangement might take more time than the school psychologist would wish to take, but one summer session followed by a combination of some teaching and study might be worked out to provide adequate knowledge of the school.

Psychologists who are looking for their first positions in school psychology might find it helpful to take positions in systems which have well-established departments of psychological services. This would give them a chance to acquire first-hand experience under direction of supervisors who could guide their footsteps. The teachers in such systems are already used to working with psychologists and would attribute mistakes to inexperience rather than to an alien attitude.

XIV

Levels of Position

THE Conference devoted much time to discussions of the question of whether or not to recommend that certification regulations recognize two levels of position and that training programs be set up on this basis. The duties which the school psychological worker performs obviously vary not only on the basis of his competence but also on the basis of many local factors: whether he is the only psychologist employed or one of several; the services which the school administration expects; the availability of other specialists; and the extent to which his position entails the supervision of psychologists and other personnel. Length of experience is also a factor. A new Ph.D. may serve an internship or begin his regular service on the same level as, or even under the direction of, a B.A. (And it behooves him to have humble respect for the experience and personalities of his colleagues, regardless of their training.)

THE CURRENT SITUATION

The certification requirements of one state, Indiana, postulate 3 levels; of 6 states, 2 levels; and of 13 states and the District of Columbia, one level. Separate cities have established levels of position with distinctive titles. The State of New York, for example, gives a permanent certificate at only 1 level, but New York City has 5 levels: chief school psychologist, supervisor of school psychologists, school psychologist, substitute school psychologist, and school psychologist in training.

A committee of the Division of School Psychologists of the APA, which surveyed certification procedures in 1950, described four levels of position based on training:

1. The supervisor or director, who possesses the doctorate or its equivalent in education or psychology.

2. The school psychologist, who possesses an M.A. in clinical or educational psychology or education and has also met specific course requirements in clinical and abnormal psychology, child growth and development, etc.

3. The school psychometrist or psychological examiner, who possesses the A.B. plus certain course requirements.

4. The psychological examiner or intern in training, who may be a "qualified" student at undergraduate or graduate level.

The Conference survey asked school psychological workers to express opinions as to whether or not requirements should be set up for different levels. Of those answering, 338, or 61 per cent, felt different levels should be defined; 215, or 39 per cent, favored a single standard. Of those favoring a single standard, six individuals pointed out that the psychometrist often worked without supervision. Detailed comments were made by 64 psychologists from 21 states. The majority of them favored three levels: the supervisor or director, the psychologist, and the psychological examiner.

The crucial question is not the number of levels but the amount of training and experience required of a school psychological worker who is to work without *psychological* supervision from a better-trained, more-experienced psychologist. Even states which certify school psychologists at two levels let the lower-level psychologist work alone. In Connecticut, 2 of the 9 top-level psychologists are working alone and 7 with staff; 6 of the 23 lower-level psychologists for whom information is available are working alone and 17 under direction. Three who are classified as "in-training" are working under psychological supervision.

THE CONFERENCE DEBATE

The question of two levels of position was considered by the Conference on the first day, during the discussion of the functions of school psychologists. The members came back to the question day after day, and it was one of the crucial issues taken up in the last two days. Two principles were constantly in the minds of the Conference members during their deliberations.

1. There should not be two levels of qualification at a given task. A person is either qualified to do a task or he is not.

2. No person, whatever degree he may hold, will ever be competent to undertake every task in the broad field of school psychology. No individual should undertake tasks for which he is not competent or which the regulations under which he is working allocate to other workers.

The arguments advanced for and against two levels are outlined here.

FOR TWO LEVELS

The proponents of two levels pointed first to the realities of current practice and particularly to the large number of psychological examiners who are giving excellent service in a wide variety of situations. They felt that these workers had not been given the recognition which they deserved nor yet that which they need for personal and professional security. Experience shows that though the majority of these workers will probably not qualify for the doctoral degree, they will make strenuous efforts to acquire the knowledge necessary to meet specific challenges which rise in their particular positions. Like members of other professions, they will not stand still or regress, but constantly strive to improve their training. Actually, the recommendations made for the training of the psychological examiner are a step up from the training now required in many places. If this proves inadequate, a future conference will raise the standards higher.

The great difficulty which school administrators face in securing adequate funds makes it unlikely that many systems will be able to afford to pay school psychologists the salaries which an individual with a doctor's degree commands. A doctor's degree is not a state requirement for any other position on the school staff except that of the school physician. Budgetary limitations may well keep schools from offering salaries to school psychologists that would attract enough people of the high ability required of the school psychologist. The number with this ability is limited, and the competition between the professions, including science and engineering, is very keen.

The proponents also argued that there were many services in the field of school psychology which a psychological examiner can perform adequately and which a psychologist with the broad and extensive training demanded for the doctoral degree might find limited. One member of the Conference was very definite in expressing the opinion that the psychologist with doctoral training would not be content to devote a major part of his time to testing. He sees a permanent need for workers who are interested mainly in individual psychological examinations and making recommendations about individual children.

Another consideration is that the school psychological worker is not an independent worker as is a clinical psychologist in private practice. The school position is a staff position, an advisory position. The worker's conclusions and advice are always subject to comment and review from the classroom teacher and the school principal and frequently from still higher authority.

AGAINST TWO LEVELS

The opponents of two levels made the following points. There is an old saying that the world accepts a man at the valuation he places on himself. Certainly the raising of requirements for admission to the professions of law and medicine has resulted in greater prestige and higher salaries. More men and women of ability have been attracted and the quality of the service has improved. There is precedent for requiring the doctor's degree in psychology. The APA requires it for Fellows. The Boulder Conference recommended that the title *clinical psychologist* should be used only by persons who have received a doctor's degree based on graduate education in clinical psychology at a recognized university (149, p. 37). If people can qualify as school psychologists with less training or less ability than they would need in other fields of psychology, school psychology may become a refuge for inferior individuals. If the Conference approves two levels, employers will consider two years of training sufficient and many people will enter the profession at the lower level and remain there. These people will be frozen in their jobs by the tenure system and because other members of the school system will like them personally and feel loyal to them. Salaries are large enough to satisfy many people, who will therefore have no urge for further training.

The school psychologist needs at least the training required for the doctoral level to take advantage of his opportunities to promote mental health. The psychological examiner often works alone and almost inevitably makes major decisions about children which he is not qualified to make. The limitation on legitimate service which limited training entails is a far more important argument against recognizing two levels of position than any loss of prestige or of salary.

THE CONFERENCE'S CONCLUSIONS

During the summary session in the last two days of the conference, a committee was appointed to draw up a statement of the Conference's opinions on the question of two levels of positions. The committe submitted a statement, which was approved by the Conference, to the following effect:

At the present time and in the foreseeable future, it is doubtful if school needs for psychological service can be met by personnel trained at the doctoral level. There are some of us who feel that even under ideal conditions there will be a need for subdoctoral personnel on the school psychologist's staffs to handle many of the tasks that do not require upper-level skills. Parenthetically, it is believed that the so-called lower-level person has not been given the recognition he needs for personal and professional security.

The psychological examiner will be under great pressure to exceed the limits of his training. Some safeguards against this are desirable. The psychological examiner should be trained to seek the help of better-qualified individuals, both those among his colleagues on the school staff and those in public and private mental-health agencies. Where skilled supervision of the psychological examiner is not provided locally, it may be possible to arrange it on a state or county basis. All workers (including school psychologists) should be encouraged to continue to improve their knowledge. In the last analysis, of course, ethics should prevent an individual's undertaking tasks which he is not competent to handle.

The Committee's statement included some remarks on training which are presented in Chapters XV and XVI. See also Chapter VIII.

THE QUESTION OF TITLES

Parallel with the discusion of whether or not there should be two levels of position, there was a discussion of what title might be attached to each.

The convenience of standard titles is enormous. For everyone to know that a person who calls himself a school psychologist has met certain definite requirements makes life simpler for psychologists in service, for employers, and for candidates for positions. Moreover, it is something of a safeguard against quackery. The Conference voted unanimously that the title *school psychologist* should be used for individuals with doctoral training.

In the summaries of the first two days of discussion, the title *psychological examiner* was used to describe the lower level of worker. This title and *Level II worker* were very generally used during later discussions, but without real approval. In the final sessions a committee was appointed to consider the problems of titles. It reported to the following effect:

We agree on the principle that the names of the two levels should discriminate clearly between them in terms of training and functions. The use of the title *school psychologist* for the upper level is approved. No title for the lower level seems to fill all the requirements. The committee does not favor the use of titles like *assistant* or *junior school psychologist*, because there is danger that the qualifying term will be dropped in practice. Common usage favors the title *psychological examiner*. APA terminology might indicate that *psychological technician* is more appropriate. A possible title would be *school psychological service worker*. In any case, the name should be such as to indicate a lower level of training and of functioning.

No formal action was taken on this report. But when the title *psychological examiner* was used at the APA meeting in September, 1954, it became the main topic of discussion by the two hundred who heard the preliminary report. Most called it unsatisfactory, but no one suggested a better title. So, until some title meets with general approval, it seems well to use the title *school psychological examiner* but to recognize that the duties of qualified workers at the lower level should, and in fact do, extend far beyond mere testing.

FUNCTIONS COMPARED

The members of the Conference felt that it would be unwise to specify or limit the functions of any school psychological worker, provided always that no one should undertake work out of line with his qualifications. The interests and training of individuals and the demands of local situations made exact statements impossible and undesirable.

In general, the *school psychologist* was expected to be competent to act as a consultant in the development of total school programs and therefore to have wide knowledge of educational organization and administration. He should be prepared to work in both elementary and secondary schools. He should have the ability to suggest and evaluate policies and procedures which would provide for good mental health. He should have expert knowledge of individual and group tests and their use in diagnosis. He will be familiar with the backgrounds, the problems, and the best methods of education of many types of exceptional children, including the physically handicapped and the gifted. He should, when it is advisable, be able to provide re-education. He should be expert in research design and execution.

Some members of the Conference maintained that a *psychological examiner* should work only under the supervision of a school psychologist. Other members of the Conference saw that it would be impractical (outside of large cities) to require that all psychological examiners work under the immediate supervision of a school psychologist. They also appreciated the excellent work being done by psychological examiners in the schools. They agreed, however, that a psychological examiner should try to maintain professional contacts with state supervision, with the personnel of local clinics, and with psychological workers of both levels in the neighborhood. He should be quick to ask for help when he has doubts about handling a case (as should the *school psychologist!*).

The Conference members agreed that the *psychological examiner* will have a less extensive repertoire of individual tests than the *school psychologist*. He should not be expected to carry on supervision of other psychological personnel. He might be prepared to serve in an elementary school or in a secondary school rather than in both. He is not expected to deal with the broad policies of the school system. He does not engage in intensive re-education. There were differences of opinion about the character of research he might undertake but no doubt as to the value of research as in-service training. Beyond this, no differentiation of functions was made at the Conference.

In current practice, the duties of *school psychologists* and *psychological examiners* overlap. Duties of the former may, of course, include all the duties of the latter. The extent to which this is true can be seen from reading the reports of the two workers in San Mateo County presented earlier (see Chapter IV).

One school superintendent, announcing an opening in the position of psychological examiner, describes the duties and qualifications as follows:

GENERAL STATEMENT OF DUTIES OF THE PSYCHOLOGICAL EXAMINER

The examiner is responsible for the administration and interpretation of a variety of psychological and educational tests to individuals and to groups of school children. He prepares reports and recommendations based on his examinations and confers with principals, school social workers, and classroom teachers. When required, he participates in conferences with staff members on individual cases. It is particularly desirable that he should be familiar with diagnostic examining of children who have educational disabilities and with clinical examination procedures. He should also be familiar with group tests of intelligence and achievement so that he can participate in the group testing program. . . . The examiner will work under the supervision of the Director of Research and Guidance, who is a certified school psychologist. In addition to those qualifications required for certification as a psychological examiner (master's degree and about two years' testing experience), experience in a psycho-educational, child-guidance, or mental-hygiene clinic, where the psychologist's study was coordinated with the findings of co-workers of professional rank, is desired. Public-school teaching experience would be valuable, but education courses, particularly methods, will be an acceptable substitute. Psychological service is well accepted in this school system, and more than test scores or IQ's is expected. There will be ample opportunity for initiative.

XV

A Two-Year Training Program

THE Conference, having agreed to recommend that school psychological workers be trained and certified at two levels, discussed what the content of the training program for each level should be. Like other groups who have struggled with the problems of professional training at a subdoctoral level, they found recommendations extraordinarily difficult to make.

A GENERAL PROBLEM

The E & T Board's Committee on Subdoctoral Education made a report in April, 1953, summarizing available information about subdoctoral training programs. The committee described existing conditions. A substantial proportion of employed psychologists have less than doctoral training. There are differences in the amount of training in different sections of the country. There is disagreement among psychologists about the amount of training required for various kinds of psychological work. There are wide differences among institutions providing training at this level. The committee found that "the effectiveness of a program is dependent upon the size of the instructional staff, the professional efficiency and teaching skill of the staff, library, laboratory, and practicum facilities available, the opportunities available for training in collateral fields, the quality of students admitted to the training program, and the individualized teaching and guidance available to students." The committee recommended further study of subdoctoral training and that individual departments be encouraged to develop and evaluate experimental subdoctoral programs (12).

Moore, in an article on the master's degree in psychology (125), reports on conferences on subdoctoral education which were held over a period of two years in connection with five regional-association meetings. The educational programs described at these meetings fall into three categories. The more traditional program is of a theoretical nature and is planned as a portion of the Ph.D. program. This was the conception of the M.A. program in nearly all Eastern departments of psychology and in many Midwestern ones. The second type of

144

program combines theoretical education with some professional train-ing and is more common in state colleges and universities. This is sometimes a two-year program. Programs of the third type are aimed primarily toward professional training for a terminal master's degree and were reported more commonly in the Southern and Rocky Moun-tain regional meetings, and to some extent in the Midwestern meeting. Professional training was reported in several fields closely related to school psychology, e.g., clinical psychology, special education, guidance, and child development.

The comments and questions Moore heard at the regional meetings were very much like those at the Conference. What kind of theoretical training is most valuable for the clinician? One person said that the M.A. degree should prepare a student for learning and not for a job. Another said that scholarly training does not necessarily lead to proficiency in the applied fields, and that psychology departments have definite responsibilities for providing service courses. It was pointed out that state aid is sometimes offered for a special-class teacher or social worker but not for a school psychologist. If sub-doctoral training is not offered in psychology departments, other ser-vice workers with less training are likely to do the psychological work. There was concern about schools of education providing the training of school psychologists. The dangers of technically trained persons' trying to do more than they were qualified to do were pointed out, but no suggestions for avoiding this were generally accepted. One suggestion made in these discussions was brought out at the Confer-ence: training should provide an awareness of limitations and responsi-bilities.

Obviously the problem of subdoctoral training is not limited to school psychology. That the profession of psychology as a whole is concerning itself with all levels of training for psychological work is reassuring.

TYPE OF PROGRAM RECOMMENDED

The Conference recommended that institutions be encouraged to develop strong programs for the initial training and further training of psychological examiners. It was felt that this should be approxi-mately a two-year program and probably include a master's degree. It should be an integrated program of courses and practical work. The final recommendation was that practical work should include the equivalent of a half year either in practicum facilities in the university or in carefully supervised experiences in a school system with a school psychological program. There was, however, a difference of opinion about the length of time of the practicum. Some of the Conference members felt that an internship of less than a year was inadequate.

RELATION TO BACKGROUND

It was recognized that the training program must be flexible in order to provide for students with different backgrounds. It seems probable that in the future as in the past many people wishing to study to be psychological examiners will have had teaching experience. Successful teachers with from one to five years of experience were thought of as desirable candidates. The two-year training program would probably be adequate for such a student. However, the kind of teacher training and experience would be a factor in his ability to complete the program in two years of graduate training. In general, training and experience in elementary school teaching would probably be better preparation than training and experience at the secondary level. The student with training only at the secondary level would probably need additional courses in curriculum materials and methods, as well as practical experience in working with younger children.

For students with no teaching experience, an additional internship experience of one year should be required. This internship should be planned to give the student a wide practical knowledge of many phases of the school program. It should probably be entirely in a school setting (see Chapter XIII).

Plans for practical experience for psychological examiners would need to be flexible because it is hoped that many persons already employed in psychological work may be stimulated by the recommendations of the Conference to increase their level of training. These people may already be psychological examiners who have had long, varied, and successful school experience. They will nonetheless seek further training, but still at the subdoctoral level, as this becomes available. Practical experience in a child-guidance clinic or neuropsychiatric institute might supplement their experience in a much more valuable way than further work in the schools. Some psychologists who have experience in institutions for the mentally retarded or for delinquents may elect to take training for work in the schools. Their previous experience would need to be carefully evaluated to make the best plans for them. Whatever training is offered should be the most effective program which the institution can plan for the individual.

PART-TIME STUDY

For the teacher who wishes to become a psychological examiner and for the psychological examiner who wishes to improve his training and perhaps become a school psychologist, part-time work must be offered. Few school employees can afford to give up their salaries for long periods.

Moore (124) states that there are part-time students in clinical training programs, although he does not give their number. He says the number of students in urban universities seems excessively large because it includes both full-time and part-time students. The Teachers College, Columbia University, program for diploma candidates offers course work on a part-time basis, but requires candidates in their second year to study full-time for one semester, preferably in the spring.

THE CONFERENCE OPINION

The Conference opinion about training programs for psychological examiners is summed up in a statement approved unanimously in one of the closing sessions. This reads:

> The training program for psychological examiners must be planned to meet their needs rather than as a preliminary to a doctoral program. Only where the needs of workers at the two levels coincide should the programs be the same. The institutions best equipped to give training for psychological examiners should undertake it, both because of the need of well-trained workers and also because less-well-equipped institutions might otherwise enter the field. In any case, there should be a strong national program of accreditation of training institutions and definite control of workers by adequate state certification regulations. Where a psychological examiner is not under the immediate supervision of a fully qualified school psychologist, an attempt should be made to provide such supervision on a regional basis. Training programs for psychological examiners should always include a sound foundation of general psychology and indoctrination in ethics, and should emphasize the need for future training.

DIFFERENCES BETWEEN TWO- AND FOUR-YEAR PROGRAMS

The specific differences between the recommended two-year program and the recommended four-year program depend on the differences in the functions of the psychological examiner and the school psychologist, which were described in the previous chapter. The psychological examiner would very likely not have time to prepare for work in both the elementary and secondary levels. He would have skill in a less extensive repertoire of tests, he would not be prepared to give intensive re-education, he would not have advanced preparation for work in research, he would not be prepared to supervise psychological interns, and he would not be prepared to advise on over-all school policy and its mental-hygiene aspects.

He would be trained to undertake the assessment of intellectual, educational, and emotional difficulties of all children, with special attention to the problems of exceptional children. He would acquire skill in gathering basic information, conducting interviews, establishing rapport in test situations, working with parents, and working with small groups, e.g., of personnel from school and community agencies. He would learn to integrate the information he gathers and to make adequate verbal and written reports. His training in re-education would include practice in making recommendations about changes in situations. He should be skilled in brief interviews with school children, parents, and teachers. His training in research would include the ability to evaluate and interpret research. He should attempt to perceive opportunities for research growing out of his own interests and his activities in the school.

TWO-YEAR TRAINING

The University of Michigan's two-year training course, though designed to meet special conditions in Michigan, may be of general interest. The folder which describes it is quoted at length to show how the ideas expressed in this chapter may be implemented.

Training Program for School Psychological Diagnosticians

A two-year training program for School Psychological Diagnosticians has been set up by the University of Michigan under the joint sponsorship of the School of Education and the Department of Psychology. Students may include the graduate courses taken in this program in satisfying the requirements for the degree of Master of Science in Education or in Psychology. The courses making up the sequence are selected with a view to developing a certain degree of understanding of both educational and psychological practice and procedures. On this foundation, training in individual testing is provided, to be followed by a semester of practice under supervision.

Satisfactory completion of the program will qualify the candidate for approval as School Psychological Diagnostician for the reimbursable educational programs for special services for mentally handicapped children. (A Michigan plan for the education of the mentally handicapped, under which the local schools are reimbursed for the costs of certain types of services.) The chief responsibility of the School Psychological Diagnostician is that of determining by means of various psychological techniques the intellectual, emotional, and social characteristics of pupils and their educational potentials, in order that an informed judgment may be made as to the kind of school program that would best fit their needs. The findings of the diagnostic study will be utilized to assist the school screening committee, the teacher, the parent, and the community in meeting the needs of mentally handicapped pupils.

Equivalent courses may, in certain cases, be substituted for those listed. Variations in the program of courses offered by the applicant, however, must be approved by the joint committee and when so approved will be accepted by the Department of Public Instruction. The Department must give either its "temporary" or "full" approval of the credentials of the candidate before he can participate in the reimbursable program.

The sequence of courses necessary for approval assumes certain undergraduate prerequisites and consists of four parts: (1) a measurement core, (2) background courses, (3) related electives, and (4) an internship. For full approval candidates must present a total of thirty six hours exclusive of prerequisites and the internship. Units are indicated in semester hours.

Prerequisite
Elementary General Psychology—3
Introductory Educational Psychology—2
Note: Either a valid Michigan teaching certificate or Associate Membership in the American Psychological Association is required for full approval. Those who do not hold a teaching certificate are required to elect a minimum of four semester hours in two of the following three fields: educational history, curriculum, and administration.
It is suggested that selection be made from the following courses:
History of Education—2
Elementary School Curriculum *or* Modern High School Curriculum—2
Elementary School Organization and Administration *or* Secondary School Administration—2

Measurements (required: 9 or 10 hours)
Appraising Student Progress *or* Human Traits and Abilities—3

Educational Statistics—2, *or* Elementary Statistical Methods in Psychology—3

Individual Testing—4, *or* Basic Methods in Psychology—2 and Individual Mental Testing—2

Background courses (required: 13 hours)

Psychology of Child Development—2
Mental Hygiene of Childhood and Adolescence—2
Personality Development—3
Education of Exceptional Children—2
Education and Social Control of Mentally Retarded Children—2
Medical Orientation of Teachers of Hospitalized Children *or* Medical Information for Social Workers—2

Related electives (13 or 14 hours)

In the general fields of psychology, educational psychology, mental hygiene, and child development. Election from the following list is recommended.

Clinical Study of Atypical Children *or* Socio-Emotional Development of Children: at University Fresh Air Camp—2-4
Note: Those who have not had practice-teaching experience are required to elect both of these courss.
Educational Statistics—2
Social Learning—2
Psychology of the High School Subjects—2
Psychology and Teaching of Reading, Writing and Spelling—2
Psychology and Teaching of Arithmetic—2
The Deviant Individual—3, *or* Mental Hygiene—2
Physical Growth of the Child—2
Experimental Study of Personality—2
Basic Methods in Psychology—2

Internship (supervised experience in individual testing)

Prerequisites: At least two-thirds of the program of required and elective courses including Individual Mental Testing. The arrangement for the Internship must provide for practice in administering and interpreting tests under supervision in an institutional setting. The total minimum time required is fifteen weeks full time or the equivalent in part time work (or one semester, or two summer sessions, in college-connected centers). Arrangements will be made either in a school system employing a qualified supervising psychologist or in a custodial institution or center or clinic in which the clientele is primarily children (175).

XVI.

A Four-Year Training Program

THE Conference discussions on training were mainly devoted to a doctoral training program in which three years would be devoted to study and research and a fourth year to internship. This amount of training was considered necessary to equip the school psychologist to offer the many psychological services which are essential for the best development of all children. The demand for school psychologists with this kind of training exceeds the supply. The principal stumbling block has been the lack of well-developed training programs. At present such programs are few in number and not easily accessible to everyone.

REORGANIZATION OF GRADUATE TRAINING

School psychologists who have spent many years in the schools and have seen the developments in psychology which demand further education are puzzled as to how a student can learn enough to be qualified for his responsibilities when he is first employed. Training institutions find it difficult to plan a program which is adequate in four years. But members of the conference were definite that it should be a four-year program not a five- or six-year program, although these might be easier to plan. School psychologists are not alone in this dilemma. President Charles W. Cole of Amherst discussed this in his Spaulding Lecture at Yale University in 1953. He pointed out that two developments make a drastic redirection of higher education necessary: the tremendous growth of facilities for making information readily accessible, such as dictionaries, encyclopedias, and card catalogues; the tremendous increase in factual knowledge in the last two hundred years. It is no longer possible for anyone to master even a narrow specialty within his chosen subject before he is 28 or 30. To keep up with all the developments in a broader field would be a full-time job. This has resulted in our becoming a nation of specialists. It could push specialization to absurd limits.

Cole observed a group of doctors trying to compress medical knowledge into a four-year curriculum. This was impossible. They decided to place less emphasis on memory work and put greater stress on clinical training. Even the first-year student might work with a doctor in the care of the sick. The objective of the education of the medical student will not be the acquisition of all medical knowledge but learning to think like a doctor. Cole illustrates from other fields. For example, the graduate schools cannot attempt to pass on any considerable fraction of the accumulated knowledge of psychology. But they can teach young men and women to think like psychologists. This requires the psychologist to have an understanding of the materials for thought, where they may be found, and how they may be analyzed. He must also know how to organize and use these materials in solving problems. These objectives entail a reorganization of higher education, with emphasis on laboratory and field work (54).

PROGRAMS MUST BE EXPERIMENTAL

Creative, imaginative planning on the part of the faculties of colleges and universities, working in close collaboration with advisory committees of practicing school psychologists and school administrators, will be needed to determine the best type of program. Members of the Conference hope that major colleges and universities will see the importance of providing full training in this area and that smaller institutions will insist on high standards in any courses which they offer.

The discussions on training were approached with all the humility which it was said school psychologists should have. No one knows just what the training program should be. It is impossible to list the specific abilities and skills which the school psychologist should have. Such a list would be endless, far longer than can be listed here, or than could be compressed into any reasonable training program. Members of the Conference were aware, too, that they were dealing with a growing body of knowledge. Abilities and skills that are needed now will be changed by the deepened and sharpened understandings and techniques which the future will bring. The well-trained school psychologist will find before and after employment that he will need to increase his skill and understanding in specific areas. Skill in assessing the intelligence of the blind or of infants might be examples. All school psychologists should have awareness and understanding of such areas, but only a few need be intensively trained in each special skill.

The training program should definitely not try to train the school psychologist to perpetuate what is being done. It should develop in the student an attitude of applying his abilities and skills both in accepted and in original ways in the schools. The Conference expected that students will gain their training in course work, in laboratory experiences, and in field work. One member of the Conference, Dr. Marie Skodak, presented an analysis of the school psychologist's competencies and related areas of training which the Conference found helpful in its discussions, but no attempt was made to suggest the contents of a program in terms of courses or semester hours. This sort of recommendation might result in a collection of courses rather than an integrated program. However much help it seeks, each faculty must, in the final analysis, plan its own program. Different types of programs in various universities would provide different experiences. Faculty members in one university could profit from experiences in other universities, and, in this way, sound progress would be made. The important consideration is a carefully planned program based upon clearly defined objectives. This chapter describes the objectives which the Conference set up after ten days of discussion. It may be a guide to faculties working on the problem, but they will have to work through the problem for themselves.

So many areas of the country have no facilities for training school psychologists that it may be advisable to develop plans on a regional basis. The eight states in the Northeast, which have reciprocal certification regulations, have been making regional plans for the training of special-class teachers. They may form a good precedent to follow for training school psychologists.

A Program of Psychology and Education

The members of the Conference foresaw difficulties in organizing a program of training which would include both psychology and education. The training requires cooperation by departments of psychology, education, child welfare, social welfare, and perhaps other departments. The important considerations are the content of courses and the qualifications of the persons teaching them. For example, an adequate course in the psychology of learning might be offered either as psychology or as education. The qualifications of the person who teaches the course will determine its adequacy, not the department in which he teaches. The Conference unanimously agreed that, in whatever department he is teaching, the person teaching a course in psychology should be a qualified psychologist.

In large universities the broad patterns are set up by a graduate school which awards the degree. It must rely on some department to administer the program and recommend candidates for degrees. Insofar as the graduate school is concerned, the recommending unit may be a matter of indifference. However, the amount of participation of individuals and departments and the type of experience to be provided for students is of concern to the units supplying the preparation. A simple quantitative definition of hours of education and psychology will not resolve the difficulty because of differences in organization.

Wherever there are several highly developed departments, e.g., of psychology, education, and child welfare, concerned with this training, it is recommended that interdepartmental committees be organized to set up the requirements for the doctor's degree. Such committees might involve whatever university persons and resources might be helpful.

For example, the University of Illinois set up a joint committee on school psychology. The original statement read:

> In order to facilitate the operation of this program it is necessary that there be appointed by the Dean of the College of Education and the Head of the Department of Psychology a continuing Joint Committee on School Psychology of not less than four members, two from education and two from psychology. The chairman of this committee could be elected by the members of the committee. (Further administrative plans regarding tenure of the committee members, possibly of rotation of membership, reporting procedures, manner of operation, etc. can be worked out at the time the committee is constituted, or shortly thereafter.)
>
> This committee should have these official responsibilities:
>
> a. recommending the approval of applicants for admission to the program, over and above the respective college or department requirements;
>
> b. individual program counseling of students working in this program, not necessarily including dissertation supervision;
>
> c. recommending, for approval by the College of Education and the Department of Psychology, situations in which internship experiences may be acquired; and
>
> d. continued responsibility for the over-all improvement of the total program for the training of school psychologists (174).

Members of the Conference felt that a thoroughly competent school psychologist with good experience in the schools should be on the steering committee planning a program of training. If possible, such a person who has the full confidence of his colleagues should be responsible for organizing, directing, and coordinating the training program.

PREREQUISITE COURSES

School psychological workers have a variety of undergraduate backgrounds. Some who were liberal-arts-college graduates majored in psychology, some minored in psychology, and some took only one or two courses in psychology. Teachers-college graduates have devoted varying proportions of their time to liberal arts (or general education), to psychology, and to education.

The trend in higher education today is definitely toward giving students a broad general background and away from early specialization in a subject and particularly from courses designed to train students in the techniques of a specialty. A succession of committees of lawyers, doctors, and engineers have found their own education too narrow and have advised the inclusion of more liberal arts in the preprofessional and professional curriculums. These men, outstanding in their professions, feel that when study is too narrow, the product is likely to be a limited perspective in world affairs and a rigidity in professional matters. The Conference felt that an undergraduate who looked forward to specializing in any field of psychology might well limit his preprofessional courses to those required for admission to the graduate school of his choice. Certainly the able graduate student can acquire the techniques which he needs more quickly and thoroughly than the average undergraduate.

One Conference group outlined four basic understandings that students should secure either as undergraduates or graduates. The reader should remember that many of the topics suggested may be covered in a single course or in general reading.

BASIC UNDERSTANDINGS

A broad foundation in psychology very similar to that outlined for clinical psychology (see Chapter XII). This will include an understanding of the principles and facts of human growth and development, especially in children and adolescents; an understanding of basic psychological concepts underlying behavior, with emphasis on the extent of individual differences, learning theories, personality structure, the theory of assessment, test construction, and statistics.

Comprehensive understanding in the field of education. This includes

156   SCHOOL PSYCHOLOGISTS AT MID-CENTURY

practical familiarity with teaching in the classroom and school organization (see Chapter XIII).

Social and cultural background. This should emphasize the sociological study of the community, social sciences, and the humanities.

Biological background. This should give the student a foundation in physiological psychology which would be basic to his understanding of mental defect, speech pathology, the cerebral palsies, epilepsy, and sensory defects, as well as other physical conditions which have a pronounced bearing on general behavior and particularly on learning.

The program for basic understandings should be flexible. It should be based on the previous background of the student. Some students would require greater training in some areas and less in others.

PSYCHOLOGICAL BACKGROUND FOR GRADUATE WORK

In the Conference's discussion of preprofessional background, most of the emphasis was on the need to understand educational procedures and how that training might be accomplished. But the teacher who wishes to become a school psychologist wants to know what training he lacks, and some of the psychologists at the Conference were fearful that a thorough training in psychology would be overlooked.

The majority opinion was that the graduate school would set up prerequisites for graduate training in psychology. For example, most initial graduate courses in psychology presume undergraduate work in general and experimental psychology and statistics. It is to be expected that there would be some deficiencies in undergraduate work and that each graduate institution would arrange that these be made up adequately in accord with its own regulations.

GRADUATE COURSES

With the exception of courses designed to fill in the gaps in the students' undergraduate program, all the courses in the graduate training program should be specifically designed for graduate students, and, under usual circumstances, the enrollment limited to graduate students. There are many institutions, particularly smaller ones, where courses are offered for either undergraduate or graduate credit. In these courses there is very little strictly graduate work. It is possible in many places to get a master's degree by taking such courses. This has not been approved by the APA in evaluating clinical programs. The Conference unanimously agreed to define a graduate course as one in which the majority of students are graduate students. The assumption was that the majority would pace the course.

Training for Promoting Mental Health

The student should acquire an understanding of the principles of mental health, what contributes to it and what interferes with it. As a school psychologist, he will need ability to observe signs of maladjustment in its early stages in children and faculty members and to plan with others methods of overcoming the difficulties. He will need knowledge of the theories about mental health and familiarity with pertinent literature. He will need an understanding of the influence of the home and the community in furthering or preventing the development of mental health. He must be competent to assist in the development of the educational program and procedures so that they will contribute to mental health. This may include skill in curriculum planning, over-all school policy, teacher selection and promotion, evaluation policies, and report-card and cumulative-record development.

The training in school psychology should indoctrinate the student with the idea that mental health is one of the most important areas of his work and that he should strive for opportunities to develop it, even if it is not expected of him and even if he is overwhelmed with other duties. His work in this area will make demands upon all the skills he is able to develop in techniques and personal relations required in other areas of his work.

Research

The training program should stress the value of research. The student should develop a research point of view, so that he sees tasks needing research, and sees opportunities to work into a busy service schedule some time for carrying out research. Every effort should be made during the training program to prepare him for his maximum research contribution.

The school psychologist should have sufficient understanding of research design to be effective in several phases of research. He should be able to plan and carry on systematic studies of practical school problems and to prepare research reports in both technical and popular form. He should occasionally make brief research reports to professional journals. He should learn to write readable and interesting reports for the annual school report, for use in the schools, for use in the local newspapers, and for use in the popular magazines.

He should be able to interpret, evaluate, and use the research of others and interpret it to the school staff. He should form the habit of reading research studies regularly. He should also form the habit of looking for articles in the local newspapers reporting speeches or articles which touch on his field. Educational personnel and the general public will depend on him to tell them whether what they read or hear on the radio or see on television is scientifically accurate or nonsense. It would be a waste of his valuable time to keep up with all of the popularization of research, but he should keep his eyes and ears open and be ready to answer questions.

He should be able to stimulate and assist other school personnel in carrying out research studies which may clarify the problems with which they are struggling. He should encourage and participate in cooperative efforts to secure dependable evidence on debatable issues of school policy and procedure.

His own experience in graduate work should teach him how to cooperate with university researchers who may carry on projects in the schools. He must learn how to keep a balance between pupil and teacher welfare and the promotion of research plans of university personnel. It is expected that every doctoral candidate will offer a basic research study in satisfaction of the requirements for the degree. This will provide fundamental experience in systematic inquiry and reporting.

Working With Groups

The school psychologist should be concerned with the evaluation of the abilities and achievement of all the children. As one means to this end, he should be thoroughly familiar with all types of group tests. He should be competent to select tests, and work with other school personnel in selecting them. He should be able to devise new tests when this is required. He should be capable of planning and administering a group testing program. He should be skillful in teaching others to give and score group tests, and to supervise the reports of these tests. He should be skillful in training others to take over duties of this sort which may have been originally assigned to him, but could be carried on by others equally well. He will learn to gather useful knowledge of exceptional children through the study of group-test results. He will find clues pointing to those children who need further study but have not otherwise been reported to him.

The school psychologist's training in test construction and statistics, his theoretical knowledge about intelligence, educational achievement, vocational aptitude, and personality adjustment, give him a unique responsibility for contributing to the effectiveness of the testing program through evaluating and interpreting the validity and usefulness of specific tests. He should be equipped to advise on the school system's over-all testing program.

The school psychologist should gain skill in observing children in groups on the playground, in the classroom, and in the community. Sociometric techniques furnish tools he should be able to use. A study of group dynamics will make his work with groups more effective, whether the groups consist of children, youth, parents, teachers, or other adults. He should have some familiarity with, and develop some skill in, group counseling and group therapy.

WORKING WITH INDIVIDUALS

Work with individuals is traditionally the main duty of the school psychologist. Although emphasis is now placed also on a broad scope of work, the assessment of the individual is one of the duties for which he must be prepared. If he becomes head of a psychological department, he must be able to train others to work with individuals and he must supervise their work.

He must acquire skill in collecting, evaluating, and integrating relevant background information from all areas—the child himself, parents, teachers, and agencies. He must acquire the ability to understand many different vocabularies. These will include the idioms of children and parents from various social classes, the educational terms used by school personnel, and the technical terms used by social workers, doctors, psychiatrists, and other specialists. He must have sufficient knowledge of each field to understand the concepts behind the phraseology. For example, he must have a general understanding of such diseases as epilepsy and rheumatic fever and of their educational implications.

The school psychologist will study the individual child in the setting of the information he has gathered. He will need to be competent in the selection, administration, and interpretation of individual tests of intelligence, aptitude, interests, and special abilities. He will need skill in the use of individual tests of educational abilities, potentialities, and disabilities, including the interpretation of sensory and other physical conditions in relation to educational adjustment.

In the assessment of personality, the psychologist must have a firm grounding in the theory of personality and understand how the techniques which he uses assist in disclosing personality. Assessment of personality will include the use of projective techniques as tools when these are appropriate. The psychologist needs to recognize the importance of the interaction of his own personality with that of the child. He will need skill in interviewing and observing the child in order to understand the child's potentialities and how he values himself.

He must have ability to synthesize all the information into an overall understanding. He must learn that assessment is never carried on for its own sake but must lead to action which is designed to influence the behavior of the child or set the stage for better adjustment of one or many children. This action (or planned refrainment from action) may be carried on by the psychologist or, more often, by others whose duty it is to promote the necessary adjustments.

WORKING WITH EXCEPTIONAL CHILDREN

The school psychologist must have an understanding of his responsibility in identifying those children who need special services. The broader aspects of psychology should not wean him away from this important responsibility. He must develop skill in identifying various types of exceptional children. He should be specifically competent in the assessment of the mentally retarded, including the identification of the factors which occasionally cause a child to behave in a fashion closely resembling mental retardation; of children with educational disabilities; of socially and emotionally disturbed children; of children with sensory handicaps, visual, auditory, or other; of crippled children, including the less involved cases of cerebral palsy and other physical handicaps. He need not be skilled in examining all those whose special handicaps require specialized methods of assessment, but he should be aware of the problems involved and of where more highly specialized services are available. He will need skill in making many kinds of recommendations for exceptional children. If exclusion is to be recommended, he must know the procedure and what further recommendations can be made. He will need to be able to recommend classroom modifications for exceptional children and to devise new methods of teaching such children. He will need to be able to plan and develop resources for exceptional children in school and in the community, e.g., special educational and recreational facilities. He will have to know how to work with teachers on suitable methods for special classes, and how to help the parents accept and understand the problem.

When he discovers educational disabilities, he must be able to help plan remedial programs, and to apply appropriate remedial techniques himself if necessary. For example, there will be emphasis on remedial reading programs and he will need to know how to help.

The gifted child should be one of his major responsibilities, whether the child appears well-adjusted in school or not. The psychologist should know how to help the school challenge the gifted child, how to help the gifted child who is failing in any aspect of his school life, and how to see that the child has all possible opportunities for development.

METHODS OF CHANGING BEHAVIOR

The breadth, depth, and quality of the school psychologist's skill and judgment receive their severest tests and make their greatest contributions in recommendations and actions designed to produce changes in behavior. He must see the teaching process as a group process and be able to assist the teacher in the teacher's classroom role as well as in meeting the needs of the individual pupil. To make adequate recommendations for all kinds of children, the school psychologist needs a broad knowledge of the school program in general and of the particular features of the school where the child with whom he is working is placed. He must know the resources in the schools, in the home, and the community for added help. He must know the possibilities of institutional placement. He must know the laws that govern his actions and those of the teachers. The school psychologist must be skilled in changing the situation as one means of bringing about the child's best development, educationally, socially, emotionally, and physically. He may need to engineer a change in environment. He may do this through school placement or through curriculum adjustment. He may have to bring about changes in attitudes or methods of teachers or parents. He may utilize community resources.

On the other hand, the school psychologist must also be able to work with the child needing individual treatment. He will not usually have the training which the clinical psychologist has in individual psychotherapy. He should be competent in the types of re-education which can be carried out in a school setting. The school environment may actually contribute stability and effectiveness and instill confidence which the child would not otherwise feel. The school psychologist should have skill in dealing with personal problems on an immediate basis, providing release and reorientation of the child's emotions. In short, he must understand the principles and techniques of modifying behavior and have skill in using them.

WORKING WITH OTHERS TO HELP CHILDREN

The school psychologist must have an understanding of the school's relations with parents, physicians, psychiatrists, social workers, and clergy, and must have respect for the contributions of each.

He must understand how to integrate his services with the entire school program. He must learn to respect lines of authority and responsibility and to inspire respect for his contribution. He must have skill in working as a member of teams which will be different with different children and in different situations. He must be able to utilize services and skills in areas where he has limited competence. He will need to know how to handle anxiety, uncertainty, and hostility in himself and others.

He should develop skill in case conferences focusing on the child and involving the persons directly concerned. He must have skill in staff conferences focusing on a school activity or program for the child. These skills will include the relatively simple ones of interviewing students, parents, and teachers to obtain background facts. They will also include complex tasks like conducting conferences and other group meetings, consulting with administrators, teachers, and parents, and counseling persons over repeated sessions in the effort to improve personal adjustments.

He will need the skills of a good teacher, not only to understand the problems of teachers but because he will often teach teachers and other adults. He must be a source of in-service training in his specialty. He will need competence in assisting others to acquire skills in interviewing and in individual consultation. He will need to teach others how to study individual and group behavior, write case histories, and record observations of individual and group activities. He will need skill in helping teachers and administrators to see the extent to which his services can be used in the schools. He must learn how to work with teachers so that he can be helpful in their immediate problems. And he must be able to do all of these things without arousing antagonism.

SKILL IN COMMUNICATION

The school psychologist should have an understanding of the importance of communicating in clear and forceful English both what he has learned about a child and the recommendations which he would like to make. He should be able to make himself understood by children as well as adults. This is peculiarly important and peculiarly difficult. He should have practice in making verbal and written reports to different audiences and for different purposes. He will need to have skill in the use of audio-visual techniques. He will need to have an understanding of the principles and practices of interpreting the school program to the parents and the community as a whole. He will need the skills of a public-relations expert, so far as he is able to acquire these.

ADMINISTRATION AND SUPERVISION

The school psychologist must have skill in planning his time and activities if the schools are to benefit from them. He must be able to organize the clerical and administrative procedures involved in individual case work and in all kinds of test records, with particular emphasis on incorporating these records in to the school record system. He will need to know how to plan procedures for referral and follow-up of cases and for making reports and contacts with other school personnel.

He will neeed skill in supervision. The school psychologist will frequently have to supervise psychological examiners and psychological interns. He will need to develop a vigorous sense of his ethical responsibility. He should be a leader in work with educational personnel in professional matters such as certification policies and the organization and management of professional groups.

PRACTICAL EXPERIENCES

Plans for the training of the school psychologist are going through some of the phases that the training of teachers has passed through. At one time few teachers received any specific training in teaching and none was required. But leaders in education recognized the advantages of specialized study and of practical training under supervision, and the present system of courses in education, practice teaching, and certification developed. School psychology parallels this development in many ways. The teacher turned psychologist, or the psychologist himself went into the schools without much specific preparation, and learned by hard experience how to apply a limited number of techniques. Now, with the complexity of the school situation, multiplicity of school personnel, and many more techniques to use, the need to have the school psychologist's training include supervised practice in schools, clinics, and institutions has become apparent.

The report of the Boulder Conference states that lack of agreement on terminology to describe different kinds of practical training was one of the most persistent problems. Three levels of experience were identified and a majority agreement obtained on terminology. A sizeable minority disagreed. The first level was called laboratory experience. The second and third levels were called practicum. These had previously been called clerkship and internship (149, p. 107). The APA Committee on Counselor Training also indicated three levels: laboratory experiences or prepracticum, field-work experiences, and internship (10, p. 183).

The Thayer Conference struggled with this problem also. There was particular objection to the term "clerkship" in a school setting because the clerks usually assigned for duty in principals' offices are clerks in the usual sense of the word. The terminology finally adopted was similar to that used in the counselor-training program: laboratory, field experiences, and internship. It was decided to use the term practicum as a general term covering all three types of applied experience.

POLICIES ON THE PRACTICUM

The Conference felt strongly that the practicum should be considered an integral part of the graduate program. The total practicum should be broad rather than limited in scope. Insofar as possible the student should gain experience with people of different age groups from preschool to adulthood, in different types of schools and agencies, and representing a range of social backgrounds. The experiences should be carefully planned and varied in nature. There should be sufficient flexibility so that a student can be given practice to supplement deficiencies and to have good all-round preparation for his work. Students will vary as to undergraduate majors, social and cultural origins, and past experience in teaching, work with children, and other sorts of employment.

The quality of supervision at each stage of the practicum was thought to be of paramount importance. The experiences should be carefully supervised and organized into a meaningful sequence. Persons with a broad practical background in school psychology should have a major part in planning, and especially in supervising, the practicum. This is important in order that the student may have good training and because the school is a large institution with teachers involved in a difficult task with many children. The graduate student's work in the school must be carefully planned to protect the teachers and children from wasting time and to prevent the educational program from being unduly interrupted.

It was recognized that it would be hard to find school psychologists, broadly trained, who could give the time that was necessary for supervision. It was suggested that Division 16 might canvass the field and find persons who were well-qualified and willing to serve in this capacity and were located in situations where practicum experience might be obtained. The internship may have to be served at some distance from the university.

The major portion of the practicum should be placed in the last two years of the training period. The Conference also felt that some practical work beginning early in the total program was desirable.

The Conference saw a need for the development of model internship centers which would serve to set standards. These models should be established in schools recognized as providing a fine educational experience for the children. Model centers aided the development of other comparable fields, such as medicine, social work, and clinical psychology, during the period of rapid expansion of those training programs.

LEVELS OF PRACTICUM

Laboratory. The student has his first actual experience in the use of techniques as a part of a laboratory course in the training institution. There he learns how to administer, score, and interpret tests, make observations of the child and integrate such observations with test findings, and write reports. Such laboratory experiences should obviously be a part of introductory courses in testing. The student may test children in a school setting, but the test results should not be used by the school. A university school or clinic on the campus would be an ideal place in which to undertake such training.

Field experiences. The second level of experience is also integrated with work in courses, but makes the child the central issue and develops the student's feeling for the child as an individual human being. The purpose is to provide training in making judgments, in the interpretation of the test data, and in integrating such information with other data which are available about an individual child. The reports should be in a form which could be used by the school, though the school should treat them with special caution. At this level, the student is trained in using psychological information in a school situation and with a broader range of problems. Case studies should involve conferences with the teacher, social workers, and others who may have information about a child.

It is essential that field experience be gained in a psychological-service agency under the supervision of a competent psychologist. A student who is sent to a school, clinic, or institution where there is no psychologist, or who searches out subjects for his own practice, even though his instructor provides supervision, does not satisfy the requirements of field experience. It should be a significant experience but one with limited responsibility.

Internship. The internship lies between field experience and the full responsibility of the school psychologist on the job. The university is responsible for exercising care in selecting agencies to be used for internship and for maintaining close liaison with these agencies, particularly with the supervisor of the intern.

The internship should be sharply differentiated from mere experience on the job. It involves a high level of continuous and active supervision and is designed to develop, as rapidly and as efficiently as possible, high-level competencies. In this sense it is an essential step in the development of a professionally oriented person. It is much more than a maturing experience. It attempts to provide training and instruction of an advanced sort in those areas which cannot be properly taught in courses. It includes the development of feelings of responsibility and loyalty toward the school as well as the skills in communication and judgment which characterize the well-trained professional. From the school's standpoint, the internship is not to be considered as an inexpensive source of labor. Rather, it involves a perhaps costly investment in the training of a person who can be trained no other way, and who will repay the investment through a much higher return when he is later employed in some school system as a school psychologist.

The internship is expected to be carried on full-time for an academic year. It will require ingenuity to provide all of the required training in the one-year period. The APA committee on practicum training studied internship training in clinical psychology (11). In a questionnaire survey of 176 agencies, the chiefs of the training programs stated that it was impossible to give adequate training in the three areas of diagnosis, therapy, and research, in a one-year internship. The experience in schools which was suggested in Chapter XIII will be added to the training in diagnosis and research for the school psychologist. Less training in therapy will not balance the time needed for school experience.

The student obviously cannot have practical training in all areas. He should certainly have intensive experience in a school psychological program. The major part of the internship should be in a school setting or in an agency or institution dealing with children and with problems related to education. It was suggested that at least the later stages of the internship should be in school. Other types of experience might be obtained in child-guidance clinics, community-health clinics, vocational-guidance centers, institutions or schools for exceptional children, and a children's section of a mental hospital. A suggestion was made that experience in these other agencies might be obtained in the summer vacation.

Internship planned for the student who has no teaching experience will have to include the training suggested here and also provide sufficient familiarity with schools to overcome his lack of teaching experience. The student will need to check certification requirements in the state in which he wishes to work, to be sure that actual classroom teaching for a specified number of years is not required. The training of school social workers offers some suggestions for planning an internship without providing for teaching experience. There a carefully planned alternative is substituted for teaching. Other suggestions are made about methods of providing familiarity with school procedures in Chapter XIII.

Experiences in the development of internship training in clinical psychology (8) and in counseling psychology (10, 37, 141) will be helpful in making plans for the training of school psychologists.

Further study of the practicum should be made by a committee familiar with the problems of internship and the work of the school psychologist.

An intern might expect to be paid. He is rendering service to the system in which he works. He wants to begin earning as soon as possible. But he may not have certification as a teacher or may have it in states other than those in which internships are available. This might prevent his receiving any public-school reimbursement during his internship. It is therefore recommended that steps be taken to obtain grants for stipends for such trainees during the internship period. A grant from a nonschool source, for example a foundation or governmental agency, would have the advantage of permitting an intern to serve part of the time in a school and part in an appropriate clinic, hospital, or other institution.

A CURRENT FOUR-YEAR TRAINING PROGRAM

The University of Illinois program for public-school psychologists is described in a mimeographed statement approved by the University Board of Trustees on June 24, 1953 (174). Excerpts from this are given here to show how such a program, drawing on the resources of several departments, may operate.

Essential competencies of the school psychologist. In general, a school psychologist should be capable of

a. administering and interpreting the results of individual and group, verbal, and non-verbal intelligence tests for the purpose of determining and describing the intellectual levels of children;
b. understanding the personalities of children by means of a variety of professionally accepted methods and techniques;
c. effecting, directly or indirectly, emotional and social re-education programs, both group and individual, and assisting school personnel in understanding and applying the principles of these techniques for the purpose of contributing both corrective and preventive aspects of mental hygiene in the school;
d. diagnosing educational achievement and assisting in the evaluation of eductional outcomes;
e. diagnosing educational disabilities and recommending and accomplishing remediation;
f. identifying psychologically, educationally, and socially exceptional children and recommending and effecting for them adequate educational and social programs and placement;
g. conducting case conferences both for the purpose of working in the interest of individual children and for the purpose of training those working with children;

h. diagnosing group difficulties and working with teachers, other personnel, and parents on curriculum committees, and on other school problems, for the purpose of assisting in improving learning and in facilitating better mental hygiene conditions in a school system; and

i. conducting, supervising, and advising with respect to research on
problems related to his work.

Requirements for admission to the program

a. Course requirements for a teacher's certificate (elementary or secondary) must be satisfied before the end of the first year of the program.

b. At least fifteen hours in the subject matter of psychology must have
been earned prior to admission, whether taken in education or in
psychology. These shall include statistics and experimental psychology.

c. An applicant without previous graduate work shall have attained a
minimum grade-point average of 4.0 for the last two years of his
undergraduate work.

d. Each applicant for admission to this program will be expected to meet
the requirements of that department or college in which he plans to
take his major work.

e. In addition to the above requirements, all applicants will be required
to be recommended for approval by the Joint Committee on School
Psychology.

General nature of the program

Either the degree of doctor of education or the degree of doctor of
philosophy in either psychology or education may be obtained in this
program. The nature of the work of the school psychologist being as described, it is particularly important that a significant part of the student's graduate work consist of training in research. In connection with
this aspect of his work it is anticipated that he will become competent
in both educational and psychological research methodologies as they
apply to the problems of the individual child and teacher in the school
system and that his dissertation will be a report of an original empirical
investigation.

It is at least a four-year program involving a minimum of three years
of related graduate work and twelve months of properly supervised
internship experience. The internship experience shall consist of not less
than one semester's full-time work in a school system under the supervision of a competent school psychologist and the remainder of the
experience is to be obtained in one, or preferably, two more of the following agencies: a community mental health clinic, a state colony for the
feebleminded, a state hospital for the mentally ill, an institution for
orthopedic cases, an institution for delinquents, or in an agency such as
the Illinois Institute for Juvenile Research. The internship year should
not precede the passing the preliminary examinations for the doctorate;
all internship experience must be under the supervision of persons and
in situations recommended by the Joint Committee on School Psychology
and having appropriate administrative approval by the University.

Interspersed throughout this four-year program will be (1) observation and participation in campus clinic and remedial programs, with experience in observation, clerical experience, shared responsibility for work with individual cases (both educational and psychological) and major individual responsibility for cases, and (2) participation in group screening and remedial procedures.

A minimal program of twenty-four units is proposed, these units to be distributed among the following areas as indicated:

a. General orientation—at least three units;
b. Educational and psychological diagnosis—at least four units;
c. Dynamics and development of individual behavior—at least four units;
d. Group and interpersonal relationships—at least three units; and
e. Research planning and execution—at least four units plus a dissertation for the Ed.D., or at least ten units including a dissertation for the Ph.D.

[Each of these areas is divided into education courses and psychology courses. There is sufficient opportunity for choice in each area to meet the needs of individual students. All courses are graduate-level courses, and students who have not had the prerequisite undergraduate courses must make them up outside of the program. The courses offered in the area of General Orientation indicate how the plan operates.

General Orientation (at least 3 units)

Education Courses

Preferred—Modern Theories of Education, Psychological Theories Applied to Education, Psycho-Educational Problems of Exceptional Children, Educational and Vocational Guidance, Fundamentals of Curriculum Construction, Educational Administration, Seminar for Advanced Students in Education.

Optional—Advanced Philosophy of Education, Seminar in Theories of Education and Social Changes, Elementary School Organization and Administration, Social and Psychological Factors in Elementary School Curriculum Development.

Psychology Courses

Preferred—History of Psychology, Systematic Psychology, Experimental Psychology (in learning), Contemporary Behavior Theory.

Optional—None.

Contacts with counseling and psychotherapy occur in courses in the area of "group and interpersonnel relationships." Remedial-education content is included as an integral part of the area, "educational and psychological diagnosis."]

XVII.

Accreditation of Training Programs

THE need for some evaluation and direction of training programs for school psychologists is obvious. There are already many inadequate courses—not all of them in second-rate institutions—purporting to provide the necessary knowledge. As more people become aware of the demand for psychological services and seek instruction, more colleges and universities will enter the field of training. Even with the best intentions, some of these are likely to lack experienced faculty or proper practicum facilities or both. Many students may find that they have spent time and money more or less in vain. State departments of education may find that they have been wrong in accepting degrees as a basis of certification. Superintendents may be misled into employing unqualified personnel. Worst of all, children will be subjected to dangerous bunglers. And, of course, psychology as a profession will suffer ill repute.

Setting up standards is difficult in any profession, and particularly in a relatively new profession like school psychology. The pioneers in the field have different backgrounds. They have picked up their training piecemeal, much of it by trial and error on the job. There are, in short, no precedents of proved worth, and, because of the need for flexibility and experimentation, precedents will grow slowly. A further difficulty is that courses in a school-psychology program may be given partly by teachers of education and partly by teachers of psychology. There is danger that neither department will make itself responsible for the total program, either as to content or as to standards. Moreover, institutions may find it hard to conduct simultaneously a two-year program and a four-year program differing somewhat from each other in content and design. Many Conference members feared that the best-equipped institutions might refuse even to attempt this, and that psychological examiners would be able to obtain training only in ill-equipped colleges and universities.

Accreditation does more than serve as a convenience to individuals and certification agencies. It means that an accredited program is meeting a high standard; it discourages institutions who cannot meet this standard. The credential or degree awarded to the student be-

171

comes a symbol of quality. The graduate who receives it is a member of a select group.

ACCREDITING AGENCIES

A multitude of systems of accreditation have been tried, and several are still in effect. The medieval tradesmen's guilds, the eighteenth-century medical profession, the modern trades-union admitted as new members only those who had served an apprenticeship under a member in good standing and been certified by him as competent. At least one state now grants a certificate as school psychologist upon the basis of membership in the APA, but such membership does not guarantee competency in any special field. Institutions of a given type or in a given region unite to set and enforce standards of admission, graduation, the award of graduate degrees, and the recruitment of football players. So we have the New England Association of Colleges and Secondary Schools, the Ivy League, and the American Association of Colleges for Teacher Education, all acting as accrediting agencies of a sort. State departments of one kind or another may inspect institutions or particular programs in institutions in other states as well as their own before granting certificates to graduates. The power of accreditation, which is second only to the fund-granting power as a means of making institutions measure up to standards, may actually or in effect be granted to professional associations, like a bar association.

When an institution fails to secure accreditation and the resulting publicity and standing, it may enter politics. It may secure the power to grant degrees by an act of legislature, it may bring pressure to bear on existing organizations, or it may set up a new organization to grant approval.

Proper accreditation entails large expense. A considerable staff is needed to evaluate materials and to visit and revisit institutions. Of course, the total expense increases in proportion to the number of institutions applying for accreditation. Naturally, more institutions will offer two-year training programs in school psychology than four-year programs in school psychology.

The agencies wishing to offer accreditation and the institutions wanting to receive it have become so numerous that university and college presidents have set up the National Commission on Accrediting—an accrediting of accrediting. But the word "approved" still means little unless it states by what agency approval has been given and unless this agency happens to be one which not only sets high standards but also maintains periodic inspections.

The APA and Accreditation

The situation being what it is, the directors of the APA are understandably loath to turn the Association into an accrediting agency. The directors have decided that they will consider requests for accreditation only when they come from an agency outside of the APA.

One such request has been approved. The Veterans Administration requested the APA to establish standards and approve institutions to which the government might award funds and provide internships for the development of training programs in clinical psychology and counseling psychology. As a result, the E & T Board of the APA, on recommendation of the Committee on Evaluation and with the concurrence of the Board of Directors, has approved the doctoral training programs in clinical and counseling psychology at certain institutions (71). The list is published in *The American Psychologist* and reported to the United States Public Health Service, to the Veterans Administration, and to the Surgeon General's Department of the United States Army.

The Conference Statement

The Conference, during its final session, unanimously approved a statement on accreditation, to the following effect:

> There is agreement that accreditation of training centers of school psychologists should be available. This accreditation should follow a pattern of development similar to that used in clinical and counseling psychology but distinctly different in ways appropriate to school psychology. The request for inaugurating a program of accreditation for school-psychology training programs might best be directed to the E & T Board of the APA from some national organization like the American Association of School Administrators. In the meantime, Division 16 should take steps to discuss the matter of accreditation with the E & T Board.
>
> Accreditation should be available for institutions offering a two-year graduate program as well as for those offering training at the doctoral level. The two-year program will presumably award successful candidates an M.A. or some other credential, but accreditation for the program should not require this.
>
> There is agreement that there are two types of individual certification, that by the ABEPP and that by state authorities. Division 16 should promote both types (see Chapters IX and X).

XVIII.

Summary of Conclusions and Recommendations

THE Thayer Conference on the functions, qualifications, and training of school psychologists reached general agreement on several broad issues. It did not succeed in solving all of the problems before it. Individual members continued to view some issues from different standpoints, but most of the recommendations as to policy and action received unanimous support. The discussions in the Conference and the materials on which the discussions were based have been considered in the previous chapters. Only the major conclusions, recommendations, and dissents are presented here.

DEFINITION

A school psychologist is a psychologist with training and experience in education. He uses his specialized knowledge of assessment, learning, and interpersonal relationships to assist school personnel to enrich the experience and growth of all children and to recognize and deal with exceptional children.

FUNCTIONS

There are innumerable ways in which the school psychologist can apply his knowledge. The details of what he does and of how he does it will depend on the particular situation in which he finds himself, on the special needs for his service inherent in the situation, and upon his training and qualifications. But the commonly accepted goals of education, especially the goal of promoting sound mental health in all children, make it possible to classify in general terms the ways in which he can apply his knowledge of psychology.

Assessment of the individual and of groups is one of his primary concerns. His knowledge of individual and group tests of intelligence, achievement, aptitude, and personality enable him to discover and gauge the needs of individuals and to evaluate changes.

Facilitating the best *adjustment* of the largest possible number of children lies at the core of all of his functions. His expert knowledge of the principles of learning, child development, individual differences, and group organization is applied to help each and every child make the most of his opportunities and acquire healthy attitudes and feelings.

The school psychologist's special knowledge of both psychology and education places him in a strategic position to *advise* on a school's objectives, curriculum, and methods, and especially as to how these may affect the mental health of children.

Exceptional children of all types—the gifted, the retarded, those with sensory defects and other physical handicaps, and those who are emotionally maladjusted—come within his province. He must help plan how the school is to provide for these children; for example, by individualizing instruction in the regular classroom or by setting up special classes.

Remedial measures will be needed by many children. He is equipped not only to discover which children require special help but also to determine what help is needed and how it can best be given. He will not usually have the time to do much remedial teaching himself. Rather he will advise and plan with other personnel how remedial measures can best be carried out.

Emotionally disturbed children will be referred to him. The members of the Conference were not agreed on the extent to which he should deal with these children and their parents. Some thought he should take much responsibility, others little. Most agreed that he will not usually have the time and that he may not have the training to engage in intensive psychotherapy. But he will need to consider the problems of disturbed children and at least suggest how these problems can be attacked. He may help individual teachers to understand the nature of the interaction between their own personalities and those of children in their classes. He must work continually for the promotion of the over-all mental health of his community and for clinics and other specialized services to help care for more-or-less seriously maladjusted children and adults.

Research is both a practical tool and a moral obligation of the school psychologist. He endeavors to discover facts and principles which have a bearing on the progress of the children in the schools which he serves. His research may help all psychologists and educators discover better means of promoting general mental health. But some members of the Conference continued to feel that the school psychologist, when he had fulfilled his other duties, would not have sufficient time to undertake much in the way of research.

In all he does, the school psychologist keeps in mind the idea that his function is to help the classroom teacher, the administrator, and other school personnel help children. The school psychologist's duties are *staff, not line.*

QUALIFICATIONS

Successful fulfillment of the broad range of functions which may engage the school psychologist requires an individual of the highest *personal* and *professional qualifications.* He should be a person of high intelligence. He should be emotionally mature and secure. He should have a sincere human interest in children and a desire to become more expert in his field so that he can serve all children with increasing efficiency. His professional training must be of a high order, and it must be correlated with the duties which he expects to undertake.

THE LEVELS OF POSITION

The broad range of the possible applications of psychology to education makes several types of specialized service practicable and desirable. The question of levels of service is of particular interest. There is now, and for the foreseeable future will be, need not only for school psychologists with doctoral training but also for individuals with somewhat more limited training in the field. In general, the individual with less training will function on a narrower base than the school psychologist. He will have a smaller repertoire of skills and less acquaintance with types and causes of deviations. He will be able to recognize maladjustment, but will refer individuals to fully trained psychologists or psychiatrists, or to clinics or other agencies, for re-education or treatment. He will not be equipped to give expert advice on policies. He will not be trained to supervise other psychological personnel. He will not have training in advanced techniques of research. He must be qualified to undertake the duties of his position. Above all, he must know his own limitations and avoid attempting functions which exceed his competence.

The Conference was unable to recommend a suitable title for the worker with limited training. The title *school psychologist* was approved for the fully trained individual. Several states employ the title *psychological examiner* for the individual with limited training. Members of the Conference used this title or spoke of the *Level II* or *lower-level* worker, but no one was satisfied with any title suggested.

SAFEGUARDS

There is a definite need to establish controls which will prevent the employment of unqualified individuals to give psychological service in schools. This is not just a problem of levels of service. It will be remembered that only 20 states and the District of Columbia have certification arrangements for school psychological personnel. State boards of education should *certificate* school psychological workers as they do teachers and other school personnel. It is hoped that the recommendations of this report can serve as at least a partial guide for those who wish to develop criteria for such certification. The less-qualified psychological worker should work under *supervision* or at least have ready access to the advice of fully qualified psychologists. When supervision is not available on the local level, it might be provided on a regional or state basis. An authoritative system of *accreditation* is necessary to ensure the adequacy of training programs for school psychologists. But in the final analysis the *ethics* of the individual will determine whether or not he undertakes a task for which he is not qualified. A course in ethics should be included in all training programs.

GENERAL PRINCIPLES OF TRAINING

The professional training of all psychological workers should be at the *graduate* level. The instructors in each course should be specialists in their fields, and the majority of students in each course should be graduate students. The functions of the school psychologist presuppose training in both education and psychology. A *committee with representatives from all interested departments* might well be responsible for setting up a program and recommending individuals for degrees. The committee should include an experienced school psychologist, perhaps as chairman. All training programs should include a practicum, i.e., applied experience, well integrated with the training program. Practical knowledge of the school situation and a realistic appreciation of the teachers' task is essential to the school psychologist. Actual *teaching experience* is such an asset to a school psychologist that it is now required by some education authorities. However, a majority of the members of the Conference felt that the school psychologist who had a good theoretical background in the history and philosophy of education and specific instruction in such subjects as curriculum and methods might acquire practical knowledge of the school situation by very carefully planned experiences in the classroom without having held a position as a teacher. Some members continued to believe that only considerable experience as the teacher in charge of a classroom would give the necessary background.

Certain basic understandings should be ensured by all training programs. These are a wide cultural background, a broad foundation in psychology, a comprehensive understanding of education, and a good grounding in the social and biological sciences.

TRAINING AT THE DOCTORAL LEVEL

Only a few universities in the United States have reported specially designed programs, with an internship, leading to a doctor's degree in school psychology. But many others have indicated an interest. Each university will set up its own requirements as to prerequisites, required courses, and electives—all subject only to the controls established by accreditation and certification agencies. The probable diversity in current training programs will help establish a sound basis for future programs. The exploration of many patterns of training designed to meet the essential objectives was favored. Faculties who are working out programs will naturally provide training in each of the main areas into which functions were classified above. Training at the doctoral level should equip a candidate to work in both elementary and secondary schools. Provision should be made for varying the programs to fit the needs of individuals with different backgrounds. Candidates will have had varying training and experience in education and in psychology. Some will be graduates of teachers colleges and some of liberal-arts colleges. Some will come direct from college. Some will have had responsible teaching experience, and some experience in clinics. The members of the Conference were emphatically agreed that doctoral training would require at least four years, one year of which would be devoted to an internship. It was assumed that candidates for the doctor's degree would be required to make a major research contribution as part of their doctoral program.

The *internship* was a matter of special consideration. It should be well integrated with the program. It should be served in a school or in a clinic or institution dealing with school children and with problems related to education. Experience in both schools and clinics has much to recommend it. Every intern should be carefully supervised by a school psychologist. A part of the internship for the candidate who has not had teaching experience should require him to serve in a classroom in ways which will enable him to identify himself with the teacher in his perception of a classroom problem.

A TWO-YEAR TRAINING PROGRAM

Assuming adequate undergraduate training, two years of specialized graduate training should qualify able individuals to perform many services in the field of school psychology. Such a program should be designed to equip the individual for the functions of the lower level described above. If it is to do this, there must be some differences in kind and in quantity from the first two years of doctoral training. It should include at least half a year of supervised practical experience. It will give a thorough grounding in assessment, but will not, for example, devote the time to projective techniques that doctoral training should give to them. It will give no more than limited training in re-education or therapy. It may prepare a candidate to work in either an elementary school or a secondary school rather than in both. The training in education will not of itself qualify the student to advise on over-all educational policies and methods. The Conference expressed the belief that to provide an adequate two-year program is as difficult as to provide the doctoral program. No university should undertake a two-year program lightly, nor should it be attempted at all unless good resources are available. Ill-trained workers in this field can do more harm than even the present lamentable shortage.

IN-SERVICE TRAINING

There are many individuals actively working in the field of school psychology who sincerely desire further training but are unable to take time off to reside at a university. In the future, many of those who have had two-year training will wish to continue their studies. And in a field that is so vast and growing so rapidly, no worker, whatever his background, should rest content. But specialized training for workers in service is not available in many communities. Universities which are equipped to offer part-time work in this area would supply much needed service by doing so. School psychological workers should explore the possibility of organizing in-service training on a regional basis.

THE PRESENT AND THE FUTURE

What does this report mean for the present and the future?

Twenty-five years ago, when school psychologists were just beginning to stake out their field, it was said that the future depended upon the quality of service given by the pioneers. The current demand for trained school psychologists far exceeds the supply. The Conference recognized this as a tribute to the pioneers. The members expressed their professional debt to those who had built so well, often under handicaps.

The future of school psychology now depends upon the qualifications and training of those who enter the field and the ability of these persons to become integral parts of the schools. The Conference suggested ways for raising and maintaining standards. Each member of the profession has a personal responsibility to contribute to the new goals as opportunities present themselves. The Division of School Psychologists of the APA and professional organizations at the local, state, and national levels must do their part. The faculties of institutions which undertake to train school psychologists must try out the programs which have been suggested and evaluate the results.

The Thayer Conference can give no exact and detailed blueprint for the future. It knows it has settled no problems in a final manner, but it hopes that it has indicated some lines of development that will result in continually better service to all the children in all of our schools.

Appendixes

Appendix A.

School Psychological Services in Europe

by W. D. WALL, PH.D.

Department of Education, UNESCO, Paris, France

(The information which follows is a summary of a survey which UNESCO is just completing of the school psychological services in the European member states. The full survey will be published in 1955 in *The Yearbook of Education,* Teachers College, Columbia, Institute of Education, London, and this part of it appears in French in the January-February, 1955, number of *Enfance,* vol. 5. The close parallels in development and in problems of organization and training between school psychological services in Europe and the United States give us perspective. Dr. Wall's survey helps us to be objective about our own difficulties by showing that they are not peculiar to us. Some of the solutions our European colleagues suggest may be models for us, and the others are at least possibilities. N.E.C.)

HISTORY

Among the countries of Europe as in the United States of America there exist differences in the underlying conceptions and marked variations in the degree of development of services of psychology for schools. Moreover, the apparent confusions, the partial initiatives, and the interprofessional conflicts which mark the European scene spring from similar causes. Not until comparatively recently has a coherent picture begun to emerge of the aims and organization of an effective service; and it will probably be many years before blueprints such as that arrived at by a European expert group (101) earlier this year are put into operation.

It is often alleged (36) that psychological services in Europe are based on the concept of child guidance which was imported from America in the late Twenties and early Thirties. However, this represents only one, and a relatively recent, form of service, and the idea of a practical service of psychology to schools can be traced at least as far back as the Child Study Association (founded in 1893) in the

183

United Kingdom, to the Laboratoire Pédagogique (1905) of Binet and Vaney in Paris, and to the work of the first official psychologist's office, that of Cyril Burt under the London County Council beginning in 1913 (170 III). Centers for study of the psychological problems of children and for advice to teachers and parents were set up on a voluntary basis in London, Oxford, and Liverpool in the first decade of the 20th century.

It is partly for these reasons of history and partly because the growth of services has been and rightly remains experimental that no hard and fast organization or set of basic concepts has grown up. Somewhat schematically, however, we may present the three types which seem at the moment to prevail in Europe.

PRESENT TYPES OF ORGANIZATION

The first of these is the school psychologist proper. Under this method of organization, the psychologist has his office in one large school (1,000-1,200 pupils) to which his attention is exclusively devoted; or he works with a restricted group of schools, primary and secondary, usually on the same campus. Forms of this solution are found in France, Belgium, and Denmark and are beginning in Sweden. Quite frequently, as for example in the Department of the Seine in France, the psychologist works alone or with the aid of a secretary-tester. In other cases, as for example in certain of the large colleges or lycées in Belgium, the psychologist has as members of his team a school social worker and a school medical officer.

In France, the service of school psychologists grew out of the plans for the post-war reform of French education (the Langevin plan) and in particular from the underlying ideas of the *éducation nouvelle,* which placed great stress on the adaptation of the school to individual differences. In Belgium, the development was closely associated with vocational guidance, a service which preceded by some years. In the second of these cases there was the consequent tendency to concentrate upon the secondary stage of education. Where, however, as in Copenhagen, the psychologist operates in a school district, his preoccupations embrace the primary as well as the secondary schools. The more strictly Anglo-Saxon point of view tends to concentrate upon the primary school, often at the expense of work with the secondary-school pupils.

As might be expected from his close association with the schools and from the relatively small population with which he has to do, the school psychologist has as a primary aim the improvement of the atmosphere of the school, the improvement of methods of teaching, and the guidance and adjustment of the ordinary child. Only secondarily is he concerned with "cases"—with failing, maladjusted, or delinquent children. He is usually a part of the staff of the school to which he is attached and advisor to the head and to his colleagues on all the multifarious psychological problems which arise. It is he also who maintains the contacts with the outside agencies who may become involved with individual children—with the juvenile courts, the social-welfare agencies, psychiatric units, and the like—and with the parents. In many ways, notably in the numbers of staff which would be involved if the service were extended on the basis of one psychologist to 1,000-1,500 pupils, this is a solution de luxe. In no country which applies it, is it universal, and indeed in some there is a strong move toward a more thinly spread service, operating from the local education authority. Those who see in the present form of service an ideal which allows the psychologist truly to work for the improvement of education of normal children and to engage in the ongoing research upon which development depends, are strongly opposed to such a change in policy. Their argument is that it is better to have a few good services at the present stage than, by spreading thinly over a wider area, to oblige the service, through lack of staff and direct contact with the schools, to undertake a first-aid role at the expense of more constructive activities.

A version of the conventional child-guidance clinic is the second main solution. It is found in most countries, either alone or alongside other forms of service. These clinics are variously (and barbarously) called medico-psychological, medico-pedagogical, medico-psycho-pedagogical, or psycho-pedagogical centers. Usually such clinics, under medical direction, with a strongly psychiatric slant, have no administrative relation with schools. They tend to concentrate upon the diagnosis—less frequently on the treatment—of problem cases referred by the schools, by the medical services, by the courts, and by parents. Frequently, if not usually, they are financed by the health or welfare authorities rather than from the education budget. Here and there, however, a more novel and constructive formula is emerging. For example, the Centre Psycho-pédagogique du Lycée Claude-Bernard is situated in the premises of a large academic secondary school in Paris and, while retaining a bias toward the needs of problem children, takes a considerable interest in general educational problems and in the guidance of adolescents. This center has an educational as well as a medical director and engages not only in the usual case activities but also in the work of parent and public education through its functional association with the École des Parents et Éducateurs. At the other extreme, however, are found very many centers whose activities are almost exclusively psychiatric and where the role of the psychologist—if indeed there is one on the staff—is confined to the administration of tests.

A coordinated service is the third type of solution. It is like that which has existed in the United Kingdom for many years and which bids fair to become the preponderant pattern in the English and Scottish educational systems. It aims to coordinate the preventive, research, and guidance activities of the school psychologist with an advisory service on special educational treatment, with direct remedial work in the educational field, and, in the cases where this is necessary, with psychiatric diagnosis and therapy. Under this system in its ideal form, the service is directed by an educational psychologist and is attached to and financed by the local education authority and extends to all schools, primary, secondary, and technical, and to all problems to the solution of which the science of educational psychology may be expected to contribute. The main unit in such a service is the child-guidance center, staffed by psychologists, specially trained remedial teachers, social workers, and sometimes play therapists. Closely associated with such a center or centers (a large authority like the city of Birmingham may plan to have as many as six or more) are the special educational services dealing with maladjusted, physically handicapped, or mentally subnormal children and with other children with particular educational needs and difficulties. The staffs of such centers are charged to build up close relationships with the schools in their area and undertake a good deal of preventive and constructive work. They aid in educational and vocational guidance, in the further training of teachers, in the organization and conduct of special courses, and the like. Such services have usually either a psychiatric consultant to deal with the cases of seriously maladjusted or psychotic children or they contain or work in close association with a child-guidance clinic which has the usual team of psychiatrist, psychologist, and social worker. Not unusually the link between the two services is provided by the educational psychologist, who works both in the broad service of school psychology and as the educational-psychological member of the clinic team.

This very brief account of three types of solution conceals two facts about the countries of Europe. The first is that services of any kind are by no means sufficient for the needs, even when these are considered in their narrowest sense. Some countries have few if any services; in most, there are large areas where little or no help for problem children is available and where the more general but equally important problems of the ordinary pupil at school are handled by the teacher alone, if at all. The second is that the quality and extent of the service given to schools depends at least as much upon the training, outlook, and quality of the staff of the psychological unit as it does on the form of organizational structure adopted. Nevertheless, the truth remains that a truly school-centered service develops with difficulty where it is medically oriented or not financed and administered by the educational authorities.

FAMILIAR PROBLEMS

The problems to be resolved are thus the familiar ones. The outstanding one, on which differences of opinion are sharp even among educators, concerns the form that the service should take, if indeed such a service is necessary at all! There are those who maintain that all the aspects of the mental health of normal children in school should be assured by improving the training of teachers and, perhaps, by having one specially trained teacher as an educational-guidance counselor on the staff of each school. According to this view, there would then be need (at most) only for some kind of diagnostic or treatment center for the very serious cases (36). Such an attitude with its implied or overt hostility lasts usually only so long as no service exists or where a clinic fails to make effective contact with the schools. There are others who assert that a psychological service, however it be staffed, should concentrate upon remedial and therapeutic work and as such should be outside the school system entirely. Finally there are those who insist that the main weight of effort should be towards a preventive role, and that the essential aim is, through constant cooperation with the teachers, to make of education a process whereby not only is maladjustment prevented or treated in an early stage, but also the whole educational process is used consciously and deliberately to build a better and more balanced personality for each child. The advocates of this view underline, as a necessary organizational corollary, the functional but not administrative integration of the service with other services working in the educational field, with the provision for special education, and with the social and medical services of the community.

Clearly, different conceptions involve differences in finance and the chain of responsibility. Here, too, views are markedly divergent. Many of those who think of the service as appropriately preoccupied only with severely maladjusted children advocate that it be placed in the medical services and financed from the health budget. Those who on the other hand emphasize its educational role—which includes re-education and remedial work of varying kinds—emphasize its primary responsibility to the schools and school system and stress that it should be financed as an educational service. In practice, it seems that where, as in many countries child-guidance *clinics* (centres médico-pédagogique) exist side by side with school psychological services or the psychologist attached to a single school or school group, the former are financed on a case-load basis by the health and welfare authorities and the latter as part of the total finance of compulsory education.

Some at least of the differences described above spring from a deeper interprofessional schism. From the very outset, in almost every country in Europe, the application of educational psychology has met with medical opposition. There are those who would reduce the role of the nonmedical psychologist to the routine application of tests and who would insist that all forms of "treatment"—whether this is remedial education, remedial play, or individual discussions with children or adolescents or their parents—should be carried out only under medical supervision. There are others who maintain that psychological treatment, and still more all forms of special education—such for example as work with children who experience difficulties in learning to read—are a matter for a psychological specialist with an educational background whose training does not necessarily include medicine. They contend that the psychiatrist is biased by his training towards the abnormal and pathological, whereas, to quote the words of Sully, "during childhood the vast majority of cases consist of deviations, *within* the normal rather than aberrations from the normal" (163). The difficulties of such cases can be overcome by environmental manipulation coupled with some re-educative help. In this view, the psychologist with training in education and in normal child development is better qualified than the medical practitioner to understand the real nature of the child's difficulties (170 **VII**, 177).

In particular services and under good conditions, such interprofessional tensions resolve themselves at the personal level. At the national level, however, in many countries, they have led to a split in the services offered, to one-sided developments, or, in some, to legislative action which has considerably hindered the development of educational psychology as a direct aid in the task of education.

The emphasis which has grown since 1930 on teamwork is also meeting with some challenge. This criticism is based partly on the grounds of excessive cost of the threefold psychiatrist, psychologist, social worker pattern and partly on sounder considerations of what in fact is needed in the variety of circumstances in which psychological aid has to be given. The conventional team concept is adapted particularly to the study and treatment of *severe* cases of maladjustment. It is less obviously necessary, for example, in cases of educational retardation or of mental subnormality. In other circumstances, for example when one considers the problem of a cerebral-palsied child, a team of a different composition seems likely to be more effective— perhaps a specialized teacher, a psychologist, an orthopedic specialist, and a physiotherapist. For many other problems, the social worker, the remedial teacher, or the psychologist might well be expected to work alone, at least in the stage of preliminary screening and subsequently in carrying out whatever form of purely supportive or direct remedial work may seem to be required. Thus the view is beginning to gain ground that, while the child-guidance team should be maintained in the background for cases where its services are clearly necessary, it should not be the only form of team nor should it be applied rigidly in all cases; further, for a large proportion, if not the majority, of cases, the services on a team are expensive and unnecessary. Counseling and remedial work can and should be carried out by the psychologist working with the teachers.

Clearly these and other considerations raise problems of responsibility and, in particular, of the role of the psychologist. Where a service of psychology exists in the education service or in a particular school, it is now usually directed by a psychologist. In some countries, and in some individual units, the solution of having coequal psychological and medical directors has been tried. Under both of these solutions, it is usually the psychologist who is the coordinator and who maintains liaison with outside services, except the purely medical ones. In others, there is insistence upon a medical director and the genuineness of the teamwork depends upon the kind of personal relationships which are established. The suggestion has been heard in official quarters that the service should be directed not by a representative of any particular profession but by the best available person no matter what his discipline.

TRAINING

As might be expected, problems of the selection and training of psychologists are closely bound up with the differences in conception outlined above and with the nascent state of comprehensive services. Most at least of the larger universities in Europe have undergraduate and postgraduate courses and degrees in psychology. In many cases these courses lean towards philosophy rather than psychology as it is now coming to be understood, or concentrate, for the practical work, mainly upon the older laboratory methods. Relatively few include intensive and extensive work in child study as an essential part of the undergraduate course, though most include psychopathology, theoretical social psychology, and such matters as the theory of education, mainly in terms of learning theory. Men and women trained in this way do take up work as school psychologists and as psychologists in industry, in psychiatric units, and the like.

On the other hand there are a number of centers in Europe where the training is more comprehensive and practical. As well as including child study, considerable time is devoted to the theory and construction of tests of all types, to practical work under supervision with individual children and adults, and to research techniques applicable to problems outside the narrower fields of experimental psychology. Such a center is the Institut des Sciences de l'Éducation in the University of Geneva, where, in addition to the *Licence en psychologie,* students who propose to work in the educational field also take a *Diplôme en pédagogie.* There are others of a similar kind, for example the Institute of Psychology at the Freie Universität of Berlin West, the Institut de Psychologie of the University of the Saar, and the departments of psychology of the Universities of Amsterdam and Utrecht. A considerable proportion of the psychologists working in the educational and clinical fields have no further training than this, although a number, and especially those who are in charge of services, have pursued studies at a doctoral level.

Here and there, university centers are developing postgraduate courses of practical training, specifically for educational or school psychologists, the most highly developed of which are to be found in France and in the United Kingdom. The French conception of the training of school psychologists is best represented by the courses given in the Institut de Psychologie at the University of Paris and leading to the *Diplômes de psychologie pédagogique* and *de psychologie appliquée*. Such students already have had at least five years of experience as school psychologists and may have been recommended by the school authorities or, in the case of those who will work in the secondary system, may have gone through a probationary month at the Institute during which the implications of the course are explained and guidance can be given. They pursue in the Laboratoire de Psychologie de l'Enfant, which forms part of the Institute, a course of two years' study, much of which consists of supervised practical work in the school system, of cooperative research into educational problems, as well as of basic courses in child development, test construction, psychopathology, statistics, and the like. In the United Kingdom, minimal standards as laid down by the Committee of Professional Psychologists (Mental Health) of the British Psychological Society are: graduation with at least second-class honors in psychology or its equivalent; training and at least one year's experience as a teacher (or equivalent experience with normal children or adolescents); one year's practical training as an educational psychologist which, as well as theoretical studies, shall include six weeks' experience in a child-guidance center or clinic; and finally an internship of one year in a recognized service under supervision. This committee also insists upon the attainment of the minimum age of twenty-five, and most of the training centers reserve the right to refuse candidates considered to be unsuitable on personality grounds.

It should be emphasized that these are desirable minima. In practice they are often exceeded. For example, candidates for the Diploma in Educational Psychology in the University of Birmingham, a course for which the Ministry of Education grants substantial fellowships, are not accepted for training unless they have had *at least five years of successful* teaching experience; and most of the students are aged at least thirty. Men and women are only accepted for training after exhaustive inquiries and careful personal interview. The training given concentrates upon the problems of the schools, upon remedial educational techniques, upon advisory work with teachers, parent education, and the like; and, while not neglecting the diagnosis and treatment of maladjustment of all types, is not at all psychiatric, still less psychoanalytic, in its approach. Most of the practical work is carried out in the University Service operated from the Remedial Education Center of the University Institute of Education and in close association with ongoing research.

University College, London, provides a similar training, and historically the oldest, which qualifies for the University Diploma in Educational Psychology. Somewhat similar in emphasis is the training given in the Scottish universities, many of which have university psychological services for research, demonstration, and training purposes. Here students who have already graduated, usually in some subject other than psychology, and qualified as teachers under the Scottish regulations, pursue a course of two years in educational psychology for the postgraduate B.Ed. degree.

In marked contrast to these university centers, are the London Child Guidance Center, the Tavistock Clinic, and the Maudsley Hospital. The first two of these are not university centers but operate child-guidance clinics within the Health Service. Students are financed by grants from the National Association for Mental Health, a semipublic body, and many of them enter hospital services, psychiatric units, and the like rather than the educational services. The Maudsley Hospital training is recognized by the University of London, but the standards of prior educational experience, training, and age are not as strict even as those demanded by the Tavistock or London Child Guidance Training Clinic. There is strong emphasis on a strictly, even classical, psychoanalytic approach.

Between the conceptions underlying the services which are developing in Europe and the forms of training which university and other centers are beginning to provide, there is of course a close connection. In countries like Belgium, Denmark, France, and Britain, the day of the brilliant pioneer is passing, and as services like those of the Department of the Seine in France, of Glasgow or Leicester in the United Kingdom, and of Copenhagen in Denmark crystallize and gain experience, they affect the kind of qualifications and training demanded of the psychologists who staff and direct them. It is for this reason that an international group of experienced psychologists, social workers, educators, and school medical officers was able to reach agreement recently upon the minimum level of training, experience, and prior qualifications toward the acceptance of which we should work in Europe. The conclusions of this group mark something of a milestone, in comparison for example to the state of affairs that was revealed by the inquiry of the International Bureau of Education in 1948 (99). They are therefore given here in résumé as follows:

Selection and training of school psychologists. Clearly even to dis-charge minimal functions effectively and with a full sense of the re-sponsibilities which he may have to assume, the school psychologist should be carefully selected and have a training of the highest quality both theoretical and practical. The committee is firmly of the opinion that it is better to have too few psychologists and those highly trained than to multiply those whose competence and personality are doubt-ful. The following minima seem to meet with general agreement (though far from universally realized) in those countries where psy-chological services are effectively functioning.

Basic training and qualifications. (a) A university qualification in psychology at a high level, e.g., *Licence en psychologie* (France) or an Honors degree in Psychology (U.K.); (b) a teaching diploma or other professional qualification as teacher; (c) at least five years of teaching experience, preferably varied, should be required for those who wish to work in schools. A minimum of three years of work with normal children should be demanded of those who wish to work more particularly in the clinical field.

Selection for professional training. It may be agreed that there should be little or no selection (other than is customary for entry to other university schools) of those who wish to study psychology at the undergraduate level. It is, however, essential that a rigorous selection should subsequently be made of those who wish to become school psychologists. The committee agrees that the criteria should be at least as follows:

a. In those countries where different levels or classes of university degree exist, a high level of academic attainment (1st- or 2nd-class honors for example) should be demanded for professional training.

b. The candidate should satisfy the training institution that he has a good level of capacity and has achieved a good professional adjustment in teaching or any other acceptable type of work with children.

c. By means of a preliminary period of at least one month devoted to observation and information, the training institution should satisfy itself that the candidate possesses the personal qualities necessary to the profession of educational psychologist, and that he is well acquainted with its demands (101).

It will be noticed that these requirements are comprehensive and similar to those which are gaining acceptance in America. Many psychologists practicing in the educational field in Europe possess a higher qualification, usually the equivalent of the Ph.D., which in many university centers it is now possible to take with marked emphasis on clinical training and research.

Appendix B.

The School Psychologist in the Private School

by W. Mason Mathews, Ph.D.

The Merrill-Palmer School, Detroit, Michigan

(The following pages are from an account of Dr. Mathews' work as a school psychologist in a private school. They supplement this report, which was primarily concerned with public education. Dr. Mathews, a diplomate in clinical psychology, was a member of the Thayer Conference. The Merrill-Palmer School, he says, has, since 1920, "slowly developed into an extremely complex institution which devotes its entire time to the study and teaching of child development, family life, human growth, and human relations. Its school population groups range from infancy to adulthood and are drawn from families with various socio-economic and cultural backgrounds in various types of communities. Its philosophy is that all people will learn best in situations providing experience and interaction with actual people." The school has a staff of about fifty members, representing about half as many separate fields of learning and professions. N.E.C.)

Private schools and public schools must adhere to the same standards in teaching, but private schools have much greater freedom to choose curriculums, programs, students, teachers, and other staff personnel. Frequently, public school systems do not have the latitude of private schools in establishing with other institutions cooperative projects for research or education. It would seem that the knowledge gained in such a setting would amplify our approach to this multi-faceted problem of the school psychologist. Because of the fewer restrictions placed on private schools, in general, they vary in program and personnel even more widely than do public schools, especially those established with special nondenominational objectives (172).

The total program of the Merrill-Palmer School places responsibilities and demands upon the psychologist which are as broad as any conceived of in the deliberations of the Thayer Conference. The

195

School is organized administratively on a functional plan. It has an area of School services, an area of teaching, an area of community services, and an area of research.

SCHOOL SERVICES

As chairman of School services, the clinical psychologist has an administrative responsibility as well as a responsibility to serve in the capacity of school psychologist for the various service units within the school. The administrative responsibility is in general similar to that of any head of a department or large school unit. In some ways it is not unlike that of a school principal. It does not seem important to describe the administrative functions in great detail; however, one facet, I believe, has considerable importance. Since the philosophy of the School is that most of the teaching, research, and service be carried on cooperatively with teams of staff people, we have come to believe that administration should be conducted with as much cooperative discussion and democratic interaction with the staff as can be achieved. This, of course, requires considerable study and examination of the way we administer the different school areas, to see how they should be modified individually for greater effectiveness and collectively to better accomplish the purposes of the broad general philosophy.

Because the school population is selective and rather small, more of the work with individual children is as a clinician, and the service to related disciplines and groups is a consulting role. The types of services carried on range from those for the usual preschool, elementary, and adolescent groups, to dealing with a wide variety of deviations from normal behavior. In this setting, for individual children, the school psychologist is expected to do all kinds of assessment work, administer and interpret a wide variety of psychological tests, and use other means of appraising personality. One aspect of this must be rather carefully developed and managed—writing reports. Since so many different disciplines are represented on the staff at the Merrill-Palmer School and since findings are subject to such a variety of uses, it is important that results be translated into solid, logical interpretations written in language that will be helpful to students and professional readers.

In addition to assessment work, the School psychologist has children and adults for counseling and treatment. The kind of counseling and treatment that is important in the Merrill-Palmer population varies considerably from that carried on in many treatment centers: it is more like the demands in most school systems for child guidance and the help that is expected of visiting teachers by parents. Most of this work involves a clear, sensitive understanding of personality growth and development and reasons for different kinds of adjustment. Treatment-wise the problem mainly consists of manipulating the environment in ways which will allow the child to make a better adjustment in his daily living and learning. However, the types of cases range from appraisals of infants for adoption to differential diagnostic studies of both children and adults to determine whether they should be referred to medical resources or carried for intensive treatment in the School counseling service.

The consulting role involves working with other staff people in the Merrill-Palmer setting as well as with staff people of other agencies and school systems. Most of the requests and expectations are in the field of mental health and family and child psychology. Frequently, consultation rests upon the interpretation of material given in a conference or through discussion, with the direct expectation that an opinion of the findings will be given and a recommendation follow. This is a very difficult role, since to handle such "second-hand" material in a thorough way without mistakes requires extreme care. This consulting role frequently produces requests to participate in group discussions among parents and others in the community and to conduct these in such a way that they will derive as much in mental health and therapeutic value as possible. This type of activity borders closely on different types of counseling and group therapy.

Teaching

The discussion of service and consulting responsibilities of the clinical psychologist at Merrill-Palmer leads directly to consideration of his role in teaching, since one of the School's major purposes is teaching college students, graduate and undergraduate, with the belief that this can best be done by providing real experiences; by relating theoretically practical approaches; and by helping them gain a good understanding of themselves. Thus, the clinical practitioner becomes a very useful person as a teacher. Discussions of the use of supervision and face-to-face dealing with students in terms of their experiences have been presented elsewhere (119, 120). A considerable amount of teaching time is required for small discussion seminars

198

with graduate students and direct individual supervision of clinical-psychology trainees who are at the School for a large section of their practicum training leading to the Ph.D. degree. This time is devoted to intensive work with the students, in small groups or in person-to-person relationships. It is expected that through this amplified method of teaching, students can learn more extensively, with more security, and with greater understanding than they could in larger groups and with less person-to-person contact. This factor seems important and warrants further study, since any training program for school psychologists is greatly enriched and facilitated by different types of experiences, and a thorough understanding of methods to use around them, providing they apply well to that field of training.

Another facet of teaching responsibility is to cooperate in many small, summer, graduate seminars on human relations, where the principal goal is to have a team of staff people working with eight to twenty advanced students rather intensively for a period of six weeks. The belief has grown that, no matter what the content theme of the seminars, the way the members relate to each other and the resultant feeling of group belongingness, with a clear perception by each participant of equality in the value of his ideas, is of basic importance to the growth and development of the student in the area of personal understanding and general human relations.

Another important teaching role is in connection with the School's summer camp, at which a small group of students is placed in a child-and-family-camp setting. There, through discussions around theoretical material and practical experiences with groups of children, with which each student has at least two 24-hour experiences per week, learning can occur. Close supervision of the students enables them to become good observers, to understand and interpret the meaning of a child's behavior, and to connect the facts clearly in reporting. Working with their counseling teammates proves extremely valuable in teaching about the group process, child development, and other kinds of child and family dynamics. The main intent of this experience is to allow students to learn all they can from the situation and translate it into a projected modification of whatever their regular work will be. Many are classroom school teachers. Small groups of children are allowed to operate around projects in relation to which the teachers probably can "tie-in" a variety of methods which would apply in a school home-room situation. Application of such methods, with understanding, presumably will in many ways increase the mental-health atmosphere of the classroom, thus reducing the number of children with behavior disturbances. This still is unproved, but many such teachers give personal reports that the experience has been of considerable value to them in this way.

COMMUNITY SERVICES

Many requests from the community are received by the Merrill-Palmer School to conduct different types of adult and parent education courses. The belief of the School is that a single lecture is not very useful and that most of such efforts should be confined to series of small-group discussions. These allow utilization of the knowledge gained from seminars and workshops within the School and facilitate understanding in the areas of growth and development and human relations by community groups. Some of these projects are geared to develop community lay leaders; others are geared to incorporate understanding by parents of their roles of living in their own families and dealing with their own children. All require of the psychologist who may be the group leader an understanding knowledge of human personality, the group process, and group dynamics. These groups are exposed to a curious combination of the teaching of facts and dealing with interpersonal relationships in a considerably modified therapeutic way. They serve as excellent occasions for students to gain experiences, for lay people to gain further understanding of the many problems of human relations, and for the staff, too, to gain new and varied experiences. Educational television offers promise of becoming a major factor in such programs and providing a rich opportunity for education of professional students and the laity.

RESEARCH

The expectations for the clinical psychologist at Merrill-Palmer to accomplish research are less than for other categories of responsibility. However, the interpretation of research material for service use and the cooperative planning with the staff and children in setting up research projects in human relations is a reasonably large part of the responsibility of the School psychologist at Merrill-Palmer. In any situation, no matter how service-oriented the clinical or school psychologist may be, he still is in a position where much may be expected of him in terms of contribution to the research efforts of his school or institution. From experience in working with research people it seems that those who are highly trained in a rather narrow, orthodox research direction find it very difficult to utilize their training and skill in doing research with human beings in a multidisciplinary setting. If the school psychologist, particularly in a private school, is to carry on research, one of his important graduate training needs is supervision by a sensitive, highly trained practitioner who, in addition, is an experienced research person. This implies that a broad, thorough grounding in research approaches and thinking should be one important part of a school psychologist's training.

Appendix C.

Preliminary Propositions

SOME months before the Conference, the Steering Committee compiled a tentative list of topics for discussion. This was sent for criticism to the 296 school psychologists who were then members of the Division of School Psychologists of the APA and to about 300 other people whose names had been suggested by state directors of school psychological and special-education programs and by other interested persons. Responses were received from 175 people. Moore, Chairman of the Steering Committee, used these responses to draft the following list of "Issues and Propositions on the Functions, Qualifications, and Training of School Psychologists." Two months before the Conference, this list was distributed to all the participants in order to stimulate their thinking on the issues.

I. General Issue.—Definition of the functions of school psychologists. What are the things which psychologists do, can do, and should do in the schools?

   A. Propositions on definition.

      1. A school psychologist is a specialist in bringing the contributions of psychology toward better development and learning on the part of school children.

      2. There are no unique functions of school psychologists, but rather an area of employment in which there may be service from clinical psychologists, child psychologists, educational psychologists, guidance counselors, supervisors of special education, etc.

   B. Propositions on functions. A school psychologist, or psychologists working in the schools, should perform the functions of assisting in:

      1. Measuring the intellectual and other potentialities and limitations of individual children.

      2. Understanding and interpreting the personalities of children by means of a variety of professionally accepted methods and techniques.

      3. Diagnosing educational achievement and evaluation of educational outcomes.

      4. Identifying exceptional children and effecting for them adequate educational and social programs and placement.

5. Identifying and measuring aptitudes and interests and counseling the pupil in educational and vocational guidance with the completion of (junior) (senior) high school.
6. Diagnosing educational disabilities and accomplishing remediation.
7. Diagnosing situation difficulties and working with school personnel and parents for the purpose of improving learning and facilitating better mental-hygiene conditions for school children.
8. Effecting emotional and social re-education programs, both group and individual, and assisting school personnel in understanding and applying techniques for the purpose of contributing to both corrective and preventive aspects of mental hygiene in the school.
9. Carrying on research toward solution of general problems and of specific local problems of school psychologists.
10. Supervising the training of interns and of younger staff members in school psychology.
11. Consultation services—staff and case.

C. Propositions on levels of functioning and distinctive titles for each.

1. The work of a school psychologist involves such broad comprehensive preparation at a high level that these responsibilities can not be met with less than doctoral education or its equivalent. Any person with less preparation in this field should work only in prescribed areas or under supervision, and should not be called school psychologist but be given a title at an assistant's level.
2. It is impossible for all the psychological work needed in the schools to be done by, or even under the supervision of, persons with doctoral education. Moreover, persons with experience in education plus training in psychological techniques can use these techniques very competently in much of the work of school psychologists.

II. General Issue.—Specification of the competencies of school psychologists. To what extent should school psychologists have competence in each of the following, and if there are levels of workers, what should be the minimum competencies for each level?

1. Administration and interpretation of group measures of intelligence, special aptitudes, interests, personality, and achievement.
2. Administration and interpretation of individual tests of intelligence, special aptitude, and specific educational disabilities.
3. Administration and interpretation of screening tests of vision, hearing, and speech.
4. Administration and interpretation of projective techniques in analyzing and measuring personality.

5. Skill in interviewing or conferring with children, parents, teachers, and other professional workers with school children.
6. Conducting case conferences, handling groups, and understanding group dynamics.
7. Knowledge of, and skill in, therapies—group, individual, etc.
8. Curriculum planning, particularly for special groups and individuals.
9. Functional knowledge of occupations, world of work, and of aptitudes needed for job families, to the extent necessary to give or supervise vocational guidance.
10. Knowledge and skill for teaching, especially remedial teaching of exceptional children.
11. Statistical techniques and other scientific methodologies for research.
12. Basic understanding of psychology, especially of developmental psychology and learning.
13. Basic understanding of the history, philosophy, objectives, and methods of education.

III. General Issue.—Selection, training, and experience of school psychologists.

A. Propositions on undergraduate education and on selection.
   1. A school psychologist should have had a basic or undergraduate education that would qualify him for certification enabling him to get teaching experience.
   2. A school psychologist should have had either an undergraduate major in psychology or at least twenty semester hours in psychology to enable him to begin graduate study of psychology in many departments of psychology. If this has not been done, such prerequisite work should be made up without graduate credit.
   3. The school psychologist should have had a broad, liberal undergraduate education. No specific courses or major need be required, except as necessary to meet the prerequisites for graduate study in a particular university. High-level academic aptitude or intelligence is most important.
   4. Both interest in scientific approach to human problems and interest in service to mankind are important, but the (former) (latter) is more important.
   5. The school psychologist should be well-adjusted and free from personality defects that interfere with his effectiveness.

B. Propositions on graduate training.
   1. The school psychologist is primarily a leader of teachers, and should be trained as an educational leader, with mastery of psychological techniques applicable in a school situation.

2. The school psychologist should be trained first as a psychologist and then to apply his knowledge and skills to meet school needs.

3. The school psychologist should be familiar with the basic principles of both psychology and education, but as a psychologist he is primarily responsible for applying the knowledge, techniques, and research methodology of psychologists to the needs of children in a school situation.

4. The education of a school psychologist should include courses or supervised experience such as:

   (a) General (experimental) psychology.
   (b) Developmental psychology (child and adolescent).
   (c) Theories and principles of learning.
   (d) Theory and dynamics of personality.
   (e) Individual differences and their measurement: Statistical and psychometric techniques.
   (f) Measurement and evaluation of educational achievement.
   (g) Objectives and methods of education.
   (h) Education of the exceptional child.
   (i) Social organization and community service agencies.
   (j) Counseling and therapeutic techniques.

C. Propositions on experience and practicum training.

   1. Before undertaking the responsibilities of a school psychologist, the candidate should have experience in teaching for at least (three years) (one year) (one semester) (six weeks).

   2. As preparation for his work, the school psychologist should complete a part-time clerkship followed by the equivalent of a full-time internship for eight months. These practicum experiences should be in a public or private school and in at least one of the following: psychological clinic, guidance or counseling center, child-guidance clinic, children's hospital or ward, correctional or remedial institution for children or youth.

IV. General Issue.—Administrative and professional relationships of school psychologists.

A. Propositions on utilization of school psychologists.

   1. There should be fairly exact specifications of problems which are to be brought to the school psychologists, at least in a particular school system. The purpose of this is to inform teachers, administrators, parents, and public agencies of the service available from school psychologists. This would also minimize misunderstanding in professional and service relationships.

   2. The work of a school psychologist is so new and the local

situations differ so much that it would be premature and
unwise to prescribe his functions. Moreover, his own competencies and interests will vary, making it advisable to permit him to function most effectively as primarily a clinician,
educational consultant, child psychologist, guidance counselor, etc.
3. It is feasible to have a school psychologist for each school
population of (10,000) (5,000) (1,000) (500).
4. There should be a carefully planned and versatile program
to educate the potential consumers in how they can use the
services of school psychologists.
B. Propositions on relationships and ethics.
1. The school psychologist should work as a member of a
team.
2. The school psychologist should be sensitive to other agencies
and make referrals whenever it is consistent with good service to the child.
3. The APA *Ethical Standards of Psychologists* is an adequate
basic code for school psychologists.
4. APA *Ethical Standards of Psychologists* needs to be supplemented for school psychologists; for instance, as follows:
(a) The school psychologist has a responsibility for involving parents, teachers, or others in a recognition of
maladjustment which has not heretofore proven disturbing.
(b) What is the ethical relationship of the school psychologist to the maladjusted teacher, or to a teacher-pupil
relationship which, in the psychologist's opinion, is
harmful to the child?
(c) What is his position with respect to privileged communication?
(d) What is the school psychologist's position with respect
to general school policy or practices which he deems
destructive of personality development?
(e) Is it important or essential that the school psychologist
always use democratic educational procedures in cor-
recting evils or bringing about better practices?

V. General Issue.—Professional development, recognition, and accreditation.
1. How may school psychologists be kept sensitive to needs for professional development as individuals and as an organization?
2. How can in-service training be organized, financed, and conducted?
3. Should school psychologists find their professional literature in
the publications of related fields, or should they also have their
own professional journal?

4. How can research be encouraged, financed, and conducted?
5. Is there need for more formal accreditation of school psychologists and of training centers, and if so, what kind and by whom?
6. Should there be a certificate (ABEPP diploma) independent of credentials which may develop in state departments?
7. Should accreditation be permanent or reviewed periodically?
8. Should there be any statement of minimum standards for working conditions of school psychologists?

Appendix D.

Participants in the Conference

Ackerly, S. Spafford, M.D., Chairman of Department of Psychiatry and Mental Hygiene, and Director of Louisville Child Guidance Clinic, University of Louisville, School of Medicine, Louisville, Kentucky.

Bice, Harry V., Consultant on Psychological Problems, New Jersey State Crippled Children's Commission, Trenton, New Jersey.

Birch, Jack W., Director of Special Education, Board of Public Education, Pittsburgh, Pennsylvania.

Bobbitt, Joseph M. (Guest), Chief, Professional Services Branch, National Institute of Mental Health, USPHS, Bethesda, Maryland.

Bordin, Edward S., Associate Professor of Psychology, University of Michigan, Ann Arbor, Michigan.

Boston, Opal, Supervisor, School Social Workers, Indianapolis Public Schools; President, National Association of School Social Workers.

Burdette, Esallee, Washington High School, Washington, Georgia; representing the National Education Association Department of Classroom Teachers.

Carter, Jerry W., Jr. (Guest), Chief Clinical Psychologist, Community Services Branch, National Institute of Mental Health, USPHS, Bethesda, Maryland.

Cook, Walter W., Dean, College of Education, University of Minnesota, Minneapolis, Minnesota.

Cornell, Ethel L., Associate in Educational Research, State Education Department, Albany, New York.

Cutts, Norma E., Professor of Psychology and Education, New Haven State Teachers College; Lecturer in Educational Psychology, Department of Education, Yale University.

Driscoll, Gertrude P., Professor of Education, Teachers College, Columbia University, New York, New York.

Dunlap, James M., School Psychologist, University City Public Schools, University City, Missouri.

Elliott, Merle H., Director of Research, Oakland Public Schools, Oakland, California.

Fite, Mary D., Psychologist, Gilbert School, Multonomah County, Oregon. Address: 12500 S. E. Ranona, Portland, Oregon.

Gates, Robert, Consultant, Education for Exceptional Children, State Department of Education, Tallahassee, Florida.

Gowan, May Seagoe, Professor of Education, University of California, Los Angeles, California.

Gray, Susan W., Associate Professor of Psychology, George Peabody College, Nashville, Tennessee.

Harris, Dale B., Professor and Director, Institute of Child Welfare, University of Minnesota, Minneapolis, Minnesota.

Hobbs, Nicholas, Chairman, Division of Human Development & Guidance, George Peabody College, Nashville, Tennessee.

Kelley, Noble H., Chairman, Department of Psychology, Director of Psychological Services, Southern Illinois University, Carbondale, Illinois.

Kirk, Samuel A., Professor of Education and Director, Institute for Research on Exceptional Children, University of Illinois, Urbana, Illinois.

Krugman, Morris, Assistant Superintendent of Schools in charge of Guidance, Board of Education, City of New York.

Langhorne, M. C., Chairman, Department of Psychology, Emory University, Emory University, Georgia.

Lantz, Beatrice, Consultant, Division of Research and Guidance, Los Angeles County Schools, California.

Levin, Max M. (Guest), Psychologist, Training and Standards Branch, National Institute of Mental Health, USPHS, Bethesda, Maryland.

Luckey, Bertha M., Supervisor, Psychological Service, Cleveland Board of Education, Cleveland, Ohio.

McCandless, Boyd R., Professor and Director, Iowa Child Welfare Research Station, State University of Iowa, Iowa City, Iowa.

Magness, Guy N., M.D., Director, School Health Service of University City Public Schools, University City, Missouri. (School Physician)

Mathews, W. Mason, Chairman, Laboratory Services (School Services), Merrill-Palmer School, Detroit, Michigan.

Moore, Bruce V., Executive Officer, Education and Training Board, American Psychological Association, Washington, D.C.

Mullen, Frances A., Assistant Superintendent of Schools in charge of Special Education, Chicago Public Schools, Chicago, Illinois.

Myers, C. Roger, Professor of Psychology, University of Toronto, and Psychologist, Department of Health, Toronto, Ontario, Canada.

Newland, T. Ernest, Professor of Education, University of Illinois, Urbana, Illinois.

Ojeman, Ralph H., Professor of Psychology and Parent Education, Iowa Child Welfare Research Station, State University of Iowa, Iowa City, Iowa.

Olson, Willard C., Professor of Education and Psychology, and Dean, School of Education, University of Michigan, Ann Arbor, Michigan.

O'Shea, Harriet E., Associate Professor of Psychology, Purdue University, Lafayette, Indiana.

Raimy, Victor C., Chairman and Professor, Department of Psychology, University of Colorado, Boulder, Colorado.

Roberts, S. Oliver, Professor of Psychology and Education, Chairman, Department of Psychology, Fisk University, Nashville, Tennessee.

Robinson, Francis P., Professor of Psychology, Ohio State University, Columbus, Ohio.

Rodnick, Eliot H., Chairman, Department of Psychology, Director of Clinical Training, Duke University, Durham, North Carolina.

Saffir, Milton A., Director, Chicago Psychological Guidance Center; Principal of Marshall Elementary School, Chicago, Illinois.

Skodak, Marie, Director, Division of Psychological Services, Dearborn Public School, Dearborn, Michigan.

Strother, Charles R., Professor of Psychology, Professor of Clinical Psychology in Medicine, University of Washington, Seattle, Washington.

Tulchin, Simon H., Consulting Psychologist, 30 East 60th Street, New York, New York.

Wall, William D., Department of Education, UNESCO, Paris, France.

Weiss, Emalyn R., Supervisor of Special Education, Berks County Schools, Reading, Pennsylvania.

Young, Albert T., Jr., School Psychologist, City of Falls Church Public Schools, Falls Church, Virginia.

VISITING THE CONFERENCE

Ewalt, Jack R., M.D., Commissioner, Department of Mental Health, Massachusetts, and Professor of Psychiatry, Harvard Medical School.

Ewing, Palmer L., Superintendent of Schools, Buffalo, New York.

Kelly, E. Lowell, Professor of Psychology, University of Michigan, Ann Arbor, Michigan; President-elect, American Psychological Association.

Sanford, Fillmore H., Executive Secretary, American Psychological Association, Washington, D.C.

Bibliography

Bibliography

1. American Association of School Administrators. *Health in the schools;* Twentieth Yearbook. Rev. ed., 1951. Washington: The Ass., NEA, 1951.
2. American Association on Mental Deficiency. *Standards brochure,* 1952. AAMD Business Office, P.O. Box 96, Willimantic, Conn.
3. American Psychological Association, Committee on Graduate and Professional Training. Clinical training facilities: 1947. *Amer. Psychologist,* 1947, **2**, 199-205.
4. American Psychological Association, Committee on Intraprofessional Relationships in Psychology. Fields of psychology and their implications for practice and training. *Amer. Psychologist,* 1951, **6**, 90-93.
5. American Psychological Association, Committee on Training in Clinical Psychology. Recommended graduate training program in clinical psychology. *Amer. Psychologist,* 1947, **2**, 539-558.
6. American Psychological Association, Committee on Training in Clinical Psychology. Doctoral training programs in clinical psychology: 1949. *Amer. Psychologist,* 1949, **4**, 331-341.
7. American Psychological Association, Committee on Training in Clinical Psychology. Annual report of the Committee on Training in Clinical Psychology: 1950. *Amer. Psychologist,* 1950, **5**, 585-593.
8. American Psychological Association, Committee on Training in Clinical Psychology. Standards for practicum training in clinical psychology: Tentative recommendations. *Amer. Psychologist,* 1950, **5**, 594-609.
9. American Psychological Association, Division of Counseling and Guidance, Committee on Counselor Training. Recommended standards for training counseling psychologists at the doctorate level. *Amer. Psychologist,* 1952, **7**, 175-181.
10. American Psychological Association, Division of Counseling and Guidance, Committee on Counselor Training. The practicum training of counseling psychologists. *Amer. Psychologist,* 1952, **7**, 182-188..
11. American Psychological Association, Education and Training Board, Committee on Practicum Training. Internship training in clinical psychology. *Amer. Psychologist,* 1954, **9**, 760-764.
12. American Psychological Association, Education and Training Board, Committee on Subdoctoral Education. Report of the committee on subdoctoral education. *Amer. Psychologist,* 1954, **9**, 78-79.
13. Anderson, Rose G. Concerning school psychologists. *Psychol. Clinic,* 1933, **22**, 41-47.
14. *Annual Report of the Superintendent of Schools.* New Haven, Conn. September 1, 1871.

15. *Annual Report of the Superintendent of Schools*. New Haven, Conn. For the year ending December 31, 1898.

16. *As we do it: a handbook for school psychologists*. Oakland, California: Alameda County Schools, 1953.

17. Association for Supervision and Curriculum Development. *Mental health in the classroom;* Thirteenth Yearbook. Washington: The Ass., NEA, 1940.

18. Association for Supervision and Curriculum Development. *Organizing the elementary school for living and learning;* 1947 Yearbook. Washington: The Ass., NEA, 1947.

19. Association for Supervision and Curriculum Development. *Fostering mental health in our schools;* 1950 Yearbook. Washington: The Ass., NEA, 1950.

20. Association for Supervision and Curriculum Development. *Guidance in the curriculum;* 1955 Yearbook. Washington: The Ass., NEA, 1955.

21. Bailard, Virginia. The teacher works with the specialist. *Educ. Leadership,* 1953, **10**, 338-341.

22. Baker, G. D. What the public school needs from the psychologist. *J. consult. Psychol.,* 1942, **6**, 177-180.

23. Baker, H. J. Clinical service as related to public schools. *Childhood Educ.,* 1933, **9**, 345-349.

24. Barker, L. F. The wider field of work of the National Committee for Mental Hygiene. *Ment. Hyg.,* N.Y., 1917, **1**, 4-6.

25. Barker, Margaret. The duties of the school psychologist. *J. consult. Psychol.,* 19?3, **2**, 180-183.

26. Barr, A. S. The measurement and prediction of teaching efficiency: a summary of investigations. *J. exp. Educ.,* 1948, **16**, 203-283.

27. Beers, C. W. *A mind that found itself*. New York: Longmans, Green, 1908.

28. Bernard, H. W. *Mental hygiene for classroom teachers*. New York: McGraw-Hill, 1952.

29. Bordin, E. S. (Ed.) *Training of psychological counselors*. Ann Arbor, Michigan: University of Michigan Press, 1951.

30. Bowley, Agatha H. A psychologist looks at educational reconstruction. *Ment. Hlth, London,* 1944, **5**, 1-3.

31. Brewer, J. M. *Education as guidance*. New York: Macmillan, 1932.

32. Brewer, J. M. *History of vocational guidance*. New York: Harper, 1942.

33. Brotemarkle, R. A. (Ed.) *Clinical psychology; studies in honor of Lightner Witmer to commemorate the thirty-fifth anniversary of the founding of the first psychological clinic*. Philadelphia: University of Pennsylvania Press, 1931.

34. Brown, M. F. A psychologist comes to Chelsea. *High Points,* 1949, **31** (1), 61-63.

35. Brownell, S. M. Need for services to exceptional children. *Except. Child.,* 1955, **21**, 138, 152.

36. Burbury, W. Mary, Balint, Edna M., & Yapp, Bridget I. *An introduction to child guidance.* London: Macmillan, 1945.
37. Burnett, C. W. Selection and training of school and college personnel workers. *Rev. educ. Res.,* 1954, **24**, 121-133.
38. Burnside, Lenoir H. Psychological guidance of gifted children. *J. consult. Psychol.,* 1942, **6**, 223-228.
39. Buros, O. K. (Ed.) *The nineteen thirty-eight mental measurements yearbook.* New Brunswick, N.J.: Rutgers University Press, 1938.
40. Buros, O. K. (Ed.) *The nineteen forty mental measurements yearbook.* Highland Park, N.J.: Mental Measurements Yearbook, 1941.
41. Buros, O. K. (Ed.) *The third mental measurements yearbook.* New Brunswick, N.J.: Rutgers University Press, 1949.
42. Buros, O. K. (Ed.) *The fourth mental measurements yearbook.* Highland Park, N.J.: Gryphon Press, 1953.
43. California Association of School Psychologists and Psychometrists. *Report of Research Committee of C.A.S.P.P.,* 1952-53. Report available from State Dep. of Educ., Sacramento, Calif. (Mimeo.)
44. California Conference of Psychologists and Psychometrists. *Proceedings:*
   I. California State Department of Education and College of the Pacific, Stockton, May, 1950.
   II. California State Department of Education and San Jose State College, San Jose, April, 1951.
   III. California State Department of Education, Fresno State College and Fresno County Schools Office, Fresno, April, 1952.
   IV. California State Department of Education and California Association of School Psychologists and Psychometrists, Long Beach, April, 1953.
   Available from State Dep. of Educ., Sacramento, Calif. (Mimeo.)
45. California State Committee on School Personnel Workers Credentials. *Report of the sub-committee on the psychologists' and psychometrists' credentials.* May 5, 1950. Available from the State Dep. of Educ., Sacramento, Calif. (Mimeo.)
46. California State Department of Education, State Committee on Credentials for Pupil Personnel Services. *The preparation and training of pupil personnel workers.* Bulletin of the Dep., 1952, **21** (5).
47. Cason, Eloise B. Some suggestions on the interaction between the school psychologist and the classroom teacher. *J. consult. Psychol.,* 1945, **9**, 132-137.
48. Cattell, R. B. The practicing psychologist in the educational system. *Human Factors, London,* 1935, **9**, 54-62.
49. Clark, K. E., Metzner, Norma R., & Shellow, Sadie M. *The utilization of psychological techniques in the United States: I. Survey of psychological activities in Milwaukee County.* Washington: APA, 1953.

50. Clark, K. E., Metzner, Norma R., & Rogge, Genevieve O. *The utilization of psychological techniques in the United States: II. Survey of psychological activities in Providence, Rhode Island.* Washington: APA, 1954.

51. Claytor, Mae P. State certification requirements for public school psychologists. *J. Psychol.,* 1950, **29**, 391-396.

52. *Code of ethics of National Education Association of the United States.* Washington: The Ass., 1952.

53. Coladarci, A. P. A note on the role of the school psychologist. *Calif. J. Sec. Educ.,* 1952, **27**, 445-446.

54. Cole, C. W. The redirection of higher education. Paper read as a Spaulding Lecture, Yale University, April 24, 1953.

55. Connecticut Advisory Pupil Personnel Committee dealing with the Role of School Social Workers, School Psychologists, and School Counselors. *Pupil personnel services in Connecticut schools.* First draft, unofficial, April, 1954. Hartford, Conn.: State Dep. of Educ. (Mimeo.)

56. Connecticut Association of School Psychological Personnel. *Survey of school psychological workers in Connecticut.* March 3, 1954. Available from E. A. Ricciuti, chairman, Waterbury, Conn. (Mimeo.)

57. Connecticut Special Education Association. *History of special education for mentally deficient children in Connecticut.* New Haven, Conn.: The Ass., 1936.

58. Connecticut State Department of Education. *Revisions of regulations concerning certificates for professional personnel in Connecticut public school service.* Hartford, Conn.: The Dep., May 5, 1954.

59. Cooperative Study of Secondary-School Standards. *Evaluative Criteria.* 1950 edition. Washington: The Study, 1950.

60. Cornell, Ethel L. The school psychologist's contribution. *Nat. El. Prin.,* 1936, **15**, 561-566.

61. Cornell, Ethel L. Certification of specialized groups. *J. consult. Psychol.,* 1941, **5**, 62-65.

62. Cornell, Ethel L. *The work of the school psychologist.* Albany, N.Y.: University of the State of New York, Bulletin No. 1238, 1942.

63. Cornell, Ethel L. The psychologist in a school system. *J. consult. Psychol.,* 1942, **6**, 185-195.

64. Cornell, Ethel L. What is the school psychologist's place in a program to prevent delinquency? *Understanding the Child,* 1943, **12** (1), 22-25.

65. Council of Superintendents of New York State, Committee on Research. *Preliminary report of the study of psychological and psychiatric services in the public schools of the state.* Sept. 29, 1953. Available from D. G. Salten, chairman, Long Beach, New York. (Mimeo.)

66. Crawford, J. E. Better basis for guidance. *Ind. Arts & vocational Educ.*, 1945, **34**, 145-148.
67. Crow, L. D. & Crow, Alice. *Mental hygiene* (2nd Ed.). New York: McGraw-Hill, 1951.
68. Cutts, Norma E. Development of a certification procedure for school psychologists. *J. consult. Psychol.*, 1943, **7**, 45-49.
69. Cutts, Norma E., & Moseley, N. *Practical school discipline and mental hygiene.* Boston: Houghton Mifflin, 1941.
70. Cutts, Norma E., & Moseley, N. *Bright children.* New York: Putnam, 1953.
71. Doctoral training programs in clinical psychology and in counseling psychology. Approved by the APA Education and Training Board with the concurrence of the Board of Directors, May, 1954. *Amer. Psychologist*, 1954, **9**, 258.
72. Doll, E. A. (Ed.) *Twenty-five years, The Vineland Laboratory, 1906-1931.* Vineland, N.J.: The Training School, 1932.
73. Driscoll, Gertrude P. Community leadership role of the school psychologist. *Teach. Coll. Rec.*, 1950, **51**, 204-211.
74. Dudycha, G. J. School psychologist. *Occupational Abstract* #125, 1949. Personnel Services, Inc., Sydney F. Austin (Ed.), Main St., Peacock, N.J.
75. Educational Policies Commission. *The purposes of education in American democracy.* Washington: The Commission, NEA and AASA, 1938. Out of print; reprinted in *Policies for education in American democracy,* 1946. Washington: The Commission, NEA, 1946.
76. Elonen, Anna S., Onken, Mary A., & Slight, D. Training the clinical psychologist: externeship in medical school clinics. *Amer. Psychologist,* 1946, **1**, 50-54.
77. *Ethical standards of psychologists.* Washington: APA, 1953.
78. Falick, M. L., Peters, Mildred, Levitt, M., & Rubenstein, B. O. Observations on the psychological education of teachers in a school-based mental-hygiene program. *Ment. Hyg., N.Y.,* 1954, **38**, 374-386.
79. Fenton, N. *Mental hygiene in school practice.* Stanford University, California: Stanford University Press, 1943.
80. Fernberger, S. W. The American Psychological Association: a historical summary, 1892-1930. *Psychol. Bull.*, 1932, **29**, 1-89.
81. Fine, B. Dr. Fields (Harold). *The New York Times News of the Week,* Nov. 14, 1954.
82. Frampton, M. E., & Rowell, H. G. *Education of the handicapped.* Vol. I. *History.* Yonkers, N.Y.: World Book, 1938.
83. Goddard, H. H. A revision of the Binet scale. Vineland, N.J.: *The Train. Sch. Bull.*, 1911, **8**, 56-62.
84. Group for the Advancement of Psychiatry, Committee on Preventive Psychiatry. *Promotion of mental health in the primary and*

secondary schools: an evaluation of four projects. Report No. 18, January, 1951. The Committee, 3617 West 6th Ave., Topeka, Kansas.

85. Guidance, counseling, and pupil personnel. *Rev. of Educ. Res.,* 1954, **24** (2).

86. Haggard, E. A. The proper concern of educational psychologists. *Amer. Psychologist,* 1954, **9**, 539-543.

87. Hall, Margaret E. Current employment requirements of school psychologists. *Amer. Psychologist,* 1949, **4**, 519-525.

88. Haskell, J. M. School psychologist counsels. *Calif. J. Sec. Educ.,* 1946, **21**, 88-91.

89. Healy, W. *The individual delinquent.* Boston: Little, Brown, 1917.

90. Hildreth, Gertrude. The psychologist investigates reading disability. *J. consult. Psychol.,* 1942, **6**, 212-217.

91. Hildreth, Gertrude. Services of the school psychologist. In D. H. Fyer and E. H. Henry (Eds.), *Handbook of applied psychology.* Vol. 2. New York: Rinehart, 1950. Pp. 383-388.

92. Hilgard, E. R. *Introduction to psychology.* New York: Harcourt, Brace, 1953.

93. Hilleboe, G. L. *Finding and teaching atypical children.* New York: Bureau of Publications, Teachers Coll., Columbia University, 1930.

94. Hollingworth, Leta S. Psychological service for public schools. *Teach. Coll. Rec.,* 1933, **34**, 368-379.

95. Holmlund, W. S. Flint's plan for the in-service training of teachers in child growth and development. *J. Teacher Educ.,* 1952, **3**, 50-52.

96. Horrocks, J. E. State certification requirements for school psychologists. *Amer. Psychologist,* 1946, **1**, 399-401.

97. Huseman, Mary. Psychological services to the mentally handicapped in Chicago public schools. *Amer. J. ment. Defic.,* 1947, **51**, 632-636.

98. Hutt, R. B. W. The school psychologist. *Psychol. Clinic,* 1923, **15**, 48-51.

99. International Bureau of Education, Geneva. Publ. No. 105. *School psychologists.* Paris: UNESCO, 1948.

100. Jacobsen, C. F., Carter, J. W., Jr., Perkins, K. J., Richards, T. W., Zander, Alvin, & Macfarlane, Jean W. Symposium: Psychology in the field of community services. *J. clin. Psychol.,* 1950, **6**, 111-132.

101. Joint WHO, UN, UNESCO Expert Committee. *Psychological services for schools.* Hamburg, Germany: UNESCO Institute for Educ., 1955.

102. Jones, A. J., & Miller, L. M. The national picture of pupil personnel and guidance services in 1953. *Nat. Ass. Sec.-Sc. Prin. Bull.,* 1954, **38**, 105-159.

103. Kearney, N. C. *Elementary school objectives.* New York: Russell Sage Foundation, 1953.

104. Kelley, T. L. *Interpretation of educational measurements.* Yonkers, N.Y.: World Book Co., 1927.

105. Ketcham, W. A. *A school staff looks at mental health in the class-*

room. Paper read at AAAS, St. Louis, December, 1952. Available from Author, School District, Ferndale, Mich. (Mimeo.)

106. Kitzinger, H. Certification. *Psychol. Exch.,* 1935, **4,** 21-23.

107. Krugman, M. The psychologist's role in pupil classification. *J. consult. Psychol.,* 1942, **6,** 205-211.

108. Larkin, Alice. School psychologist—another member of the team. *Tex. Trends ment. Hlth.,* 1953, **9** (3), 22-24.

109. Levine, Edna S. The work of the school psychologist. *Volta Rev.,* 1946, **48,** 728-734.

110. Lehner, G. F. J. Defining psychotherapy. *Amer. Psychologist,* 1952, **7,** 547.

111. Lindgren, H. C. *Mental health in education.* New York: Holt, 1954.

112. Lowrey, L. G., & Sloane, Victoria (Eds.) *Orthopsychiatry 1923-1948; Retrospect and Prospect.* Amer. Orthopsychiatric Ass., 1948.

113. McClure, W. E. The status of psychological testing in large city public school systems. *J. appl. Psychol.,* 1930, **14,** 486-496.

114. McDaniel, H. B. Organization and administration of guidance in elementary and secondary schools. *Rev. educ. Res.,* 1954, **24,** 109-112.

115. Macfarlane, Jean W. Interprofessional relations and collaboration with medicine and other related fields. *Amer. Psychologist,* 1950, **5,** 112-114.

116. McNally, H. J. Organizing school curricula to meet individual differences. *J. consult. Psychol.,* 1942, **6,** 200-204.

117. Martens, Elise H. *Clinical organization for child guidance within the schools.* Office of Educ., *Bull.,* 1939, No. 15. Washington: U.S. Government Printing Office, 1939.

118. Martens, Elise H. *State supervisory programs for the education of exceptional children.* Office of Educ., *Bull.,* 1940, No. 6, Monogr. No. 10. Washington: U.S. Government Printing Office, 1941.

119. Mathews, W. M., & Wineman, D. The psychologist and his role. *Amer. J. Orthopsychiat.,* 1952, **22,** 170-176.

120. Mathews, W. M., & Wineman, D. Problems of supervision and training in clinical psychology. The supervision of clinical diagnostic work. *Am. J. Orthopsychiat.,* 1953, **23,** 301-306.

121. *Meeting the needs of the mentally retarded.* Bulletin, 420. Harrisburg, Pa.: Dep. of Pub. Instruc., 1939.

122. Memoirs of the National Academy of Sciences, Vol. XV, *Psychological examining in the United States Army,* Vol. 1. Washington: U.S. Government Printing Office, 1921.

123. Miller, J. Program of a psychologist in a high school. *Sch. & Soc.,* 1927, **26,** 367-368.

124. Moore, B. V. Some data on faculty and graduate students in departments with approved training programs in clinical psychology. *Amer. Psychologist,* 1953, **8,** 200-201.

125. Moore, B. V. The master's degree in psychology. *Amer. Psychologist,* 1954, **9,** 120-122.

126. Moore, B. V. Faculty and students in departments with graduate programs in psychology. *Amer. Psychologist,* 1954, **9**, 255-257.
127. Mullen, Frances A. Fifty years of service to the mentally handicapped children of the Chicago schools. *Chicago Principal's Club Reporter,* 1949, **39** (5), 11-17.
128. Mulrine, C. L. Psychologist goes to school. *Amer. Sch. B. J.,* 1945, **110** (2), 29.
129. Munson, Grace. *Bureau of Child Study and the Chicago plan of adjustment service.* Chicago: Board of Education, 1947.
130. National Association of Secondary-School Principals. *Planning for American youth.* (Rev. ed.) Washington: The Ass., NEA, 1951.
131. National Education Association, Research Division. Personnel and relationships in school health, physical education, and recreation. *Res. Bull.,* NEA, 1950, **28**, 83-111.
132. National Society for the Study of Education. *The education of exceptional children;* Forty-ninth yearbook, Part II. Chicago: University of Chicago Press, 1950.
133. National Society for the Study of Education. *Mental health in modern education;* Fifty-fourth yearbook, Part II. Chicago: University of Chicago Press, 1955.
134. *New Haven's schools: an investment in your city's future.* Report of a survey of the public school system. 1947. Available from the Board of Educ., New Haven, Conn.
135. New York State Association for Applied Psychology, Special Committee on School Psychologists. Report on the functions, training and employment opportunities of school psychologists. *J. consult. Psychol.,* 1943, **7**, 230-243.
136. New York State Education Department. *Removing blocks to mental health in schools.* Albany, N.Y.: The Dep., 1954.
137. Nolan, W. J. A survey of practices in meeting pupil adjustment needs. *J. educ. Res.,* 1948, **42**, 268-278.
138. Oberholtzer, K. E. The school psychologist. *The Sch. Executive,* 1938, **58** (2), 16-17, 48.
139. Office of Education. *Statistics of special schools and classes for exceptional children, 1939-1940.* Washington: U.S. Government Printing Office, 1942.
140. Office of Education. *Education in the United States of America.* Special Series, No. 3. Washington: U.S. Government Printing Office, 1951.
141. Office of Education. *Supervised practice in counselor preparation.* Misc. 3314-6, April, 1952. Washington: U.S. Government Printing Office, 1952.
142. Office of Education. *Statistics of special schools and classes for exceptional children, 1952-1953.* Washington: U.S. Government Printing Office, 1954.
143. Ojemann, R. H., Nugent, Anne, & Corry, Martha. Study of human behavior in the social science program. *Social Educ.,* 1947, **11**, 25-28.

144. Parsons, F. *Choosing a vocation*. Boston: Houghton-Mifflin, 1909.
145. Pennsylvania Bureau of General Education, Department of Public Instruction. *Biennial report of the work of the county supervisors of special education, 1949-51*. Available from the Dep., Harrisburg, Pa. (Mimeo.)
146. Pennsylvania Bureau of General Education, Department of Public Instruction. *Biennial report of the work of the county supervisors of special education, 1951-53*. Available from the Dep., Harrisburg, Pa. (Mimeo.)
147. Perkins, K. J. Consultation service to public schools by a mental health team. *Ment. Hyg., N.Y.*, 1953, **37**, 585-595.
148. *Psychology and its relations with other professions*. Washington: APA, 1954.
149. Raimy, V. C. (Ed.) *Training in clinical psychology*. New York: Prentice-Hall, 1950.
150. Redl, F. & Wattenberg, W. W. *Mental hygiene in teaching*. New York: Harcourt, Brace, 1951.
151. *Report of the school committee, 1899-1900 centennial*. Providence, R.I.
152. Roberts, A. D. The cooperative personnel approach for the school psychologist. *Occupations*, 1952, **30**, 599-600.
153. Rosebrook, Wilda M. Psychological service for schools on a regional basis. *J. consult. Psychol.*, 1942, **6**, 196-200.
154. Ryan, W. C. *Vocational guidance and the public schools*. Office of Educ., *Bull.* 1918, No. 24. Washington: U.S. Government Printing Office, 1918.
155. Ryan, W. C. *Mental health through education*. New York: Commonwealth Fund, 1948.
156. Shartle, C. L. Occupations in psychology. *Amer. Psychologist*, 1946, **1**, 559-582.
157. Smith, E. R., & Tyler, R. W. *Appraising and recording student progress*. New York: McGraw-Hill, 1942.
158. *Standardized testing: an adventure in educational publishing*. Yonkers, N.Y.: World Book, 1954.
159. Stevens, G. D. 1940-1950 developments in the field of mental deficiency. *Except. Chil.*, 1954, **21**, 58-62, 70.
160. Stevenson, G. S., & Smith, G. *Child guidance clinics: a quarter century of development*. New York: Commonwealth Fund, 1934.
161. Stiles, Frances Smythe. Developing an understanding of human behavior at the elementary school level. *J. educ. Res.*, 1950, **43**, 516-524.
162. Strang, Ruth M. *Personal development and guidance in college and secondary school*. New York: Harper, 1934.
163. Sully, J. The service of psychology to education. *Amer. educ. Rev.*, 1892, **4**, 312-324.
164. Sundberg, N. D. A note concerning the history of testing. *Amer. Psychologist*, 1954, **9**, 150-151.

165. Super, D. E. Transition in the U.S.A.: from vocational guidance to counseling psychology. *Bull. de l'Asoc. Internationale de Psychotechnique,* July-Dec., 1954. In press.

166. Symonds, P. M. Every school should have a psychologist. *Sch. & Soc.,* 1933, **38,** 321-329.

167. Symonds, P. M. *Mental hygiene of the school child.* New York: Macmillan, 1934.

168. Symonds, P. M. Contribution of the school psychologist. *Proc. Eastern-States Assoc. Professional Sch. Teachers,* 1938, **13,** 164-172.

169. Symonds, P. M. The school psychologist—1942. *J. consult. Psychol.,* 1942, **6,** 173-176.

170. Symposium on psychologists and psychiatrists in the child guidance service. *Brit. J. educ. Psychol.,* 1951-1953.
    I. Kennedy, A. Psychologists and psychiatrists and their general relationship. 1951, **21,** 167-171.
    II. Davidson, May. The relation between psychologists and psychiatrists in the service of maladjusted adults and children. 1952, **22,** 1-4.
    III. Keir, Gertrude. A history of child guidance. 1952, **22,** 5-29.
    IV. McCallum, Catherine M. Child guidance in Scotland. 1952, **22,** 79-88.
    V. Moody, R. L. A conflict of disciplines and personalities. 1952, **22,** 155-159.
    VI. Banks, Charlotte. Research in child guidance, 1953, **23,** 1-7.
    VII. Burt, Cyril. Conclusion. 1953, **23,** 8-28.

171. Terman, L. M. *The measurement of intelligence.* Boston: Houghton Mifflin, 1916.

172. Thayer, V. T., Psychological services needed in a private school. *J. consult. Psychol.,* 1942, **6,** 181-184.

173. Thorndike, E. L. *An introduction to the theory of mental and social measurements.* New York: Bureau of Publications, Teachers Coll., Columbia University, 1904.

174. University of Illinois, College of Education. *Program for public school psychologists.* Available from T. E. Newland, Urbana, Ill.: University of Illinois, June 24, 1953. (Mimeo.)

175. University of Michigan, School of Education. *Training program for school psychological diagnosticians.* Available from W. C. Trow, Ann Arbor, Mich.: University of Michigan.

176. Vaughan, W. F. *Personal and social adjustment; foundations of mental health.* New York: Odyssey Press, 1952.

177. Wall, W. D. Psychological services for children. *The Times* [London] *Educ. Supplement,* April 13 and 20, 1951.

178. Wallin, J. E. W. Certification requirements for psycho-educational examiners by municipal school systems. *J. consult. Psychol.,* 1941, **5,** 252.

179. Wallin, J. E. W. Forum; the "school psychologist" in retrospect. *J. consult. Psychol.*, 1942, **6**, 309-312.

180. Watson, G. The demand for psychological counselors in education. *Ment. Hyg., N.Y.*, 1931, **15**, 542-549.

181. Watson, G. Psychology in the emerging education. *J. consult. Psychol.*, 1946, **10**, 57-62.

182. Weiss, Emalyn R. & Myer, L. N. Psychological services in the rural schools of Pennsylvania. *Except. Child.*, 1952, **19**, 15-19.

183. White House Conference on Child Health and Protection, Subcommittee on Vocational Guidance and Child Labor. *Vocational guidance*. New York: Century, 1932.

184. Wilkins, W. L. Some effects of 10 years of psychological service in a public school system. *Psychol. Bull.*, 1941, **38**, 554 (abstract).

185. Wilson, C. C. (Ed.) School health services: a report of the Joint Committee on Health Problems in Education of the NEA and the AMA. Washington: NEA, 1953.

186. Wolfle, Dael. Annual report of the executive secretary: 1948. *Amer. Psychologist*, 1948, **3**, 503-510.

187. Yepsen, L. N. The relationship between the psychologist and the teacher. *Amer. J. ment. Defic.*, 1946, **50**, 419-424.

188. Zehrer, F. A. The school psychologist as a mental hygiene specialist. *J. consult. Psychol.*, 1942, **6**, 218-222.

Index

Index

Assessment: conflict over function, 26-27; early use of tests, 19, 22, 23; ethical responsibility in, 91-92; as function, 30, 32, 33, 35, 36, 37, 38, 40, 63, 141, 142, 168, 174, 186, 188, 196; skill in, 148, 149-150, 158-160, 165-167, 168, 179

Accreditation: accrediting agencies, 172-173; and the APA, 173; Conference statement on, 173; necessity for, 147, 171, 177

Adjustment; see Mental health

Administrative responsibility of psychologist: in a department, 76-79; in Europe, 189-190; as function, 32, 34, 35; in Massachusetts, 164-165; in Merrill-Palmer School, 196; to principal, 68, 69, 72, 75; in rural areas, 76; skill in, 163; to superintendent, 69, 75; as supervisor, 77-79, 92, 104-105, 106, 110, 136

American Board of Examiners in Professional Psychology, 99; diplomate status, 99-100, 173

Binet tests, development of, 21

Boulder Conference: on practical experience, 164; as precedent, 8; report of training, 127; on title, 139

Buildings, school: assist in planning, 40; conference rooms in, 73, 103

Case conferences; see Specialists, cooperation with

Case load; see Ratio

Certification: in California, 123-124; Conference recommendations, 111-112; and degrees, 109; levels of, 109, 136; requirements, 108-112, 177, 190, 193; surveys of, 6, 12, 108, 111; teaching requirement, 110, 130, 169; types of, 100, 173

Characteristics desired; see Selection of students

Child study departments, establishment of, 19-20, 23

Child-guidance clinics; see also Specialists, cooperation with: in Europe, 183, 185, 186, 188, 189; establishment of, 24-25, 49, 52; internship in, 146, 167, 192; number of, 25; team concept in, 80; use of, 39, 55, 60, 77, 78

Clinical experience: amount reported, 121; required, 110, 143, 146, 167

Clinical psychologists: attending conference, 10; internship training for, 167; a new profession, 18; and school psychologists, 82, 116-117;

serving child-guidance clinics, 25; training of, 8, 127

Committee on Certification and Training; see Conference survey of psychologists

Conference conclusions: on accreditation, 173; appreciation of pioneers, 15; on case load, 80; on certification, 110-112; on cooperation of departments, 154; definition of case load, 80; on diplomate status, 100; on ethics, 92, 93; on experimental programs, 152-153; on functions, 30, 31; on graduate courses, 156-157; on a growing field, 14; on internship, 31, 165; on knowledge of education, 129, 135; on levels of position, 31, 139-140; on membership in organizations, 97-98; on mental health of all children, a major goal, 53, 77, 80, 86, 90; on organization of services, 86; on overlapping fields 86; on qualified professors, 153; on research, 43; on school psychologist active in training, 154; on teaching requirement, 134; on teams, 86; tentative, 14; on therapy, 48-49; on training, two-year, 31, 145, 147, four-year, 31, 151

Conference survey of psychologists: conducted, 5, 13; of degrees obtained, 119; of essential courses, 121; of fields of concentration, 120-121; of functions, 32, 41, V; number found, 5, 13; of previous experience, 115, 121, 130; questions included, 13; of requirements for levels, 137; of titles, 6

Confidential information, ethical standards about, 89-92

Conflicting opinions among participants: critical issues, discussion of, 14; on diplomate status, 100; expected, 11-12; on length of internship, 146; on levels of position, 137-139; on research, 41, 45-46, 175-176; on substitute for teaching, 135; on teaching requirement, 132-134, 178; on therapy, 48-49, 175; on titles for positions, 140, 176

Consultant to staff; see also Teacher, classroom: desired by teacher, 71; as function, 32, 33, 37, 39, 50, 51, 59, 61, 185; responsibility to administrator, 69, 76-78; salary as, 105; skill in, 159, 161, 162, 192; staff, line, relationship, 36, 71, 75-76

Counseling, individual; see also

secretarial help needed, 103; skill in, 148, 160, 163, 166, 196

Research: consulting on, 44-45, 158; ethical responsibility in, 88, 91, 92; as function, 30, 41-46, 63-64, 142, 175-176, 185, 186, 199-200; skill in, 148, 157, 158

Retarded children; see Exceptional children; Special education

Rochester Plan for Mental Health, 130

Salaries, 103-107

Selection of students: characteristics, 66, 69-71, 113-114, 176, 191-192; in Europe, 193-194; responsibility for, 114

Small school, functions in, 38, 59, 76

Social worker: comparison with psychologist, 84; at Conference, 10, 13; cooperation with, 58, 84, 162; in Europe, 184, 186; training in education, 167

Special education; see also Exceptional children: department of, 76-78; development of, 16-17, 20, 79; as function, 21, 30, 32-35, 38, 39, 51, 56-58, 168-169, 188; training for, 124, 150, 160-161

Specialists, cooperation with; see also Teamwork: ethical responsibility, 89; as function, 33-34, 37, 39, 50, 56, 58-59, 78, 185, 197

Standards: accreditation aids, 171-172; need to maintain, 6; raising of, 15, 115, 180

State psychological associations: assist with salaries, 105; with certification, 110, 111

Steering Committee, 9, 14

Subdoctoral training; see also Master's degree; Degrees: accreditation of program, 173; Conference conclusion about, 147; descriptions of, 145-150, 179; institutions offering, 6, 122, 144, 148; other reports on, 144-145; required, 127, 138-140

Superintendent of schools: address by, 10; annual reports of, 101; criticisms by, 68-70; on degrees, 120; ethical responsibility, 88; on functions, 35-38, 84; interviewed, 13, 35; on research, 41-42; responsibility of, 66-67, 69, 76; on salaries, 104-105; on teaching experience, 116, 131-132; on therapy, 47-48

Surveys; see also Conference survey of psychologists: Superintendents of schools: of certification, 6, 12, 108-110; of chief psychologists, 77-79; of internship, 167; in Milwaukee County, 79, 98; in Providence, 98, 105, 124; of salaries, 103-106; of

teaching requirement, 131; of training, 5, 12, 121-122

Teacher, classroom; see also Consultant to staff; In-service training of school personnel: assisted with difficult children, 50-52, 59-62, 71; at Conference, 10, 13; responsibility of, 68

Teaching in the classroom: of college classes, 82, 197-199; required or not, 70, 77, 110, 115, 131-135, 143, 146, 177-178, 191-193; substitute for, 135, 167, 178

Teamwork; see also Specialists, cooperation with: Conference conclusion about, 86; in Europe, 184, 186, 189; as function, 24, 41, 69, 71; purposes accomplished by, 80-81, 90; skill in, 162

Testing; see Assessment; Evaluation

Therapy; see also Re-education: Conference conclusion about, 32, 48-49; as function, 30, 32, 35, 36, 46-52, 175, 186, 196-197; psychiatrist on, 61

Titles: in certification, 109; of chief psychologist, 78; Conference conclusion about, 31, 140-141, 176-177; number of, 6, 67; school psychologist first used, 23-24

Training; see also Graduate training, Subdoctoral Training; Universities: In California, 122-124; Conference committee on basic, 155-156; Conference conclusions on, 31, 139-140, 147; Connecticut statement of, 124-125; Differences between two- and four-year, 148; Division 16 studies of, 125-126; flexible, 146, 152, 155, 178; in-service, of psychologists, difficulty in obtaining, 94, ethical responsibility for, 88, informal training, 95-98, necessity for, 94, 152, 179-180; thorough, 37, 65, 147, 179

Undergraduate training: courses desired in, 155-156; in Europe, 190; recruitment from, 117-118

United States Department of Health, Education, and Welfare: approved institutions reported to, 173; supplied funds, 9; support of meetings, 97

Universities offering training, 5-6, 12, 21, 94-95, 121-122, 151, 178, 190-193; Brown University, 124; ethical responsibility of, 91-92; participants' degrees received from, 11; part-time study in, 80, 147, 179; regional planning for, 153; responsibility for selection, 114, 194; University of Illinois, 6, 154, 168-170; University of Michigan, 148-150